MARITIME ARCHAEOLOGY

MARITIME ARCHAEOLOGY

HISTORICAL DESCRIPTIONS OF THE SEAFARINGS OF THE KALINGAS

SILA TRIPATI

Kaveri Books
New Delhi-110 002

Edition 2017

ISBN: 978-81-7479-038-5

Published by
Kaveri Books
4832/24, Ansari Road
New Delhi-110002 (India)
Tel: 011-4707 2321
E-mail : kaveribooks@gmail.com
Website: www.kaveribooks.com

Typeset by
Delta Book World, New Delhi - 110 002.

PRINTED IN INDIA

Dedicated to

Great Seafarers of Kalinga

Acknowledgements

I record my deep sense of gratitude to Dr. L.N. Raut, Reader, Department of History, Berhampur University for not only suggesting that I work on this topic but also for guiding me all through. Dr. E. Desa, Director, National Institute of Oceanography, Goa has extended all the facilities and constant encouragement which made publication of this work a possibility. It is not possible to carry out any form of scientific work without the co-operation, help and guidance from many people. Throughout my tenure at the National Institute of Oceanography I have been inspired, helped and taught Marine Archaeology by Dr. S.R. Rao, former Advisor of Marine Archaeology Centre. Shri. K.H. Vora, Scientist-in-Charge, Marine Archaeology Centre has been constantly facilitating with all necessary help for carrying out the work. Many scientists of the N.I.O. have provided sincere and involved help for quite some time. It is with pleasure and gratitude that I name a few of them: Dr. Shyam Prasad, Dr. M. Dileep Kumar, Dr. V.S.N. Murty, Dr. Rahul Sharma. Also, I have benefited immensely in association of Dr. Subrata Kumar Acharya, Lecturer in History, Dhenkanal College, Orissa, who has laid the foundation of my knowledge in this field. It is indeed my privilege to say thanks to him for all he has done. I am also thankful to all my colleagues of Marine Archaeology Centre for their help at every stage of this work. The book contains many figures, photographs, half tones etc. Shri S.B. Chitari, Shri Sheikh Ali Karim, Shri U.S. Shirsat and Shri Susanta Kumar Patnaik have shown tremendous patience and have provided me with wonderful prints. I am thankful to the scholars and institutions involved in the related research for permitting me to reproduce their figures and plates in the present work. I am also grateful to Shri Rakesh Goel, my publisher, for his encouragement and co-operation. I remain grateful to them. My parents, with the foresight that parents are endowed with, had suggested that I take up the fascinating of archaeology. Today I have a strong reason to express my thanks to them. During the course of the work I have received unflinching support from my wife Smt. Sila Suma Rani no less from my daughter Sila Naveena who have put up with my long absences during my field trips. For all of which I can only say thanks in print.

Sila Tripati

Foreword

Peninsular India has a long coast line on the west, south and east, bordering the Arabian sea, the Indian Ocean and the Bay of Bengal. In the *Vedic* literature there are references vague and scanty, to the sea voyages of which Bhujyu's the son of Tugra's military expedition by sea and his rescue by Asvins, the gods, is in the recent years highlighted. The Harappans trade in all probability with West Asia, was by sea route as well. Dwarka, as the *Bhagavata* narrates, was built in the sea at the instance of Sri Krishna that later was said to have been submerged. The long distance vast Roman trade over centuries from about 1st century onwards over at least five centuries with South India, Southeast Asian Islands is too well known from the literary sources. From sometimes before the beginning to the Christian era people from Eastern and South India migrated to Sri Lanka, and Southeast Asian islands as religious missionaries, political and commercial entrepreneurs to make fortune probably by sea. And there were many sea ports along the coast at least from Broach (ancient Bharukachha) in Gujarat to Tamluk (Tamralipti) in West Bengal known from the indigenous and foreign accounts. Thus all these substantially indicate the significant role the coastal ports and the sea routes played in the cultural history of our country almost uninterruptedly. However, but for the stray and scrappy literary references, there were hardly any archaeological evidences till recently, with the exception of scanty Harappan material remains such as a terracotta boat with probably mast, the dockyard in Lothal.

Marine archaeology in India that began in late 1981 mainly at the instance of Dr. S.R.Rao, a reputed and distinguished archaeologist in the field, in the National Institute of Oceanography (NIO), Goa is attaining adolescence. Yet, it has already made a brilliant mark in the field owing to the sustained, and committed efforts of the team under the efficient and able guidance of Dr. S.R.Rao. Shri. Sila Tripati since then being one of the members of the team participating in the arduous work of underwater explorations and onshore explorations and excavations at the sites Dwarka, Bet Dwarka, Somnath, Poompuhar, Tranquebar, Lakshadweep etc., gained invaluable experience and in depth knowledge all through, is certainly competent to handle successfully a subject like "Maritime Archaeology: Historical Descriptions of the Seafarings of the Kalingas". He has proved more than a match in this task. He has displayed his intimate familiarity with every technical aspect of the study. As a result, the study is indeed exceedingly scientific and convincing.

Orissa known for its unique and stately monuments of architectural grandeur, is equally great in its maritime activities over centuries particular with Southeast Asia that from a substantial part of the glorious history and culture of the land. The splendid monuments in Konark seem to stand as colossal witness to the maritime activities.

Ably dealing with the subject in five well planned chapters the author displays his thorough knowledge and comprehension particularly in handling the technical aspects such as the behaviour of the Indian coast line; types of maritime ports, trade routes particularly the water routes, classification of ships and boats and their principal parts such as mast, sail, rudder, ship-building involving right from the selection of wood to the construction by ordinary and reversible clinker and inter fingering tongue techniques, currents and winds etc as known from the literary works ranging from the *Rig Veda* to the medieval works such as the *Yuktikalpataru* as well as foreign accounts and archaeological relics particularly in chapters II to V. The study is exhaustive, critical and updated and the language is simple and lucid. Thus, the scholar has left no stone unturned. I am of the opinion that this fine work is a valuable, welcome addition to the Maritime History of India in general and of Kalinga in particular and will serve as a model to similar works on the coastal states of our country.

Prof. A. Sundara
329, Saundaryashri
Bharati Nagar
Dharwad - 580001

Preface

Of late, scholars working in the fields of History, Economics, Geography, Archaeology and Maritime Archaeology have shown interest in the studies on ports and their maritime importance which goes a long way to establish emphatically that India had a hectic and intimate contact with other flourishing empires/regions of the world. The present work is devoted to the study of ancient Kalingan maritime activities which centred around a good number of flourishing ports.

As a matter of fact such a study presupposes a brief general discussion at the outset. Right from the prehistoric times, India has been approachable by sea from West, South and Southeast and the Southern peninsula had a natural inclination for seafaring activity. The *Vedic* literature refers to the boats, ships and sea voyages. The *Rig Veda* refers to Varuna, the Lord of the sea. It is learnt that the Vedic people were knowledgeable about the ocean and use of ships and boats. It also mentions merchants plying ships to foreign countries in quest of wealth. The *Rig Veda* states that the merchants knew no bounds, not even the ocean, and that they went everywhere in search of wealth. There is also a passage which gives a graphic account of a naval expedition undertaken by one Bhujyu, the son of King Tugra. Further this prayer in the *Rig Veda* is self-explanatory, "O Lord, take us in a ship across the ocean for our well-being". The Eastern and Western Oceans are referred to in the *Rig Veda*, which are evidently the Bay of Bengal and the Arabian Sea. The *Atharvā Veda* and *Samhita* describe the boats their faultless construction and sturdiness. European scholars have described that Rig Vedic people were aware of the ocean and probabilities of sea-borne trade during that period. The *Brihatsamhita*, mentions that the sailors were influenced by the moon. There is another reference to ships going to sea for gainful ends.

The Harappans appeared in the Northwest as early as 3000 BC with a well developed civilised life. Archaeological finds do suggest the brisk commercial contacts between Mohenjodaro, Harappa and Lothal on one hand and the Mesopotamian centres on the other. At Lothal a particular type of dockyard was found which measured 214 x 36 m lined with walls of kiln baked bricks. This is the first tidal dock of the world serving the port town of the Harappan Lothal at the head of the gulf of Cambay. This is the earliest and probably the only one of its kind discovered so far. The analysis of the core samples from the floor of Lothal dockyard prove the presence of foraminifera and gypsum crystals. It clearly illustrates that Harappans had the maritime engineering skill and knowledge of Hydrography in 3rd Millennium BC. The urban Harappans seem to have kept the sea routes in perfect stance to meet the growing maritime trade. Starting from the gulf of Cambay, along the coast of the Arabian sea, the ships entered the Persian gulf finally reaching the north Euphrates near Ur. The stone seal with ship and a cabin, a terracotta amulet with a ship motif, terracotta boat model and dockyard with perforated stone anchors from Lothal clearly point to the modes and means of transport as well. With the advent of the Christian era the civilisation of India had begun to spread across the Bay of Bengal into both island and mainland Southeast Asia. In the light of the above attempts have been made in this study to present the maritime achievements of ancient Orissa from the earliest times to the thirteenth century AD.

The term Kalinga is used in the present study to denote a region extending between the rivers Ganges to Godavari. It would be appropriate to mention here that it was only under the Imperial Gangas (10th-13th centuries AD) that the entire region experienced political unification. However during the period under review (from earliest times up to the end of 13th century AD) a good number of independent kingdoms viz the Matharas (4th-6th century AD), the

Eastern Gangas (5th-9th century AD), the Sailodbhavas (6th-8th century AD), the Bhaumakaras (8th-10th century AD), the Somavamsis (9th-11th century AD), the Imperial Gangas (10th-13th century AD) etc rose and fell in the so called Kalinga region.

The ancient ports of Kalinga were Tamralipti, Kannagara, Khalkatapatna, Manikapatna, Chilka, Palur, Dantapura, Pithunda and Kalingapatnam. Through these ports Kalinga had her trade and cultural contacts with Roman empire, Arabian and Southeast Asian countries since early historical times. The archaeological excavation findings at Sisupalgarh, Khalkatapatna, Manikapatna, Palur, Kalingapatnam throw light on this. The excavations at these sites have yielded Rouletted ware, Roman bullae, gold coins with figure of Roman emperor and iron caltrops, Ceylonese and Chinese coins, Kharoshti-Brahmi inscriptions, Chinese and celadon ware which confirm the trade relations of Kalinga with the outside world.

Although a good number of papers have been published by scholars on the History of Kalinga, limited references to the maritime history of Kalinga during the period are available. The works of D.K. Ganguly: *Historical Geography and Dynastic History of Orissa*, D.N. Das: *The Early History of Kalinga*, K.C. Panigrahi: *The History of Orissa*, H.K. Mahtab: *The History of Orissa*, N.K. Sahu: *The History of Orissa*, B.S. Das: *The Economic History of Orissa*, R.D. Banerjee: *History of Orissa*, R.L. Mitra: *Antiquities of Orissa*, G. Coedes: *The Indianized States of Southeast Asia*, H.B. Sarkar: *Cultural Relations between India and Southeast Asian Countries*, M.P. Charlesworth: *Trade Routes and Commerce of the Roman Empire* in a very limited scale discuss about the maritime history of Kalinga. However these works are very useful for further research. Besides the published works, some research articles are available in different journals and proceedings which relate to the ports and maritime activities of the early and medieval Orissa. The research publications by A.L. Basham, M.N. Das, B.N. Mukherjee, H.P. Ray, S.R. Rao, K.S. Behera, L. Gopal, K.S. Ramachandran etc serve as useful introductions to the maritime history of India in general. Besides the literary sources, a number of existing regional traditions, legends, seafaring rituals and festivals throw light on the maritime activities of Kalinga.

The present work has been arranged in the following manner. The first chapter deals with the sources for study of maritime history and historical background of Kalinga. The usefulness of the literary, numismatic, inscriptional sources, art evidences and archaeological exploration and excavation reports has been analysed for the construction of ancient maritime history of Kalinga. The historical background incorporated herein provides a general understanding of the political developments of the region. The second chapter deals with the ports and expansion of culture and its emphasis is on *(i)* the confirmation and identification of ports, *(ii)* identification of some ancient ports hitherto unattempted, and *(iii)* location of some unknown ports. Discussion is made on ports and expansion of culture together with a view to highlighting the ancient Kalingan maritime past. The third chapter highlights the trade routes and commerce along with the recognition of their maritime importance. The classification of land and water routes, pattern of trade, exchange of articles and currency system received attention in this chapter. The fourth chapter deals with ship and boat-building and navigation techniques which were followed by the ancient seafarers. Construction techniques, decoration, preservation of boat, navigational pattern, knowledge of current and wind patterns are discussed in broad detail. The causes of decline of ports and maritime activities of Kalinga are described in the fifth chapter. The primary stress here centres on natural factors like tectonic, sedimentation, riverine character etc. The generally accepted theories on decline of ports and maritime activities are not taken into account. The findings of the study are incorporated in the concluding chapter.

25 April 2000 **Sila Tripati**

National Institute of Oceanography
Dona Paula, Goa

List of Figures

List of Plates

Contents

1

Historical Background and Sources

SECTION-I

Historical Background

The geographical position of Kalinga with several rivers, long coastline with sheltered ports, provided an ideal environment for sea voyages, *Samudra Yatra*. The sailors of Kalinga developed and constructed the ports at the estuaries of the Mahanadi, the Suvarnarekha, the Rishikulya, the Mahendratanaya and the Vamsadhara. Ancient Kalinga was a great maritime and formidable military power stretching from the mouth of the Ganges to the Godavari on the shore of the Bay of Bengal. It was variously referred to as Odra, Utkala and Kalinga in the Buddhist texts and Brahminical literatures. The Vanaparva[1] of the *Mahabharata* indicates the mouth of the Ganges as the northern limits of the territory of Kalinga. Pliny[2] mentions the southern limit extended up to the Cape Calingae which has been identified with point the mouth of the river Godavari. The Western limits sometimes extended up to the Amarakantak hills as known from the *Matsya Purana*[3], while the sea formed the natural eastern boundary. The *Mahabharata*[4] describes that the capital of Kalinga was Dantakara which is identified with Dandagula by Pliny and located about 570 miles to the south of the mouth of Ganges. The political geography of this glorious land Kalinga underwent remarkable changes in the subsequent periods of history depending upon the prevailing political conditions, as a result changes also took place in the sphere of maritime activities. During the 4th century BC Mahapadma Nanda, the Magadhan emperor invaded Kalinga and brought under his suzerainty the whole of the coastal tract of Kalinga. The main reason for the attack of Kalinga was to acquire sea ports through which the Kalingan people were carrying on overseas trade as Magadha had no sea ports of its own[5]. The Hathigumpha inscription of Kharavela[6] mentions that Mahapadma Nanda after his conquest excavated an aqueduct in the centre of Kalinga, which was renovated and extended up to Kalinganagari (modern Sisupalgarh near Bhubaneswar) after three hundred years. The fact that Mahapadma Nanda conquered Asmaka situated to the south west of Kalinga beyond the river Godavari[7], is an indirect evidence of the fact that at that time the territory of Kalinga was extended at least up to the river Godavari. In 261 BC Asoka conquered Kalinga and made it a province of the Mauryan Empire. Tosali (modern Dhauli) and Somapa (modern Jaugada) were made capital and secondary capital of Mauryan Kalinga respectively. One of the basic factors that tempted and motivated Asoka to conquer Kalinga was to capture the sea coast with its rich ports for the expansion of the maritime activities of the Magadhan Empire. Prior to Kalinga war Magadha was kept within narrow limits as the entire sea coast from the Ganges downward remained under the control of Kalinga rulers[8]. Thus, it seems that by the third century BC, when Asoka conquered Kalinga, she had already acquired wealth and power through maritime trade and colonial expansion[9]. Kautilya in his *Arthasastra* provides information about the sea trade, construction of ports and trade regulations[10]. In the first century BC Kalinga became a strong power under the reign of Kalingadhipati Mahameghavahana Kharavela which is known from the Hathigumpha inscription[11]. He renovated and extended the aqueduct constructed by the Nanda king three centuries ago up to his capital Kalinganagari. It is often conjectured that the construction of the aqueduct in the heart of the kingdom by Mahapadmananda in fourth century BC and its renovation and extension by Kharavela[12] in the first century BC were the primary steps of the royal patronage for internal riverine trade, transport and irrigation. But the word *Vata* referred to in Kharavela's Hathigumpha inscription suggests a moat or a canal which was not at all suitable for any trade activities. Asoka's missionary zeal and use of sea ports of Kalinga for the despatch of convoys, spread and propagation of Buddhism seems to have indirectly contributed to the enhancement of the status of the ports and the development of maritime activities. This paved the way for the extension of attention and patronage of feudal chiefs, *Amatyas*, *Sresthis* and the ministers of Asoka in the subsequent years. From the above discussion it is evident that the age of the Nandas and the Mauryas witnessed an epoch of extensive maritime activity that brought other nations closer to India. The wise policy of international community and friendship established in the Mauryan Age laid the foundations for the building up of a lasting Indian trade with overseas countries in the later ages. K.A.Nilakantha Sastri concludes, "It is not unreasonable to suppose that these favourable conditions were attended with phenomenal development of industry as well as inland and foreign trade of the empire under the Mauryan rule".

The rise of the Satavahana dynasty (2nd century BC to 3rd century AD) in Andhra region probably put an end to the Chedi rule in Kalinga. The Satavahanas had extended their kingdom up to Magadha[13]. The Nasik Cave inscription[14] of Vasisthiputra Pulumavi of this dynasty mentions that the Mahendra mountain of present Ganjam district of Orissa formed the eastern border of the empire of Gautamiputra Satakarni. The Satavahana rule in ancient Orissa is further corroborated by the archaeological finds at Bhubaneswar having close affinity to the Satavahana art. The discovery of Satavahana coins from southern Orissa further support this fact[15]. The Satavahana rule over Kalinga probably came to an end after the death of Vasisthiputra Pulumavi, the son and successor of Gautamiputra Satakarni after AD 154[16]. After Kharavela, Kalinga rapidly shrank in territorial extent and remained an obscure land till the rise of the Matharas in the middle of fourth century AD. Simhapura identified with modern Singupuram in Srikakulam district was the capital of the Matharas. The territory was extended from the Mahanadi in the north to the Krishna river, Pishtapura, modern Pithapuram in the Godavari district in the south. With the advent of the Matharas on the political stage of Kalinga, the Orissan history becomes eventful and important after a lapse of four centuries of disintegration. The period from first century AD to fourth century AD is one of foreign predominance on Orissan soil. With the fall of Mahameghavahanas towards the first century AD Kushanas seem to have exerted their influence over Orissa. The discovery of Kushana and Puri-Kushana[17] coins from the districts of Ganjam, Puri, Balasore, Mayurbhanj, Keonjhar and Cuttack, it can be said that Kalinga in all probability came under the sway of the Kushanas for some time[18]. M.N. Das states that, "Orissa at that time might have come under the supremacy of those been a race of mercantile adventurers, also could have busied themselves in internal and external trade for which there could have been brisk circulation of Kushana coins in almost every notable port of Orissa, especially in the coastal belts"[19]. The sculptural specimens of the gate keepers with boots found in the caves of Udayagiri exhibit the cultural impact of the Kushanas. Just as the Imperial Guptas destroyed the remnant of Kushana power in northern India, so also the Matharas seem to have driven out the Kushana from the Orissan soil[20]. Another group of scholars suggest that the Murundas probably ruled over Kalinga as the feudatories of the Imperial Kushanas, they were hailing from Northwest of India[21].

The Allahabad Pillar Inscription[22] records the southern expedition of Samudra Gupta. There is no reference to Kalinga in the inscription. Instead, there are names of several kingdoms along with their rulers which were located in and around Kalinga. They were Mahendra of Kosala, Vyaghraraja of Mahakantara, Mahendragiri of Pishtapura, Svamidatta of Kottura, Damana of Erandapalle and Kuvera of Devarastra. These places have been identified with places located in the Visakhapatnam, East Godavari and Srikakulam districts of Andhra Pradesh and Ganjam, Kalahandi and Koraput districts of Orissa. The only inference to be drawn from this inscription is that after the Murunda rule Kalinga had no central authority and it was divided into small kingdoms during the first half of the fourth century AD. The Mathara rule in Kalinga seems to have encouraged the maritime activities of the people. In the sea coast of Kalinga was located the famous port Palur, which according to Ptolemy[23] was one of the most important trading stations in the second century AD. Oldham has identified Paloura with Paluru at the northern extremity of Ganjam district[24]. The

New History of the Tang Dynasty[25] mentions a kingdom of the name Holing in Central Java which flourished in the sixth century AD. Holing has been usually supposed to be the equivalent of Kalinga. From the inscriptions of Orissa it seems that the Mathara kings ruled over Kalinga from the fourth to sixth century AD. They had become the Lords of *Mahendrabhoga* centering round Mahendragiri as understood from the Dhavalapeta copper plate grant[26]. In this context, it can be said that in the opinion of Kalidasa, who flourished almost in the same period when the Matharas were in power, the king of Kalinga was not only the Lord of Mahendragiri but also the Lord of Mahodadhi. In the words of the poet: "*Asau Mahendradri Samanasarah Patirmahendrasya Mahodadhescha*". The poet further imagines that his heroine would roam with the prince of Kalinga on the seashore where the murmuring sound of the palm trees is heard and little drops of sweat are removed by the breezes which cloves from the distant islands[27]. If we consider that Kalidasa had a fair knowledge of India of his times then this piece of information cannot be ignored. The passage *Dvipantaranita lavanga puspaiah* of the *Raghuvamsa* appears to be very significant. In this poetic expression obviously there is an allusion to the seafaring activities of the people of Kalinga with the islands in the *Mahodadhi* (Indian Ocean) in the fifth century AD during the rule of Matharas. Again palaeographical similarity found in the Orissan and Javanese inscriptions of the fifth century AD also leads us to believe that under the Matharas Kalinga was the carrier of civilisation to Indonesia. A.C. Burnell[28], a competent authority on South Indian Palaeography is of the opinion that there are many inscriptions in Java which are of the same character as those of Orissan inscriptions. Moreover, A.H. Dani has also expressed his believe that the writing style prevalent in the records of the Matharas, Vishnukundis, and Pallavas have some resemblences with that of Southeast Asia[29]. Consequently, the Sailodbhava dynasty which succeeded the Matharas in Kalinga is regarded as the greatest patrons of Kalinga's maritime activities. The Sailodbhavas ruled over the territory called Kongoda or Kanyodha. It is identified by scholars with modern Ganjam and regions surrounding Chilka lake. During the rule of Sailodbhavas trade and maritime activities were carried out through the ports of Paluru, Ganjam, Kalinganagar. The Sailodbhavas of Kongoda successfully launched a colonial adventure in *Suvarnadvipa* and founded the famous Sailendra dynasty there[30]. This became possible for the Sailodbhavas due to the earlier maritime activity of Kalinga. According to R.C. Majumdar, this dynasty is the branch of the Sailodbhavas. The Sailodbhavas were the rulers of Kongoda during 7th to 8th century AD and subsequently they were driven by the Bhaumakaras. Perhaps the Sailodbhavas migrated to Java and Borneo. During later period the name of the dynasty changed and it became Sailendras[31].

About the 5th century AD a new dynasty was established around the Mahendra mountain area with its capital at Kalinganagara. The dynasty was known as the Eastern Gangas[32]. The capital of early Ganga dynasty was located on the river bank of the Vamsadhara. In the beginning, Kalinga under this dynasty denoted the same area which were under the Matharas. But it seems that other ruling families also shared the Kalinga territory along with the Eastern Gangas during 6th to 7th centuries AD. Their family deity was Lord Siva as is known from the inscriptions. The names of the Kings of the Eastern Ganga dynasty were Indra Verma, Jaya Verma, and Ananta Verma which correspond to the names of the rulers of Sri-Vijaya dynasty of Sumatra, Java and Bali. The Sailodbhavas of Kongoda were crushed by the Bhaumakaras who ruled over from the Ganges to the Mahendra mountain and the capital at Guhesvarapataka probably nearer to Viraja, modern Jajpur in Cuttack district. During the Bhaumakara rule missionary activity was started between Orissa and China. King Subhakaradeva sent a religious text to the emperor of China through Prajna and he translated the scriptures into Chinese language. During this period there prevailed well organised administration. The frequent conflict between the Bhaumakaras and the Somavamsis of South Kosala region continued for years together. The Bhaumakaras checked the aggressive force of the Somavamsis for some time. After the death of Dharmamahadevi, the last monarch of the Bhaumakara dynasty in AD 950 the dynasty was occupied by the Somavamsis. Orissa evidently derived considerable revenue from sea trade as an inscription of the Bhaumakara period refers to *Samudrakara bandha*. During the reign of Somavamsi king Yayati II, the political and geographical arena of Kalinga was strengthened and the whole of Kalinga, Kongoda, Utkala and Kosala was under the dynasty. He proclaimed himself as the Lord of all the provinces[33]. During the Somavamsi rule Orissa attained peace and tranquillity for a longer period. They substantially contributed to the art and architectural glory of Orissa. Although, till date direct evidence, (archaeological or otherwise), regarding the maritime activities of the people is not available, yet, it can be suggested that Orissa under the Somavamsis did not altogether do away with ancient Kalingan maritime traditions. The decline of the Somavamsis witnessed the rise of another powerful and glorious dynasty called the 'Ganga' in eleventh century AD. This dynasty ruled for more than three centuries by uniting the whole of Kalinga, within its traditional boundaries, i.e. from the Ganges to the Godavari and from the Amarakantaka to the Bay of Bengal. During this period all-round development took place in the fields of art and architecture, religion, trade and commerce, language and literature. This period may be described as the 'Golden Age' or 'Classical Age' in the history of Kalinga. The Ganga monarchs such as Chodaganga Deva, Anangabhima Deva II extended their patronage and contributed immensely to the growth and development of Kalinga's sea borne trade. During the reign of Chodaganga Deva (AD 1077-1147) the empire extended from the Ganges to the Godavari and declared his territory as Sakalotkala. The kings and officials of the Ganga empire always supervised the production of goods and prepared the rules for internal and sea borne trade. This period also marked the climax of material prosperity with the rise in agrarian products and flourishing inland and overseas trade and commerce. Thus, on the basis of what has been discussed above, it can be said that in ancient times the east coast played an important role in the maritime history of India and left the vestiges of its civilisation and oceanic enterprise fully imprinted on the annals of history. But the maritime activities of ancient Kalingas was not confined to Kalinga only or to the east coast but rather crossed the boundary of India and diffused Indian trade, commerce, culture, art, architecture, religion in countries abroad especially in the islands of Bali, Java, Sumatra, Borneo and Malaya. The people of Kalinga were the pioneers of Indian colonisation in furthering India and the Indian Archipelago.

SECTION-II

Sources

In order to understand the prevailing conditions for the location of ports, growth and development of maritime activities, trade routes and commerce, political, socio-economic and cultural relations with overseas countries, one must take into consideration the historical background, the geographical features, economic and political conditions of ancient Kalinga. Kalinga has passed through various phases of development through the centuries and its geographical setting has largely influenced its development. The geographical setting of Kalinga has also played a vital role in the progress of the maritime activities of the country. This favourable geographical situation of Kalinga in relation to the Bay of Bengal and Indian Ocean around her helped to develop international commerce as well as foreign relations. Besides, the navigable rivers like the Ganges, the Mahanadi, the Vamsadhara, the Godavari helped for hinterland trade and commerce. The hill tracts of western Orissa provided precious and semi-precious stones for overseas trade. It was easy for traders of north India to reach the ports of Kalinga without any difficulty. The littoral region provided suitable facilities to set up ports and the deltas served as natural harbours of Kalinga. From the available literary, inscriptional, numismatic and archaeological findings it is possible to draw a picture of the maritime history of Kalinga.

Literary Sources

The literary sources are the main tool for the study of maritime history of a country. The *Rig Veda*, the oldest scripture of India frequently mentions the word *Samudra*. It is difficult to say whether it refers directly to sea or broadly describes the big rivers of the *Sapta Sindhu* region[34]. But the sea is referred to in the expression of *Samudrarthah*[35] clearly shows that the Rig Vedic people had knowledge of the sea. There is a well known story of Bhujyu, the son of Tugra who was saved by the God Asvina when he was caught up in the mid sea. Bhujyu was stated to have been rescued in a boat with hundred ores. Sayanacharya narrates the story how Asvina went with their army in three ships and brought back Bhujyu. These ships are mentioned as *Nau* with 100 ores *sataritram navam atasthivasam*. Similarly the ancient texts namely the Vedas, and particularly the *Agni Purana* which give the Indian names found in the islands of Southeast Asia. The *Ramayana* and the *Mahabharata* mention about Burma, Malaya Archipelago which shows their contact during that time. The

Mahabharata also described the valour and grandeur of the Kalinga kings and the heroic part they and their people played on the side of the Kauravas[36].

It also mentions Dantakara as Dantapura, the capital of Kalinga. The *Sankha Jataka*, the *Samudra Jataka* and the *Mahajanaka Jataka*, mentions that the traders from central India used to come from Benaras to Tamralipti[37], the ancient port of Kalinga via the Ganges and the Bhagirathi from where they sailed to Southeast Asia. The Buddhist literature *Mahavamsa* mentions that Asoka sent his missionaries to Ceylon from Tamralipti. According to Buddhist legends, when Buddha's relics were divided after his death, Brahmadatta, the King of Kalinga, got for his share the left canine tooth of Buddha. The *Vassentara Jataka* mentions that Kalinga as a great commercial and industrial country, from which rice, fine cloth, ivory, diamonds and other goods were exported even to foreign countries[38]. The people of Kalinga were adventurous traders and they went by sea on big ships to distant countries. The oldest Buddhist legends describe the Kalinga kings as rulers of a civilised country. The *Mahavagga* of the *Vinaya Pitaka* reveals the name of two merchant brothers named Tapussa and Bhallika of Ukkala which is probably Utkala. However, it cannot be said that these two merchant brothers hailed from Utkala. But the probability cannot be ruled out altogether. The *Chulla Kalinga Jataka* mentions that Dantapura[39], the capital city of Kalinga was linked with many other kingdoms by good roads. Dantapura is also referred to in the *Mahagovinda Suttanta* of *Digha Nikaya*, the *Dathavamsa* and the *Uttaradhyayanasutra*. The Ceylonese Chronicles like the *Datha Dhatu Vamsa*, records that the sacred tooth-relic was taken from Dantapura to Sri Lanka. The *Chulavamsa* mentions that king Vijayabahu of Simhala (AD 1054-1109) married a Kalingan princess named Trilokasundari[40]. The *Dathavamsa* describes the name of Kalinga king Guhasiva, a contemporary of king Mahasena of Ceylon. It was he who protected the precious tooth-relic of Buddha from the foreign invaders, by sending it to Ceylon by sea through his daughter Hemamala and son-in-law Dantakumara[41]. The relic was received by king Sri Meghavarna, the son and successor of king Mahasena. The story clearly indicates that Kalinga had an efficient and well managed naval power. Otherwise king Guhasiva could not have trusted to send the most precious tooth-relic of Lord Buddha in the sea route to Ceylon in the hands of his daughter and son-in-law, for which he had to give up his life in the hands of the invaders in the battle. Kautilya's *Arthasastra*, contains useful information on sea borne trade and commerce. It describes different departments and officers concerning navigation, for example there was a department called Board of Admiralty under the war office of Chandragupta Maurya's administration. The *Arthasastra* describes the duties and responsibilities of *Navadhyaksha*, who exercises the duty of the superintendent of ships to inspect the accounts concerning navigation on the sea, the estuaries, the lakes, natural as well as artificial, and the rivers[42]. Varying duties were levied on different articles transported onboard the ships. The fisheries and passengers had also to pay taxes. The large ships are called *Mahanavah* and were provided with a *Shasaka* (captain), *Niyamaka* (steersman) and also with men who worked at the cordage and for bailing out water. The *Arthasastra* also codifies certain regulations to be followed in naval and mercantile marine affairs[43].

In the 3rd century BC Kalinga was a major power of Eastern India. Asoka conquered Kalinga eight years after his coronation, around 261 BC. Asoka invaded Kalinga apparently to gain control of trade centres and natural resources. Kalinga controlled the trade routes to the South which passed through its coastal tracts. The edicts of Asoka bear testimony to the travels of his missionaries to far off lands in Syria, Macedonia, and Egypt[44] to spread the message of Dharma and gospel of universal brotherhood from Kalingan ports. This was only possible because of efficient system of communication. There is also evidence about Asoka's son Mahendra and daughter Sanghamitra, who sailed from the famous port of Tamralipti to Ceylon. The location of Asoka's Major Rock Edicts at Dhauli and Jaugada suggests the existence of coastal route from Tamralipti to the present Andhra coast which formerly constituted southern part of Kalingan Empire[45]. Kharavela (1st century BC), the greatest ruler of Kalinga, developed his territory far and wide. It is known from the Hathigumpha inscription that Kharavela defeated the southern confederacy[46] and "caused the procurement of pearls, precious stones and jewels from the Pandya king". Kalinga's commercial importance and association with the Bay of Bengal is evident from the works of foreign travellers viz *The Periplus of the Erythraean Sea*[47], an account left behind by an unknown Greek author who visited India in the 1st century AD, the Natural History written by Pliny[48] and the Geography of Ptolemy[49] AD 150. These accounts contain useful information about the maritime history of that period. Pliny places Kalinga on the sea coast. He says "the tribes called Calingae are nearest the sea. The royal city of Calingae is Parthalis. Over their king 60,000 foot soldiers, 1000 horsemen, 700 elephants keep watch and ward in precinct of war". The Periplus Tes Exo Thalasses, compiled by Marcianus of Heraklea (between AD 250-500) also mentions the apheterion from which "all those navigating to Khryse leave"[50]. Paloura of Ptolemy is possibly identical with the village of Palur in the neighbourhood of Chilka lake[51], with its ideal geographical location near the sea and a hillock. Kalinga was an important maritime zone of Eastern India. Pliny describes Dantapura town as Dandaguda or Dandagula which is said to have stood at a distance of 625 miles south ward from the mouth of the Ganges[52]. Its king, according to Kalidasa, was the "lord of the Mahodadhi". In connection with the sea shore of Kalinga, the *Raghuvamsa*[53] (6: 57) mentions *dvipantara* (Indonesian Archipelago) from which breezes, filled with the scent of cloves, blew:

> ***anena sardham viharamburaseh tiresu talivana marmarresu dvipantaranvita lavanga puspeih apakrtasveda lava marudbhih***

Legends and local traditions of Java mention that '20,000' families were sent to Java by the prince of Kling. The Javanese inscriptions, dated between the 9th and 11th century, refer to foreign merchants and captains of ships. These foreigners include the Kalingas, the Arrays, the Simhalese, the Dravidians, the Pandikiras, and the Khemars. In the inscriptions the Klings or Kalinga people were clearly distinguished from people of other parts of India. Kalinga was so famous for maritime activity that Kalidasa referred in the *Raghuvamsa* to the king of Kalinga as the *Lord of Ocean*. Kalinga has also been described as the mistress of all islands in the Kalinga sea (Kalingodresu) in the *Aryamanjusrimulakalpa*[54], a text on Mahayana Buddhism. Apparently the modern Bay of Bengal was known as the Kalinga sea during ancient times, which was dominated by the maritime activities of Kalinga. The

Dasakumaracharita of Dandin mentions that the Chinese travellers Fahien and Hiuen Tsang visited the Binduvagiri temple situated at Tamralipti and subsequently the temple was destroyed by the river Rupanarayana[55]. The *Kathasaritsagara* suggests that Tamralipti was the main port for Chinese trade and commerce at that time[56]. The Arab and Persian writers of the 9th and 10th centuries AD throw valuable light on the sea borne trade and sea ports of Kalinga. Ibn Khurdah-bin, Ibn Rusta and the anonymous author of the *Hadud-al-Alam* mention the main places and ports of Orissa under the Bhaumakaras namely Mahisya (Midnapore), Jharkharo (hilly tracts), Orissa (Orissa proper), Ganjam (South Orissa) and Andhra (a part of the Telugu speaking territory) and the main ports were Kalinganagar, Ganjam, Keylkan, Al-Lava and Nubin of which last three have not been identified[57]. The *Madala Panji,* the Jagannath Temple chronicle, also bears some information on the maritime history of Kalinga. It appears that people from Greece, Rome, China, Persia came to Kalinga for trade. These people were termed as *Yavanas* or *Mlechhas* in the chronicle[58]. Orissa's cultural and commercial contact with China seems to have continued from early times to a later period. The *Chu-fan-chi* of Chau-Ju-Kua[59] written in AD 1225-26 refers to Kia-ling sea going vessels (i.e. Kalinga ships) and their system of trade organisation. Chau-Ju-Kua mentions two types of ships plying between Kalinga and Canton. The *Yuktikalpataru* a compilation attributed to Bhoja Narapati, gives the description of ships and narrates the techniques of construction, etc[60].

Inscriptional and Numismatic Sources

Numismatic sources amply testify to the overseas contacts of Kalinga. As pointed out earlier coastal navigation came into prominence under the Mauryas. The occurrence of punch marked coins and the Northern Black Polished ware (NBP) (Fig.1) from Gedige and Anuradhapura in Sri Lanka datable to the Pre and Mauryan period 600-450 BC, is of great importance. Unique type of punch marked coins with ship symbol are obtained from the earliest levels at Chandraketugarh[61] of West Bengal. In northern Sri Lanka a single mast boat coin in conjunction with a donatory inscription of 1st century BC is found. Similar archaeological finds are found in coastal Kalinga which show her ancient trade links with different countries. The excavations conducted at the stupa mound of Kalingapatnam by Bhattacharya in 1928 and subsequently by the Archaeological Survey of India between 1977 and 1979 yielded a brick wharf[62]. The wharf suggest that Kalingapatnam served as a port during 3rd century BC[63] and had contacts with Southeast Asian countries. Another Buddhist site adjacent to Kalingapatnam is Salihundam which also served as an emporium as some of the Roman coins of Tiberius[64] (AD 14-37) were found during excavations. Similarly the excavations conducted at Bavikonda and Thotlakonda in the district of Visakhapatnam reveal Roman coins of Augustus (31 BC-AD 14) and Tiberius (AD 14-37)[65]. Kalinga as a maritime power can be established from the coins issued by different ancient dynasties, viz. the Satavahanas and the Salankayanas. It is because some portions of Kalinga were under their sovereignty. To cite examples, the Satavahanas issued coins with ship motifs. This type of coins were issued by the King Vasisthiputra Pulumavi, the illustrious son and successor of Gautamiputra Satakarni[66]. These coins are made of lead and are circular in shape and depict both double (Pl. I a-b) mast and are single mast ships anchored in mid sea. Gautamiputra Yajnasri (AD 184-213), his successor, also continued this type more prominently and are known from Buddham, Vidyadharapuram, Guntur, Chebrolu and other places on the east coast of India[67]. A unique coin now in the British Museum collection shows the device clearly and what is more interesting is the portrayal of cargo vessels approaching the anchored ship. The double mast ship type coins were continued to be issued by the Salankayanas (Vijaya Devavarman, *circa* 280-293 AD) who succeeded the Satavahanas in the Vengi country[68]. The Salankayanas were also powerful kings having trade contacts. They furthered the cause of Buddhism as well as Brahminical religion beyond the shores. Samudra Gupta, the Gupta king took the east coast route and subdued all the then powerful kingdoms, for a brief period. Bull and double mast ship type copper coins were also issued by the Pallavas of Pre-Mahendra line[69]. Punch marked coins with boat motifs were also collected from the excavations of Chandraketugarh and other sites of ancient Kalinga which are similar to boat symbol coins issued by the Satavahana kings. Such coins were also found on the present Andhra coast. This confirms brisk maritime activity of Kalinga. Boat symbols have also continued on the cast copper coins on which vessel is depicted with a long oar and boatman[70]. The ship symbol is noticed on the terracotta sealings and in the graffiti on pottery found from the coastal regions, as well as the trade centres along the Ganges. Similar type of objects from Vaisali depict a boat with a prow, stern, oar, passenger decks and a female standing in the boat[71]. The Roman gold coins of Gordian, Constantine and other rulers found at Bamanghati and Tamralipti show evidence of contact with the Romans[72].

Besides coins the terracotta seals of Bangarh, Hadipur and Tamralipti Museum which were examined by B.N. Mukherjee (1989) are inscribed in Kharosthi-Brahmi script of early centuries of Christian era indirectly indicate the maritime trade with other countries. The vessel on the seal of Bangarh is a bowl shaped sailing boat filled with corn and the bows at both ends are decorated with *Makara-mukhas*[73]. A seal found at Chandraketugarh, depicts a boat with a single mast and bears Kharosthi-Brahmi inscription. The vessel resembles the ship motif on the coin of Gautamiputra Yajnasri Satakarni and the boat motif painted in the caves of Ajanta[74]. A galaxy of Buddhist teachers like Buddhaghosa, Buddhadatta, Bodhi Dharma (who flourished between AD 470 and 520) of Vajrabodhi (Tantrik Buddhism), Dinnage (Nyaya), Vinitaruchi faith took Buddhism to the Far-Eastern countries through the sea route from the East coast of India. The Far Eastern countries assumed great importance and as Lokesh Chandra[75] puts it, it was not Bengal, Orissa or Assam but Oddiyana meaning girdle i.e. Manimekhalai and Kanchi and Andhrapatha which were the chief centres transmitting Tantrika Buddhism to Indonesia and China. Ship symbol occurs on terracotta sealings from Central Thailand. Ship type coins of bronze with a cow or bull on the reverse were found from Klong Thom and Khuan Lukpad which were perhaps in circulation amongst the merchants[76]. A stone seal from Nakorn Pathom shows a two masted ship[77]. Tin used for minting coins, particularly during post Mauryan dynastic times issued by the Satavahana rulers seems to have come from Thailand (Phuket province) so also the Malayan gold and tin. Items that were exported from India included ivory, carnelian seals (a pendant of leaping lion from Ban Don Ta Phet), glass beads, and knobbed Bronze bowls of Orissa-Bengal origin. The extensive distribution of carnelian beads and seals of Indian origin in Southeast Asia shows the impact of organised maritime network between Indian ports of the Eastern coast, Southeast Asia, Sri Lanka and the Mediterranean world[78] right from early centuries of Christian era.

According to the Hathigumpha inscription, Maharaja Kharavela of Kalinga captured the market town of Pithunda, an ancient metropolis, and a port town on the East coast near Machilipatnam. Sea faring merchants were travelling by boat from Champa (Kampuchea) to Pithunda even during the time of Mahavira[79]. Kudura and Kantakossyla were also important centres mentioned by Ptolemy in the country of Maisolia. King Kharavela speaks of even a confederacy of the Tamil countries whom he confronted and defeated. The maritime activity led to extensive religious and cultural expansion along the Eastern coast and also brought Sri Lankan port towns closer. In the inscriptions of first-second century AD there are references to a master mariner residing at *Mahanagaparvata*[80] (Guntupalli) and Ghantasala. The Indo-Roman trade of this period is well known and the port towns of ancient Kalinga were humming with activity. Mahayana Buddhism through its sects spread to coastal towns of south like Mailai (Mylapur), Kanchi, Kaveripoompatinam and Sri Lanka. The Mon race now known as Tailang in Burma are believed to have come from Telingana or Kalinga on the East coast. The script of the oldest inscription found on a pillar in Mon resembles the early Pallava[81]. The earliest Tailang script is identified with the Vengi script. According to Burmese tradition the Salankayanas of Vengi were responsible for the spread of Buddhism in Burma[82]. The inscription of the time of Maharaja Mulavarma, the ruler of Malaya, refers to a Master Mariner Mahanavika named Buddhagupta, a native of *Raktamarttika Mahavihara*[83] (Rangamati district Murshidabad, West Bengal) going to Malaya Peninsula in 5th century AD. Again it is exceedingly interesting to note that a 7th century AD inscription in Kavi language and script of Java was found in Mexico which referred to a *Mahanavika* Usaluna. It appears that the *Mahanavikas* from East coast had undertaken extensive sea faring activity right from 2nd to 7th centuries AD. They were largely followers of Buddhism[84]. Historians have the impression that during the Pallava rule, south India had trade relations with Indonesia. But recently discovered terracotta religious tablets from Java, Bali, Borneo mention that the rulers of Kalinga and neighbouring provinces had established their capitals in those islands. Even the religious leaders and Brahmins were invited to those islands to spread Sanskrit and Indian culture. The names of kings, culture, religion and language might have reached to these far off islands from the Kalinga coast[85]. The inscriptions of Madhava Verma (AD 620-670) of the Sailodbhava dynasty embodies to this fact. He was also ruling over some parts of Kalinga and the islands under the supremacy of the king Sashanka. When Harshavardhana captured the territory of Sashanka perhaps Madhava Verma ruled his region independently. Java, Bali and Borneo islands were also under the supremacy of the Sailodbhavas. The inscription of Jaya Verma discovered at Funan of Indonesia which mentions Jaya Verma's wife Prabhabati was born in the Pushyabhuti dynasty. Another pillar inscription found at Borneo mentioned king Muja Verma donated one thousand cows to the Agnihotri Brahmanas. After receiving the boon from the king, those Brahmanas settled in the same island. After examining the scripts of these inscriptions it was found that similar type of scripts were used in Kalinga during 9th-10th century AD. It seems that probably the rulers of those islands invited the Brahmanas of Kalinga and permitted them to settle down in these islands. Besides, a few inscriptions found at Anuradhapura of Sri Lanka and Rameswaram on the east coast of India are in Oriya script. According to Kunha, the early Pali language of Ceylonese Chronicles originated from Kalinga and was brought to Ceylon from Magadha. Probably under the influence of the local language, it got changed into the present form[86]. The textual data for the early historical period is not adequate to give a clear picture about the role of Orissa in the navigation of the Indian Ocean. Furthermore, there is a complete lack of Oriya literary sources prior to the 15th century AD. The identification of places mentioned in the classical texts and Chinese sources, as for example Paloura, Che-li-ta-lo etc., are problematic and not out of controversy. On the whole, the literary and epigraphical data, discussed above are limited and do not provide conclusive evidence. In such a situation, the archaeological and art evidences are of paramount importance.

Archaeological Evidences

Orissa is rich in archaeological remains. Earlier works done in Orissa indicated its potentiality. However neither problem oriented studies have been carried out nor rich sites have been excavated. Since V. Ball[87] picked up the first prehistoric tools in Orissa in the last century, several prehistoric sites have been reported which provide the idea about the progress of society from hunter food-gatherer stage to settled life and food production. The excavations of Neolithic sites of Kuchai and Baidyapur in Mayurbhanj district gave positive evidence of the use of polished shouldered axes, rice and cord impressed pottery in the Neolithic age. In view of the technological affinities of shouldered adzes with those of Southeast Asia, some scholars suggested that Orissa had maritime connections with Southeast Asia from Neolithic period. But the possibility of introduction of shouldered adzes into India through land route via north-eastern India cannot be ruled out[88]. The excavations at Golbai on the left bank of Malaguri river, a tributary of the Daya which falls into the Chilka lake in Khurda district has provided evidence of Copper Age remains and a sequence of cultures from Neolithic to the Iron age[89]. The initial spade work at a place called Sankarjang in Angul district also revealed the cultural stratum of Chalcolithic period (Carbon date 2590 $\pm$ 60 B.P. = 600 BC), it concluded that barcelt from Sankarjang was the earliest musical instrument in India and it resembles the one found from Vietnam[90]. Recent archaeological discoveries in Sri Lanka, Indonesia, Thailand, Vietnam, Burma, etc. have thrown new light on India's maritime connections with those countries. Archaeological excavations in Anuradhapura proves the introduction of Indian cultural elements including Buddhism into Sri Lanka even before the days of Asoka. Excavations in Sembiran in North-eastern Bali[91] yielded Indian Rouletted ware, one rim sherd of Wheeler's Arikamedu type 10, a body sherd with Kharosthi characters and hundreds of glass beads. These evidences suggest that Bali and India had cultural interactions about the beginning of the Christian era. Scientific analysis of the samples of Rouletted ware from Arikamedu (India), Anuradhapura (Sri Lanka) and Sembiran (Bali) are very similar. Rouletted wares have also been reported in Kopak Kendal and Cibutak in north-west Java (Fig. 2). The material evidence brought to light from Don Ta Phet[92] in Thailand includes semiprecious stone and glass beads, knobbed ware, bronze vessels, etc. The knobbed ware pottery was first identified at Sisupalgarh[93] and this occurs at several sites in Eastern India and the Ganges valley. These evidences indicate the contact between Eastern India and Thailand and probably also with Orissa in view of the occurrence of Knobbed ware pottery and rich deposits of semiprecious stones in Western Orissa in Kalahandi, Bolangir, Boud and Sambalpur areas. It is interesting that an Indian ivory comb (dated 1st-3rd century AD) has been recovered from Chansen in central Thailand. The *Srivatsa* motif on it, is analogous to the motif found in the art of Khandagiri, Udayagiri caves and the Hathigumpha inscription of Kharavela (1st century BC). Later on *Srivatsa* motif became fairly common in coins from Oc-Eo in Vietnam to Arakan[94]. Kharosthi inscriptions discovered in Orissa coast from Manikapatna[95], Thailand, Bali and possible depiction of a horse on bronze bowl from Southeast indicate maritime contacts of Orissa with Kharoshti using horse merchants in lower Bengal and Southeast Asia. B.N. Mukharjee believes that activities of the Yueh-Chih horse dealers in Southeast Asia are preserved in an engraving on a drum from an Indonesian island, representing two persons clad in Yueh-Chih dress along with a horse. The prolific occurrence of NBP ware at Amaravati and Dharanikota[96] excavations (1974-75) in such early contexts has opened up fresh grounds of study. In recent years, apart from the above evidences from Dhanyakataka stupa, some sites along the coastal Tamil Nadu have yielded positive evidences. It is of great significance to note that the NBP ware and Punch marked coins were reported from the earliest levels of some Buddhist sites—specially Gedige and Anuradhapura citadel in Sri Lanka. In the light of these evidences it can be recalled with profit the Buddhist legends enshrining certain important events. According to the *Mahavamsa*[97], the Mauryan emperor Asoka came to despatch the *Bodhivriksha* (Bodhi tree) sappling to Sri Lanka in a highly religious manner. He descended into the water up to the neck and set the Bodhi tree on the ship and stood with folded hands on the shore. Again, the *Mahavamsa* narrates that King Duttagamini of Sri Lanka (177-101 BC) celebrated with pomp the lying of great stupa inviting many monks and kings from foreign lands (one Mahadeva from Pallava Bhogga and Yona Mahadharmarakshita from Alasandra, i.e. Alexandria)[98]. The *Vinaya* texts and the Jatakas inform us that merchants from Sahajati, Kausambi, Varanasi, Pataliputra and Champa brought their goods to Tamralipti for trade with South Asia[99]. The sea port towns of great importance are Tamralipti (Ganges) and Kanthi on lower Bengal coast, Kainapara (Konark), Dosarene

(Dhauli), Kalingae (Kalingapatnam) of coastal Kalinga. It is therefore becoming clear that the first ceramic, viz the NBP ware with Punch marked silver coins reached South east Indian port towns and farther beyond Sri Lanka by the middle of the 3rd century BC along with the Buddhist monks and mercantile guilds *Sreshthis* and *Nigamas*, who were converts to this popular casteless religious faith. A momentous discovery was recently made by B.N. Mukherjee[100] who recognised for the first time, numerous Kharosthi inscriptions on pot, plaques and seals earlier found from the excavations at Chandraketugarh and nearby places like Bangarh and Hadipur in the district 24 Paraganas of West Bengal. The terracotta seals from Bangarh and Chandraketugarh display sea going vessels containing corn flanked by symbols like Conch and Taurine. Such vessel types are known as *Sasyadidhrta Sthali*, a bowl shaped vessel filled with corn. The other one of same size vessel has legend in Kharosthi-Brahmi script referring to *Tridesayatra*, meaning a voyage to three countries or directions. Yet another seal from Chandraketugarh reveals a type of vessel called *Trapyaka* belonging to the wealth earning Tasvadaja family. It may be noted that *Trapyaka* is a type of ship mentioned also in the Periplus and the *Angavijja*. The above vessel types as well as flanking symbols recall the Satavahana ships. It appears that the Kharosthi script using tradesmen settled in the lower Gangetic valley of Bengal in good numbers during third to first centuries BC mixed up with the Brahmi using local merchants and developed a mixture type Kharosthi-Brahmi writing in North-western Prakrit expressions. A unique sea going vessel, single mast type with an eye socket symbol engraved thereon indicated an early trade contact with Egypt as well[101].

The term "*Suvarnadvipa*" found in Sanskrit and Pali literatures refer to Southeast Asia and the *Milindapanho* describes this as a land of ports where ships congregated. Recent archaeological excavations in the main land and peninsular Southeast Asian sites like Chansen, Don Ta Phet in west central Thailand, Myanmar, Oc-Eo in Mekong delta, Beikthano and Taungthaman, Sembiran on the Northeast coast of Bali in Indonesia, revealed certain important objects such as glass and carnelian etched beads intaglios and seals, etc[102]. Sembiran on the North coast of Bali excavated between 1987-89 yielded Rouletted ware and most significantly an inscribed sherd with three characters in Kharosthi and Brahmi script have been found atleast in four important coastal sites in Southeast Asia. The use of Kharosthi and Brahmi with typical symbols like *Srivasta*, conch and Sun clearly point to the maritime contacts with the Indian subcontinent during this period[103]. In this trade Sri Lanka had also been at the receiving end. Horses from North-western India were sent by the Sea through ancient Kalinga coast right from the Mauryan times. Religious involvement provided a cohesion and inspiration to the trading community and through these channels early Buddhism and Brahmanical religious cults found their way to the Southeast Asian countries[104]. The excavations at Kalingapatnam revealed a fortified settlement and remains of a brick wharf[105]. Excavations at Khalkatapatna has revealed the existence of a brick jelly floor which might have served as a loading and unloading platform, along with some Chinese Celadon ware, Chinese porcelain and glazed chocolate ware of Arabian origin. Other ceramic ware unearthed are the dark grey and red slipped indigenous ware[106]. The other important finds from excavations were one complete and one fragment of Chinese copper coin of 14th century AD. The circular copper coin had a square perforation in the centre and had legend in Chinese character[107]. Early historical period, Indian Rouletted ware, fragments of amphora, red-glazed ware and Puri-Kushana coins and a Kharosthi inscription were found during excavations at Manikapatna[108]. In the upper levels large quantity of Chinese Celadon ware and a damaged Chinese copper coin with a square perforation in the centre were collected. These findings indicate that Manikapatna had close trade contacts with Africa, Rome, Ceylon and China[109]. The explorations at Palur and the adjacent areas have yielded red ware bowls and a fragmentary terracotta dabber. The pottery was assigned to 12th-14th century AD[110]. Besides, there are some early medieval temples in the region which are buried up to the plinth due to siltation. The recent excavations at Palur revealed the antiquities datable to 3rd century BC to 14th century AD. Tamralipti excavations yielded copper coins, terracotta figurines of Sunga period, Rouletted ware, Red Polished ware and sprinkler. Gold coins of Gordian, Constantine and other Roman Kings are also found at Bamanghati and Tamralipti which show contact with the Roman world[111]. The Kharosthi-Brahmi script on the terracotta seals from Bangarh, Hadipur and Tamralipti suggests that certain community of people migrated from the north-western region to the territory of lower

Bengal[112]. Similar inscriptions were also noticed in Thailand and Bali further indicating that the traders went from Kalinga to far off countries.

Art

Sources of the history of ancient Kalinga are not as vocal as expected regarding its glorious maritime past. However, traces of evidences are found reflected in the works of literature like Puranas and poems; novels and short stories of various contemporary and subsequent writers. A study of the art of Khandagiri and Udayagiri caves reveals the use of West Asian decorative elements such as honey suckle, acanthus, stepped merlons, winged animals, etc. Some of the pilasters facing the doorways of the cave of Anantagumpha have *ghata* bases ornamented in the Hellenistic fashion, very similar in treatment to vessels found from excavations in Western India. A Yavana guard is shown on the pilaster of the cave in the upper storey of the Ranigumpha. The kilted foreigner is in boots and wears a fillet on the forehead, while a sheathed sword hangs from the left side[113]. The huge Bell capital from Bhubaneswar imitated from Asokan columns, also shows West Asian motifs in its ornamentation[114]. Buddhism played a significant role in the relations between Orissa and Southeast Asia. Scholars, so far have discussed Indian influence in terms of the Gupta, the Pala and the Pallava art. Comparative studies of Buddhist art of Orissa and Southeast Asia show several common elements and striking affinities. Excavations conducted in Orissa at Ratnagiri, Udayagiri and Lalitagiri have brought to light masterpieces of Buddhist art. The Buddha heads from these centres and those from central Java share common traits of massive form, sensitive modelling and spiritual expressions[115]. The Javanese Boddhisattvas from Chandi Mendut have their attributes placed on long lotuses in the style distinctive of the Lalitagiri figures of Orissa. A sculptural frieze collected from the vicinity of the Brahmesvara temple, Bhubaneswar and now preserved in the Orissa State Museum depicts a boat carrying elephants (Pl. II). Another slab depicting *Mahisasura Mardini* with a boat motif carved on the pedestal lying under a banyan tree near the Brahmesvara temple is interesting. In the temple of Konark a four headed *Martanda Bhairava* is shown dancing in ecstasy on a boat (Pl. III). An interesting sculpture supposed to have been collected from Konark and now preserved in the Indian Museum, Calcutta depicts a boat being rowed by four persons. A royal personage sits inside the boat. There is also an elephant on the boat. On the *Bhogamandapa* of the famous Jagannath temple at Puri there is a magnificent representation of a boat in chlorite stone. Perhaps the most faithful representation of an oceanic vessel is found in the sculptures of Borobudur in Java. As Kalinga's relation with Java was very intimate, it is likely that ancient Oriyas used such ships for their voyage to Java. The numerous depictions on sculptures and paintings discussed above reflect the sea-faring activities and the maritime pride of ancient Orissa. The most immediate proof of the glorious and eventful maritime past lies in the annual conduct of the *Kartika Purnima* and *Boita Bandana*, which have been in vogue among the Oriya speaking people from time immemorial till this day.

SECTION-III

Approach

While much has been said about the maritime history of Kalinga, some of the basic questions such as the identification of ancient ports, classification of trade routes, pattern of trade, ship and boat- building techniques, current and wind patterns, the natural forces like riverine character, sedimentation, and tectonic movements leading to decline of maritime activities and similar other questions have not been seriously probed into by the earlier authorities working in the field. The literary texts no doubt reveal a number of flourishing ports of ancient Kalinga which served the purpose of the sea going people of India. But excepting a few, identification of the rest of the port towns still remained in desideratum. An attempt has been made hence to identify some of them and to locate some others. The classification of land and water routes, pattern of trade, exchange of articles and the currency system that was prevalent then have also been dealt with. Adequate attention has been paid to analyse the ship and boat-building, and navigation techniques which were followed by the ancient seafarers. The terms boat, vessel and ship have been used interchangeably. Construction techniques, decoration, preservation of boat, navigational pattern, knowledge of current and wind pattern have been discussed in broad detail. The figures showing the current and wind patterns in the Kalinga coast amply justify the ship-building techniques followed there. But the most important aspect of the study is the factors leading to the decline of the ports and maritime activities of Kalinga. Although it has been generally attributed to the decline in long distance trade, yet our approach to the problem is to give more thrust on the natural factors like riverine character sedimentation and tectonic movements, in order to account for the decline of ports and maritime activities of Kalinga. The conclusions arrived at through the scientific analysis of such natural forces are more acceptable than the traditionally accepted theories.

References

1. *Vanaparva, (Mahabharata)*, CXIV. 4.
2. McCrindle, J.W., 1985 *Ancient India as described by Ptolemy*, (reprint), Delhi, 114.
3. *Matsya Purana*, Vol. CXXCIV, 12.
4. *Udyogaparva*, XXIII, 708; *Dronaparva*, IXX. 7.
5. Devi, G., 1992 "Tamralipti: The Port of Ancient Orissa", *Orissa Review*, Vol. XLIX, (4): 50-52 .
6. Mahtab, H.K., 1981 *The History of Orissa*, Vol. I, Cuttack, 76-108.
7. Sahu, N.K., 1964, Utkal University *History of Orissa*, Vol. I, Cuttack, 30.
8. Pargiter, F.E., 1913 *Purana Text of the Dynasties of the Kali Age*, London, 25-26.
9. Das, M.N., 1977 "Ancient and Medieval Empires and Kingdoms", *Sidelights on History and Culture of Orissa*, (ed.) M.N.Das, Cuttack, 86-103.
10. Shamasastri, R., 1967 *Kautilya's Arthasastra*, Mysore, 142-145.
11. Jayaswal, K.P., 1983 "The Hathigumpha Inscription of Kharavela", *Epigraphica Indica*, (reprint), Vol. XX: 71-89.
12. Das, M.N., 1977 "Ancient and Medieval Empires and Kingdoms", *Sidelights on History and Culture of Orissa*, (ed.) M.N. Das, Cuttack, 86-103.
13. Das, M.N., 1977 *op. cit.*, 90.
14. Senart, E., 1981 "The Inscriptions in the Caves at Nasik", *Epigraphica Indica*, (reprint), Vol. VIII: 59-95.
15. Panigrahi, K.C., 1981 *History of Orissa*, Calcutta, 39-40.
16. Sahu, N.K., *et al.*, 1981 *History of Orissa*, Cuttack, 56.
17. Ganguly, D.K., 1975 *Historical Geography of Ancient Orissa*, Calcutta, 150-154.

18. Das, D.N., 1977 *The Early History of Kalinga*, Calcutta, 84-90.
19. Das, M.N., 1977 *op. cit.*, 92.
20. Behera, S.C., 1964 "Origin of the Mathara Dynasty of Kalinga", *Orissa Historical Research Journal*, Vol. XII, (2): 57-59.
21. Sahu, N.K., 1964 *Utkal University History of Orissa*, Cuttack, Vol. I, 422-30.
22. Gai, G.S., et al., 1981 "Inscriptions of the Early Gupta Kings", *Corpus Inscriptionum Indicarum*, (reprint), Vol. III: 203-220.
23. Gerini, G.E., 1974 *Researches on Ptolemy's Geography of Eastern Asia*, Delhi, 743.
24. Das, D.N., 1977 *The Early History of Kalinga*, Calcutta, 247-58.
25. Chatterji, B.R., 1928 *Indian Cultural influence in Cambodia*, Calcutta.
26. Ghoshal, R.K., 1985 Dhavalapeta plates of Maharaja Umavarman, *Epigraphica Indica*, (reprint), Vol. XXVI: 132-135.
27. *Raghuvamsa*, Canto VI, Verse. 54.
28. Burnell, A.C., 1878 *Elements of South Indian Palaeography*, London, 53-56.
29. Dani, A.H., 1986 *Indian Palaeography*, New Delhi, 230.
30. Majumdar, R.C., 1955 *Ancient Indian Colonies in the Far East*, Vol. II, Calcutta, 227.
31. Rajaguru, S.N., 1993 "Prachin Abhilekhare Samudra Yatrara Suchana", *Sagar O Sahitya*, (Oriya) (ed.) K.S. Behera, Cuttack, 55-59.
32. Rajaguru, S.N., 1958 *History of the Gangas*, Vol. I, Bhubanewsar, 4.
33. Das, M.N., 1977 *op. cit.*, 95.
34. Ritti, S.H., 1988 "Shipping in Ancient India", *Marine Archaeology of Indian Ocean Countries*, (ed.) S.R.Rao, NIO, Goa, 5-7.
35. *Rig Veda*, Vol. VII. 49-2.
36. Banerjee, R.D., 1930 *History of Orissa*, Vol. I, Calcutta, ,43-58.
37. Law, B.C., 1967 *Historical Geography of Ancient India*, Paris, 310-11.
38. Rao, R.S., 1971-72 "The Historical Geography of Kalinga", *Journal of the Andhra Historical Research Society*, Vol. XXXII, (I-IV), 2.
39. Cowell, E.B., (tr.) 1895-1907 *The Jatakas*, Vol. III (301): 1-5.
40. Das, M.N., 1977 "Kalinga and Simhala: A Study in Ancient Relations", *Sidelights on History and Culture of Orissa*, (ed.) M.N.Das, Cuttack, 122-131.
41. Das, M.N., 1977 "Ancient and Medieval Empires and Kingdoms", *Sidelights on History and Culture of Orissa*, (ed.) M.N.Das, Cuttack, 86-103.
42. Das, D.N., 1977 *The Early History of Kalinga*, Calcutta, 247-262.
43. Shamasastry, R., 1967 *Kautilya's Arthasastra*, Mysore, 142-145.
44. Mookerji, R.K., 1912 *A History of Indian Shipping*, Bombay, 283.

45. Dikshit, K.N. & Pandeya, R.G., 1978 "Ancient Maritime Contacts of West Bengal - Literary and Archaeological Evidences", *L.N.Mishra Commemoration Volume*, (ed.) U. Thakur, Bodhagaya, 232-237.
46. Panigrahi, K.C., 1981 *History of Orissa*, Calcutta, 22-38.
47. Schoff, W.H., 1974 *The Periplus of the Erythraean Sea*, Delhi, 323.
48. Melmoth, W., (tr.) 1945 Pliny's Natural History, Vol. II, London, 20-21.
49. McCrindle, J.W., 1985 *Ancient India as Described by Ptolemy*, (reprint), Delhi 468.
50. Mukherjee, B.N., 1981 "The Relevance of the Periplous Tes Exo Thalasses to the History of Orissa", *Journal of the Orissa Research Society*, Vol. I, 8-9.
51. McCrindle, J.W., 1985 *Ancient India as described by Ptolemy*, (reprint), Delhi, 63-70.
52. Cunningham, A., 1963 *The Ancient Geography of India*, Varanasi, 489.
53. Nandargikar, G.R., (ed. & tr.) 1897 *Raghuvamsa*, Bombay, VI. 54.
54. Sastri, T.G., 1920-25 (ed.) *Aryamanjusrimulkalpa*, 3 Vols. Trivandrum, 168.
55. Law, B.C., 1967 *Historical Geography of Ancient India*, Paris, 310-311.
56. Kar, B., 1973 *Prachina Utkalara Nau Vanijya*, (Oriya), Cuttack, 307.
57. Panigrahi, K.C., 1981 *History of Orissa*, Calcutta, 468.
58. Mohanty, A.B., 1969 *Madala Panji*, Utkal University Publications, Bhubaneswar.
59. Ray, H.P., 1990-91 "The Identity of Huang Chih: An Ancient Indian Kingdom in intimate contact with Han China", *Indian Historical Reviews*, Vol. XVII, (1-2): 1-34.
60. Sastri, I.C., (ed.) 1917 *Yuktikalpataru*, Calcutta, 223-230.
61. Ray, H.P., 1991 "In Search of Suvarnabhumi: Early sailing Networks in the Bay of Bengal", *Bulletin of the Indo-Pacific Prehistory Association* -10: 357-365.
62. Sree Padma, B., 1991 "Kalingapatnam port through the Ages", *Recent Advances in Marine Archaeology*, (ed.) S.R.Rao, NIO, Goa, 73-74.
63. Rao, S.R., 1987 *Progress and Prospects of Marine Archaeology in India*, NIO, Goa, 68.
64. Subramanyam, R., 1964 *Salihundam*, Department of Archaeology and Museums, Government of Andhra Pradesh, Hyderabad.
65. Sree Padma, B., 1993 "Coins and Maritime Trade of Andhra Country" *Studies in South Indian Coins*, (ed.) A.V.Narasimha Murthy, Vol. III, Madras, 97-100.
66. Sarma, I.K., 1980 *Coinage of the Satavahana Empire,* Delhi, 101.
67. *Ibid.*
68. Sarma, I.K., 1989 "Salankayana Coins from Ghantasala, Dist. Krishna,

Andhra Pradesh", *Ajaya Sri, Recent Studies in Indology*, (ed.) D. Handa, Vol. I, Delhi, 313-317.

69. Sarma, I.K., 1992 *South Indian Coinage, A Review of Recent Discoveries*, Madras, 22.

70. Sarmadhikari, R.K., 1984 "Some Observations on the coins of East Bengal", *Indian Museum Bulletin*, Vol. XIX: 38-47.

71. Ray, H.P., 1991 "In Search of Suvarnabhumi: Early Sailing networks in the Bay of Bengal" *Bulletin of the Indo-Pacific Prehistory Association* -10: 357-365.

72. Warmington, E.H., 1974 *The Commerce Between the Roman Empire and India*, Delhi, 300.

73. Sarma, I.K., 1991 "Rare Evidences on Maritime Trade on the Bengal Coast of India" *Recent Advances in Marine Archaeology* (ed.) S.R.Rao, Goa, 38-40.

74. Schlingloff, D., 1988 *Studies in the Ajanta Painting*, Delhi, 195-218.

75. Chandra, L., 1980 "Oddiyana - A New Interpretations", *International Journal of Dravidian Linguistic*, Trivandrum, 127.

76. Higham, C., 1989 *The Archaeology of Mainland Southeast Asia*, Cambridge, 207.

77. Ray, H.P., 1989 "Early Maritime Contacts between South and Southeast Asia", *Journal of South Asian Studies*, Vol. XX, (1): 47-52.

78. Glover, I.C., 1990 Early Trade between India and Southeast Asia: A link in the development of a World Trading System, *Occasional Paper No. 16*, The University of Hull, London, 1-45.

79. Sarma, I.K. 1990 "Ancient Andhra Ports, Religious Centres and Sea-Faring", *Journal of Marine Archaeology*, Vol. I: 19-23.

80. Subramanian, K.R., 1932 *Buddhist Remains in Andhra and History of Andhra between 225 to 610 A.D.*, Madras, 88-135.

81. Sarma, I.K., 1988 *Studies in Early Buddhist Monuments and Brahmi Inscriptions of Andhradesa*, Nagpur, 72-85.

82. Thakur, U., 1970 "A Historical Survey of the Elements of Hindu culture in Burma", *Indian's contribution to World Thought and Culture, Vivekananda Commemoration Volume*, (ed.) Lokesh Chandra, Madras, 437-441.

83. Majumdar, R.C., 1986 *Suvarnadvipa*, Vol. I, (reprint), Delhi, 82-83.

84. Mitra, D., 1971 *Buddhist Monuments*, Calcutta, 236.

85. Chaudhuri, K.K., 1990 "South India's Contact with China: A study in the Earliest Phase from Chinese Sources", *U.Thakur Felicitation Volume*, (eds.) G. Kuppuram, K. Kumudamani, New Delhi, 217-221.

86. Rajaguru, S.N., 1993 "Prachin Abhilekhare Samudra Yatrara Suchana", *Sagar O Sahitya*, (Oriya) (ed.) K.S. Behera, Cuttack, 55-59.

87. Ball, V., 1876 "On stone implements found in the Tributary States of Orissa", *Proceedings of Asiatic Society of Bengal*, 122-23.

88. Behera, K.S., 1991 "Trade and Patterns of Commerce in Orissa (700 - 1200 AD)", *Utkal Historical Research Journal*, Vol. II, 122.

89. Sinha, B.K., 1993 "Excavations at Golbai Sasan, Dist. Puri, Orissa", *Puratattva-23*: 48-50.

90. Yule, P., & et al., 1987 "Sankarjang - A Metals period burial site in the Dhenkanal Uplands of Orissa", *South Asian Archaeology*, (ed.) M. Taddei, Rome, 581-84.

91. Ardika, I.W., & Bellwood, P., 1991 "Sembiran: the beginnings of Indian contact with Bali", *Antiquity*, Vol. LXV, (247): 221-232.

92. Brandtner, M., 1988-89 "Archaeological explorations around Bhubaneswar", *MANAV, Journal of Anthropological Society of Orissa*, Vol. III: 231-250.

93. Lal, B.B., 1984 "Excavations at Sisupalgarh", *Ancient India No. 5*, (reprint), Archaeological Survey of India, Delhi, 62-105.

94. Behera, K.S., 1994 "Maritime Contacts of Orissa—Literary and archaeological evidence", *Utkal Historical Research Journal*, Vol. V: 55-70.

95. Pradhan, D., 1991 "Manikapatna: Ancient port city on Chilika", *Kalinga, The Brave Souvenir*, Bhubaneswar, 8-10.

96. Ghosh, A., (ed.) 1989 *An Encyclopaedia of Indian Archaeology*, Vol. II, New Delhi, 15-16.

97. *Mahavamsa*, Vol. XIX, 6 & XIX, 11-12.

98. Litvinsky, B.A., 1970 "India and Soviet Central Asia", *India's contribution to World Thought and Culture, Vivekananda Commemoration Volume*, (ed.) Lokesh Chandra, Madras, 265-266.

99. Bajpai, S.G., 1989 "Mathura: Trade Routes, Commerce and Communication Patterns during Post-Mathura Period to End of Kushana Period", *Mathura, The Cultural Heritage*, (ed.) D.M.Srinivasan, Delhi, 46-58.

100. Sarma, I.K., 1991 "Rare Evidences on Maritime Trade on the Bengal Coast of India", *Recent Advances in Marine Archaeology*, (ed.) S.R.Rao, NIO, Goa, 38-40.

101. Sarkar, H.B., 1990 "Gangetic Ports of Bengal and the Western World", *U. Thakur Felicitation Volume*, (eds.) G. Kuppuram, K. Kumudamani, New Delhi, 53-58. Photograph of this is published in Bengal's Past (ed.) P.C.Das Gupta, 1987, Dept. of Archaeology, West Bengal.

102. Glover, I.C., 1990 Early Trade between India and Southeast Asia: A link in the development of a World Trading System, *Occasional Paper No. 16*, The University of Hull, London, 1-45.

103. Ray, H.P., 1987-88 "Early Trade in the Bay of Bengal", *Indian Historical Review*, Vol. XIV, (1-2): 79-89.

104. Manavid, J., 1990 "Commercial and Cultural relationship between India and Thailand during 4th-13th century", paper presented at the International Seminar on Silk Route, UNESCO, Madras.

105. Rao, S.R., 1987 *Progress and Prospects of Marine Archaeology in India*, NIO, Goa, 67-68.

106. *Indian Archaeology - A Review 1984-85*, Archaeological Survey of India, Delhi, 56-60.

107. Sinha, B.K., 1992 "Khalkattapatna: A Small Port on the Coast of Orissa", *New Trends in Indian Art and Archaeology*, (eds.) B.U.Nayak and N.C.Ghosh, Delhi, 423-428.

108. Nigam J.S., 1993 *A Brief Note on the Excavation at Manikapatna*, Bhubaneswar, (unpublished).

109. Pradhan, D., *op. cit.*, 8-10.

110. *Indian Archaeology - A Review, 1984-85*, Archaeological Survey of India, Delhi, 56-60.

111. Warmington, E.H., 1974 *The Commerce between Roman Empire and India*, New Delhi, 322.

112. Mukherjee, B.N., 1989 "Decipherment of the Kharoshti-Brahmi Scripts", *Asiatic Society Monthly Bulletin*, Vol. XVIII, (8), 4.

113. Behera, S.C., 1970 "Mathara Rule in Kalinga", *Journal of Indian History*, Vol. XLVIII: 117-127.

114. Behera, K.S., 1994 "Maritime Contacts of Orissa: the Archaeological Perspectives", paper presented at the International seminar on Techno-Archaeological Perspectives of seafaring in the Indian Ocean, NISTADS, New Delhi, (28 Feb.-3 Mar. '94), 1-20.

115. Ghosh, D.P., 1983 "Influence of Indian Art on the art of Southeast Asia", *The Aspect of Indian Art and Culture*, S.K.Saraswati Commemoration Volume, Calcutta.

2

Ports of Kalinga and Expansion of Culture

The Kalinga was dotted with a number of active and excellent ports. This coast had a prosperous and glorious maritime past and possessed a large sea-faring population, daring and adventurous sailors and seamen, who traversed countries and islands, situated beyond seas and oceans. Those ports served as the medium for not only export and import of the merchandise but also spread of Kalingan culture and civilisation on foreign land. The people of ancient Kalinga had established colonies in different parts of the world, and had contacts with Roman, Arabian, African, Far Eastern and Southeast Asian countries.

The people of Kalinga dominated the overseas trade and maintained contacts with the far off countries since remote past. Kalinga was so prominent in maritime trade that Kalidass referred in the *Raghuvamsa*[1] to the king of Kalinga as *Mahodadhipati* the Lord of Ocean. The text *Aryamanjusrimulakalpa*[2] of Mahayana Buddhism refers to "all islands of the Kalinga sea" (Kalingodresu) which establishes that in the past the modern Bay of Bengal was known as the "Kalinga Sea" being dominated by the ships of Kalinga. It is mentioned in the Sanskrit literature that people of Kalinga were very brave *Kalingah Sahasikah* evidently due to their martial character and maritime adventures[3].

In Ptolemy's Geography of Ancient India, a work of the 2nd Century AD, a vivid picture about the major and prosperous ports of Kalinga such as Nanigaina (Puri), Katikardama (Kataka or Cuttack), Kannagara (Konark), mouths of the rivers Manada (Mahanadi), Tyndis (Brahmani), Dosaron (Baitarani ?), Adams (Subarnarekha ?), Minagara (Jajpur ?) and Kosamba (Pipili or Balasore)[4] which had overseas trade relations has been obtained. But Ptolemy did not refer to the other ports of Kalinga viz. Tamralipti, Manikapatna, Palur, Che-li-ta-lo, Kalingapatnam, Pithunda, Khalkatapatna which also played a dominant role in the maritime history of Kalinga (Fig. 3). Out of these ports, some were active from the very ancient times and continued to be so for a long periods. Some ports became prominent during a particular period and perished or lost their significance subsequently. Some ports were meant for internal trade and transport by boats and others for export of commodities to far off countries. The following are the different ports of Kalinga known from existing sources. Owing to the absence of primary information about their actual operational period the ports in their geographical setting have been analysed.

Tamralipti

Tamralipti (Fig. 3), was a *Dronimukha* as it was located at the confluence of the sea and the Rupanarayana river. It was the most important port of Kalinga. Situated at the apex of the East coast of India served as the main gateway for ancient Kalingan sea-going traders, travellers and missionaries[5]. It was one of the major sea ports of India which was connected both by sea and land routes with the West and the extreme Far East[6]. It is identified with present Tamluk in the Midnapore district of West Bengal. It is an irony of history that many Indian and Western historians have stated that the port of Tamralipti as the port of Bengal[7], being on its present geographical existence but have ignored to mention the fact that Tamralipti was under the control of the kings of Kalinga for many centuries. The Kalingan sailors and traders were extensively using the port and contributed to its growth and development. The sea ports through which Kalinga carried on her overseas trade, namely Tamralipti, Palur and Pithunda were connected with the arteries of roads within the hinterland of Orissa[8].

Ptolemy and Hiuen Tsang and others have mentioned that sailors and merchants landing at Tamralipti, located on the bank of navigable river the Ganges, also could sail in the Ganges up to Champa, Pataliputra and Varanasi[9]. However, from this port, there was a regular sailing of vessels which either proceeded along the coast of Bengal to Burma or crossed the Bay of Bengal to make a direct voyage to Malaya Peninsula and to the East Indies and Indochina or even beyond that region[10].

Tamralipti was a well known port which maintained maritime relations with other countries, especially Ceylon. In the days of Asoka (273-232 BC), Indian Missions to and from Ceylon passed through Tamralipti port. Prince Mahendra made his journey by water from Pataliputra to Tamralipti and on to Ceylon[11]. Asoka, the emperor also travelled up to Tamralipti to see off Sanghamitra carrying a branch of Bodhi tree to Ceylon by ship. The *Mahavamsa*[12] also informs that the journey from Tamralipti to Ceylon covers seven days only. In the fifth century AD the Chinese traveller Fa-hien saw it as a strong maritime settlement of the Buddhists and left for China via Ceylon from Tamralipti. Hiuen Tsang who came to India during the reign period of Harshavardhana (AD 606-647) visited Tamralipti port and learnt here for the first time regarding Ceylon and the perils of the Southern voyage. I-tsing arrived at Tamralipti in AD 673 by the sea route from China[13] and learnt Sanskrit and philosophy *Sabda Vidya* in Baraha monastery where both monks and nuns were living in perfect discipline of life and conduct[14]. It was one of the important sea ports for Southeast Asian voyages[15]. It become a famous port for exporting copper ore to foreign countries. It can be said that irrespective of its geographical position which varied with time, the port of Tamralipti was utilised by the sailors, traders and merchants of Kalinga along with other Indian merchants and traders.

Archaeological findings from the excavations at Tamralipti, carried out by Archaeological Survey of India, have unearthed copper coins and terracotta figurines dated to the Sunga period. Rouletted ware and other objects like sprinkler indicate the overseas contact of Tamralipti with the Romans. Among the ancient structural remains of Tamralipti (2nd-3rd century AD) a brick built stepped tank indicates the prosperity of Tamralipti[16]. It is believed that the ancient palace of Tamralipti was built on the banks of the Rupanarayana river. Part of the city is buried under the river silt and the temple remains are now partly buried. Houses are found at 18 to 20 feet below the surface. A considerable number of silver and copper coins bearing Buddhist symbols have recently been discovered in the midst of debris from the crumbling banks of the river Rupanarayana[17].

Hatthasis

It is mentioned in the Jaina text *Naya Dhama Kaha* that once Hatthasis city was the main trade centre of Kalinga. The mariners used to go to Kalingadvipa (Java) from this city. It is also mentioned in the Jaina texts that, Mahavira halted at this place for a short duration during his travelling period. It is true that during the life time of Mahavira, Hatthasis existed as a city of Kalinga. It is known from the Tang China history that a new country called (Ho-ling) probably Kalinga come to light in Java around 7th century AD. During that time Hatthasis was the main centre of Buddhism and Buddhist saint Jnanabhadra was born here[18].

Hatthasis was the port town of Kalinga. With regard to the location of the port no clear evidence is forthcoming. After a lot of examination scholars have identified it with "Hattasisua" village situated on the bank of river Birupa in Tangi region of Cuttack district. Probably this place might be the ancient Hatthasis and later came to be known as "Hattasisua". Binaka village near Hattasisua probably provided shelter to traders on their way to and from Kalingadvipa. Due to the frequent change of the flow of the river Birupa during the last 1200 years, these two villages might have shifted to their present location. It is believed that Kandarakana (Kandarikona), name of the big mound near the village, could be the ancient Hatthasis port. During survey a number of broken sculptures and Tirthankara's images are found at Hatthasis. Undoubtedly this region was under the influence of Jainism[19].

Khalkatapatna

Khalkatapatna (Fig. 4) is situated 11 km east of Konark on the left bank of the river Kushabhadra in Puri district. As per the local and regional traditions Khalkatapatna is known as Old Palace (garh) of Langulla Narasimha Dev (AD 1238-1264) of the

Ganga dynasty. The right bank of the river forms a narrow barrier of sand between the ancient township and the bay. It served as a groin wall. Excavations carried out at Khalkatapatna in the year 1984-85 by Archaeological Survey of India have revealed the existence of a brick jelly floor which might have served as a loading and unloading platform. Pottery from excavations consists of Chinese Celadon ware, Chinese porcelain with blue floral design on white background and egg-white glazed ware besides glazed chocolate ware of Arabian origin. In both wares the main shapes are bowls, basins, vases, and miniature pots. Other ceramic ware are the dark grey and red slipped indigenous ware[20]. All the pottery belong to the wheel turned. The contact of ancient Orissa with Africa and Arabian countries can be assumed from the depiction of giraffe on Konark temple and Arabian and African costumes worn by merchants.

Important antiquities recovered in excavations included arecanut-shaped beads of terracotta, fragments of bangle of glass and copper, terracotta animal figurines, a miniature copper bowl and copper coins. Besides celadon ware and Chinese porcelain, however, the most important find from excavations are one complete and one fragment of Chinese copper coin, datable to *circa* 14th century AD. The circular copper coin has a square perforation in the centre and legend in Chinese character. The occupation at this single culture site can be dated between 12th and 14th century AD, the period which comes under the Imperial Gangas[21]. No structural remains have been encountered in the habitational area which may suggest that being on the shore of the sea the structures might have been washed away by the tide. However, in the habitational area, on either side of a brick lane a group of four to five ringwells have been noticed, each is supposed to have been connected with a house. Their proximity to each other suggests that these were used as soakage pits. This single evidence is sufficient to indicate the habitational pattern.

Wan-Ta-Yuan[22], a Chinese writer of 14th century AD states about the flourishing condition of trade and commerce during the Ganga period. Further, boat motif sculptures and location of Konark temple prove that Konark was once situated near a sea port. On the southern facade of the *Jagamohan,* there is a panel in which the king sitting on the elephant receiving gift from a group of well dressed people and in the group there is an animal motif giraffe, which is strange to Indian ports. Probably this animal was brought to Khalkatapatna as a present to the king when the temple was built. The occurrence of Chinese coins and pottery point to the fact that Khalkatapatna was one of the ports on coastal Orissa from where trade passed to Southeast Asia, China and Arab during early medieval Orissa.

Che-li-ta-lo

Che-li-ta-lo or Charitrapura was the next important sea port in ancient Kalinga on the east coast of India. During 7th century AD Chinese pilgrim Hiuen Tsang visited India and his account Si-yu-ki mentions, "near the shore of the ocean in the south east was the city Che-li-ta-lo about 20 li in circuit (6 to 7 km), which was a thoroughfare and resting place for sea going traders and strangers from distant lands in the Wu-tu country"[23] meaning Orissa. This city was naturally strong and was a great mart for rare commodities[24]. It was a great centre of culture and a famous emporium of overseas trade; during 7th century AD was also a great centre of Buddhism in Orissa. However, regarding its identification scholars differ in their opinion. Che-li-ta-lo, a major port during 7th century, probably situated in the vicinity of Chilka lake and may be tentatively identified with Chhatragada[25]. Che-li-ta-lo was a centre of Buddhism besides being an important port, and standing on its shore Hiuen Tsang could imagine of the glittering rays emanating from the gem placed on the tooth relic of Buddha at Ceylon. Waddel identified Che-li-ta-lo with Nendra on the bank of Chitrotpala, a tributary of the river Mahanadi in the district of Cuttack[26]. The existence of an old fort at this place is suggested in support of this view. The Sarala Mahabharata, an Oriya work of Sarala Das identifies Che-li-ta-lo with Chandrabhaga near Konark[27].

The references to the river Chandrabhaga in the Tugu inscription of Java and Srikshetra in Talang Tuwo inscription of Sumatra indicate that they were familiar with Puri and its vicinity[28]. Although Chandrabhaga is known to be the site of a silted river port, this view has not been widely accepted. General A. Cunningham, equated Che-li-ta-lo to Charitrapura and identified it with modern Puri, the seat of Lord Jagannath[29]. The above description is quite applicable to Puri and Che-li-ta-lo seems to be the Chinese representation of the Ksetra (religious centre). As Fang-Chih renders Che-li-ta-lo as Chiao-hsing-che which may mean "having religious observance", its identification with Puri made by Cunningham is tenable. There can be no doubt therefore that Puri was recognised as a holy place in the 7th century AD.[30]

Rhys Davis[31] while accepting the identification of Che-li-ta-lo with Charitrapur, is not convinced about Puri being the same place as ancient Charitrapur. Davis is not convinced on this matter because of the silence of the Chinese pilgrim regarding the temple of Jagannath in his account about Charitrapura. However, Che-li-ta-lo (Charitrapur) and Jagannath Puri appear to have been one and the same place and in support of Cunningham's view, it can be said that the Chinese pilgrim, visiting centres of Buddhism in India might have confined his travel accounts to centres of Buddhism only, excluding thereby reference to the place coming under a different religion[32]. In pursuance of this assumption, it can be said that the thriving of a centre of Buddhism along side the famous seat of Hinduism in Jagannath Puri appears to be a plausible probability. This is quite likely because Jagannath Puri as a confluence of different faiths has at all times welcomed to its fold all the different streams of religious movements in this country. Hence Che-li-ta-lo (Charitrapur) and Jagannath Puri appears to have been one and the same place[33]. Here it can also be mentioned that, if Chodaganga Deva built the Jagannath temple in the 12th century AD the Chinese pilgrim could not have known about it by 7th century AD when he visited Puri (Charitrapura or Che-li-ta-lo). Scholars are however of the opinion that the cult of Jagannath is more ancient than the present temple. But it can be said that probably by the time Hiuen Tsang visited Puri (Che-li-ta-lo) the cult of Jagannath might not have acquired the universal status in association with the present temple so as to motivate the pilgrim to mention about Jagannath in his account.

Che-li-ta-lo is translated in a note to the text by Fa-hien which may mean 'Setting out' that is on a voyage or journey, and the city is supposed to have received this name because it was a starting place for navigators and land travellers[34]. N.K. Sahu has tried to restore the word as Sritra indicating Srikshetra, the ancient name of Puri[35]. But if the name was Srikshetra during the 7th Century, Xuan Zang (Hiuen Tsang) would have transcribed it as Shi-li-cha-da-lo as he did in case of Srikshetra while describing it as situated Northeast of Samatata i.e. Srihatta in Bangladesh or Myanmar[36]. Kongodamandala, where Xuan Zang went from Odra is north of Ganjam, near Chilka, the country being 2000 li Southwest of Zhelidala (Che-li-ta-lo), forests intervening in between. Southwest of Kongoda is Kalinga known as Dantapura; it also included a part of modern Andhra Pradesh including Mahendra mountain where Rajendra Chola's inscription has been found. H.P. Ray thinks *dalo* is *tala* which means 'lake' in India. In that case, Zhe-li may perhaps represent Chili of Chilka, in which case the word will be Chili (ka)-tala, the lake Chilka. In Chinese transliteration it is quite normal to miss one or more sounds, as for example, Lakhanauti is Cha-na-ji, Nasiruddin is Nading, Ghiyasuddin is Ai-Ya-Si-Ding and so on[37]. If this interpretation is accepted then the location of the port will be somewhere on the southern bank of Chilka lake. No doubt Che-li-ta-lo was an important port of Kalinga but historians have suggested different locations of the port on the basis of their study. It seems that Che-li-ta-lo was located somewhere at the adjoining area of Chilka lake. So a thorough archaeological exploration and excavation is required around the Chilka lake region which is expected to be of help to identify the port and trace out its antiquities.

Manikapatna

Manikapatna (Fig. 4) was a flourishing port and an important trade centre of Kalinga. It is situated in Brahmagiri taluka of Puri district on the mouth of Satapada *ghat* of Chilka lake. Abul Fazal (AD 1595-96) described Manikapatna as a sea port where taxes on salt were collected[38]. During later period, Mughals invited the Dutch to establish a factory at Manikapatna. The place is mentioned in maps of the 16th-17th centuries and Gujarati sea manuals in the 18th century.

The Orissan Institute of Maritime and Southeast Asian Studies, Bhubaneswar carried out trial excavations in 1989-1993 and brought to light remains of early historical period such as Indian Rouletted ware, fragments of amphora, red-glazed ware, Puri-Kushana coins and a Kharosthi inscription on a potsherd[39]. In the upper levels Chinese Celadon ware made of jade green celadon occurred in huge quantity. Other finds are a damaged Chinese copper coin with a square perforation in the centre. These findings indicate that Manikapatna had close trade contacts with Arabia, Rome, Ceylon and China[40] since ancient times. It seems that Manikapatna played an important role in the maritime history of Orissa from 1st century BC to 18th century AD. The discovery of Shasamalla's coins from Manikapatna in Orissa, Polonnaruwa in Sri Lanka and Kotchina in Indonesia, prove a maritime network linking coastal Orissa, Sri Lanka and Sumatra[41].

During the joint explorations carried out by Marine Archaeology Centre of National Institute of Oceanography, Goa and Department of History of Berhampur University in 1993, terracotta ringwells were noticed on the shore of Chilka at Manikapatna. They are submerged during high tide and exposed in low tide. Huge quantities of Chinese ceramics are also encountered at the same site. Early historical pottery has been collected from nearby mounds.

Ports around Chilka Lake

Ptolemy and Hiuen Tsang provided information on ports, cities, towns and religious centres of contemporary Kalinga. Two important ports viz. Manikapatna and Palur situated on the bank of Chilka have already been discussed. Besides, there are references, literary and situational, to Chilka as having reputation as a port in ancient times (Fig. 4). The *Brahmanda Purana* describes that Chilka was an important centre of trade and commerce. Thousands of ships having a number of masts and sails were sheltered in the lake. Some of the ships had curvilinear towers with three to five stories. Ships used to go to Java, Malaya and Ceylon from the Chilka[42]. The lake was very deep and was connected to the sea through a wide mouth, which provided easy berthing for the sea going boats and ships[43]. It is locally known that the hillock on the shore of Chilka referred to as *Deepa-Adia Pahada* (Hill of Light) which had a stone built light house to guide the mariners during night navigation[44].

The people of Kalinga had established their colonies in Java and Bali islands and ships sailed to those far off places from Chilka port. In the past, people from south India used to travel to Puri by ships which were anchored in Chilka. There was a

Samudrakara bandha (Sea tax gate) on the bank of Chilka, where taxes were collected from the sea traders. The mariners of Kalinga had close relations with the people of Southeast Asia. The people adopted surnames like Rana Tunge, Singha Naik, Bandar Naik etc. which are popular in Southeast Asian countries. People with similar surnames are living around Chilka lake even at present and this was probably the outcome of a prolonged maritime contact. Ptolemy has described the Nanigainar as. a port on coastal Orissa. The village Niminagainada near Kuhudi on the bank of Chilka can be identified with Ptolemy's Nanigainar. At present, Nimina and Gainada are two separate villages. It is also mentioned that Balia and Amaravati villages on Chilka bank had contacts with Bali island and Amaravati of south India[45]. Hiuen Tsang refers 'Kung-yu-to' country situated on the sea side containing many rare precious commodities and produced large dark coloured elephants which were capable of long journeys[46]. Cunningham and Ferguson have identified 'Kung-yu-to' with the district around the Chilka lake[47]. This area is now named as Ganjam district[48].

Palur

Ptolemy refers to Paloura as an important port of the Kalinga country and a 'point of departure' (apheterion) for ships bound for Khryse. The 'Golden land' that is Suvarnabhumi (island of Southeast Asia) was immediately to the south of Paloura[49]. Khryse denotes different parts of Southeast Asia such as Khryse nesos *(Suvarnadvipa)* and Khryse Khora *(Suvarnabhumi)*. Generally it includes Sumatra, Java, Pegu, Burma and some parts of Malay Peninsula and Indonesia[50]. Paloura or Palur is identified with modern Palur in Ganjam district of Orissa and was located in the southern tip of Chilka lake. It acted as the only port of departure to the East on the Coromandel coast[51] and east coast of the Bay of Bengal and Malay region[52]. During the early centuries of Christian era, Kalinga's importance for trans-Asian maritime trade can be assessed from the fact that even large vessels did not cross the Bay of Bengal directly from Sri Lanka to Southeast Asia. Instead they sailed up to Palur from where they proceeded to Suvarnabhumi.

In the opinion of Sylvian Lèvi, Dantapura the famous sea port and the ancient capital of Kalinga mentioned in the Buddhist Jatakas, Pali texts and the Cylonese Chronicles is identical with

Palur[53]. In the words of K.S. Behera, 'Dantapura mentioned in the Buddhist literature is probably the same as Palur since 'Pallu' (Telugu term) means 'Danta' (tooth) and 'Ur' is identical with 'Pura' (city)[54]. It may be recalled here that Palur and Dantapura were two different ports of Kalinga. According to the Pali text the *Dathavamsa*[55] composed by Dhammakirtti, a tooth relic of the Buddha was presented by Thera Khema to king Bramadatta of Kalinga who deposited it in a magnificent stupa at Dantapura. It remained there till the reign of Guhasiva, who despatched it to Ceylon in the safe custody of his son-in-law Dantakumara and daughter Hemamala. It is worth noting that this tooth of the Master is worshipped even in recent times at Kandy in Ceylon.

The archaeological explorations by Archaeological Survey of India in 1984-85 at Palur and the adjacent areas have yielded red ware bowls with flaring rim and having ledge on the exterior and a fragmentary terracotta dabber in an area of half a square kilometre in sand dunes. On the basis of a comparative study, the pottery was assigned to 12-14th century AD[56]. The recent excavations by the Orissan Institute of Maritime and Southeast Asian Studies, Bhubaneswar, further reconfirm the existence of Palur port since the Mauryan period. There are some early medieval temples in Palur, buried up to the plinth due to siltation which is a continuing process due to Southwest monsoon and wind. While digging the foundation of a house at Palur, a huge quantity of pottery of early and medieval times was encountered[57].

Kalingapatnam

Kalingapatnam, the ancient port city of Kalinga, is situated at the mouth of the Vamsadhara river in the present Srikakulam district of Andhra Pradesh. In ancient times Kalingapatnam was variously called like Kannagara, Katikardana and Kartikeyadhama[58]. There is a controversy among the scholars about the identification of Kalingapatnam. Alexander Cunningham[59] suggested that the location of Ganga-Kalinganagara is at Rajahmundry. Fleet suggests the location of Kalingapatnam on the mouth of the river Vamsadhara. G.V. Ramamurti considers Mukhalingam on the left bank of the river Vamsadhara to be the site of Ganga-Kalinganagara[60]. The Eastern Ganga king, Indravarman in his Chicacole grant[61] and Hastivarman in his Narasingapalli plates[62] also refer to Kalinganagara, the capital city as situated near the sea. From this evidence it can be inferred that the port town of Kalingapatnam enjoyed the position of the capital of Kalinga.

Pliny mentioned it as a thriving port in his Natural History[63]. This is substantiated by Kalidasa in the *Raghuvamsa*[64] and the *Dasakumaracharita*[65], where he alludes the capital of Kalinga, situated on the sea shore. Ptolemy and Pliny have recorded a number of ports on the East coast like Dantapura, Palur, Kalingapatnam etc. Scholars are of the view that the capital of Kalinga was washed out by the sea and the remains are found near the present town of Kalingapatnam, which has been silted up[66] over the years.

The excavations at Kalingapatnam by Bhattacharya (1928) revealed a fortified settlement and the habitational remains ranging from 2nd century BC to early medieval period. A number of Gupta period gold coins were also found at the mound site of ancient Kalinganagara. The Asokan inscriptions indicate that by the third century BC Kalinga was a force to reckon with. According to some estimates Kalingapatnam was an emporium of trade in 8th century AD.[67] The Archaeological Survey of India carried out excavations in the Stupa mound between 1977 and 1979. Pre-stupa occupation had been dated to 300 BC. The size of the stupa and the offerings made to it in the form of gold grains suggest that it attracted a large number of wealthy patrons, probably merchants who traded in rice and other commodities. Some remains of a brick wharf and structures have also been traced[68]. The sacred scripture *Buddhagat* of the Burmese refers that there was commercial contact between Burma and the Buddhist monks of Kalinga. The textiles of Kalinga were very much in demand overseas. It must be from Kalingapatnam that Asoka's mission went to *Suvarnabhumi.* It is likely that merchants and Buddhist monks who went to Malay Peninsula sailed from Kalingapatnam. A two way traffic is revealed by ancient texts[69].

Dantapura

Dantapura in Kalinga figures prominently in Buddhist literature. The Jirjingi Plates of Indravarman of Early Ganga dynasty inform that Dantapura was more beautiful than Amaravati, the city of Gods[70]. The Pali text *Mahagovinda Suttanta* mentions that

Dantapura was the capital of Kalinga. According to Subba Rai Dantapura was situated on the southern bank of the river Vamsadhara, three miles (approximately 4 km) from the modern Srikakulam[71]. The Korni Plates of Anantavarma Chodaganga refer to Dantavarapukota as the capital situated on the banks of the river Vamsadhara[72]. Sylvain Levi has identified it with Palur. Ptolemy refers to the apheterian immediately to the South of Palur, where the vessels bound for the Malay Peninsula ceased to follow the littoral and entered the high seas. The fame of Palur or Dantapura was due to its importance as the point of departure for the Far East and Southeast Asia. Dantapura is mentioned in the Buddhist *Dathavamsa* written by Dhammakirtti[73] as the place from which the tooth relic of Buddha was brought to Anuradhapura in Sri Lanka in the fourth century AD. It was a famous international port as known from the Natural History[74] of Pliny and also from the Simhalese Buddhist Chronicle *Mahavamsa*[75].

The port of Dantapura linked with important highways had overland trade contact with Tamralipti on one hand and Burma, Ceylon and the Far East and East Indies on the other[76]. Dantapura also played a vital role for carrying the maritime relations with the outside world, particularly East Indies and Ceylon[77]. During the period of Hindu imperialism in Northern India, Kalinga, along with Bengal considerably contributed to the colonisation of the East Indies[78]. The Buddhist as well as the Jaina texts gave evidences of Kalinga's overland and sea borne trade with the outside world from Dantapura.

The *Chulla Kalinga Jataka*[79] mentions that Dantapura of Kalinga was connected with many kingdoms by road. Dantapura is also referred to in the *Mahagovinda Suttanta* of the *Digha Nikaya*[80], the *Dathavamsa*[81] and the Jaina text *Uttaradhyayanasutra*[82]. Probably Dantapura is identical with Dantakara found mentioned in the *Mahabharata* as the capital of Kalinga. Pliny speaks of a town called Dandaguda or Dandagula which is said to have stood at a distance of 625 miles south of the mouth of the Ganges[83].

The explorations and trial digging carried out in this area by the Department of Archaeology, Government of Andhra Pradesh in 1993 at Dantavarapukota on the bank of the river Vamsadhara revealed the ruins of Buddhist structures spread over an area of

500 hectares of land. The pottery included Knobbed ware of foreign origin. The geographical position and the exploration evidence corroborate the identification of Dantavarapukota with ancient Dantapura[84]. The results of the exploration and excavation concluded the long standing confusion about the location of Dantapura and Palur. Now it is clear that Dantapura and Palur were two separate ports and contemporary to each other.

Salihundam

Salihundam, was considered as a meeting place for culture and trade from the 3rd century BC onwards. It is located on the banks of the Vamsadhara river near the foot hill. It functioned as a beacon for the ships anchoring at nearby Kalingapatnam. Two inscribed conches discovered in the monastic precincts during excavations supply the names *Salipetaka* and *Salipataka*[85]. These were perhaps the ancient names of Salihundam. *Sali* means 'rice' and *pataka* or *vataka* means town or place. The name signifies 'the place where rice is stored'. No doubt Salihundam was a major trade centre for rice as well as an important market place for exchange of commodities. The presence of Rouletted ware and Roman coins of Tiberius of (AD 14-37) indicate that the port had trade relations with the Romans[86]. Also in Salihundam there are extensive Buddhist remains. These remains are datable from the 3rd century BC to the 8th century AD. Probably the port was in operation during the above mentioned period.

Thotlakonda and Bavikonda

To the south of Kalingapatnam, the Buddhist sites on the coast between Bimunipatnam and Visakhapatnam are Pavuralabodu, Thotlakonda and Bavikonda. The Department of Archaeology of Andhra Pradesh has conducted excavations at these sites. Probably the Buddhist viharas (monastery) at Thotlakonda was constructed in the 3rd century BC. The monasteries at Bavikonda and Pavuralabodu have been dated to the 1st century BC[87]. Each monastery sheltered more than a hundred monks and the dinning hall at Thotlakonda could serve more than 150 at a time. The excavations at these sites yielded black and red ware, Rouletted ware, Satavahana and Augustus and Tiberius coins[88]. At Thotlakonda, coins with double mast ship motif were discovered in which one ship is shown anchoring while another is seen sailing. On the basis of pottery and coin it is suggested that these sites were frequented by navigators and traders.

Gopalapatnam

Gopalapatnam was a Buddhist site located on the banks of the Tandava river. It is famous even today for its rice and coconut cultivation. Probably the main item of export from Gopalapatnam was rice. In and around Gopalapatnam archaeological remains such as brick structures, stone veneered stupas, brick built stupas and *viharas*, fragmentary *chhatras* and early historical pottery are found[89]. The recovery of other objects such as beads, inscribed potsherds, stone objects and Vishnukundin coins suggest that the site was under habitation between 1st and 5th centuries AD.

Pithunda

Pithunda another port of Kalinga, was a flourishing trade centre from the very ancient times. Kharavela of Kalinga (1st century BC) invaded the coastal belt of Andhra and captured the port and market town of Pithunda, the ancient metropolis. The Hathigumpha Inscription of Kharavela mentions that Pithunda a deserted port was renovated by Kharavela[90]. Ptolemy locates Pithunda in between the deltas of the rivers Godavari and Mahanadi[91]. According to the Jaina text *Uttaradhyayanasutra* Pithunda had trade relations with Champa (modern Kampuchea) even in the days of Mahavira[92]. Further the text states that Pithunda was a sea coast town. The text also mentions that a merchant of Champa named Palita came to the port of Pithunda by boat. Palita was blessed with a son on his return voyage in the ship itself. Hence his son was named Samudrapala[93]. This city of Pithunda is described as a famous seat of Jainism and probably this city was located between the Godavari and Mahanadi rivers[94].

The above discussion shows that ancient Kalinga was a maritime province on the East coast of India. A good number of ports rose with the march of time contributing to the national maritime traditions.

EXPANSION OF CULTURE

There are abundant evidences regarding the emergence of Kalingan settlements in the Southeast Asian countries in early times. The cultural contact was so effective that the local population assimilated a superior culture to their best advantage with some variations. This process began very early probably during the first few centuries of the Christian era in the Malay Peninsula and eventually spread to other areas. It would be worthwhile to indicate here the factors involved in the expansion of the Kalingan culture across the seas.

The ports of Kalinga had opened different sea routes to different lands for admittedly seaborne commerce. The adventurous mariners continued to have commercial, socio-cultural and political relations with Southeast Asian countries (Fig. 5) like Ceylon, Java, Sumatra, Bali, Borneo, China and Japan in the East and to the Roman Empire and Africa in the West. The expansion of Indian civilisation to the Southeast Asian countries during the early centuries of Christian era is one of the outstanding events in the history of the world. The Indianization on the foreign soil created a series of true Indian kingdoms in Cambodia. Champa Sumatra, Java, Bali, Burma and Thailand[95] (Fig. 6). The people of Kalinga were the pioneers in the maritime activity of India and played a leading role in the overseas trade activities[96] and expansion of Culture. The role of Kalinga in the colonisation of Southeast Asia was very important. R.D. Banerjee[97] opines that the term Kling or Kalinga, used extensively in the Malaya Peninsula and other ports of the Archipelago, denote a man going there from any part of India. Probably every Indian seemed to them as a Kalingaite, irrespective of the province from which he came. This could be because of the fact, that the earliest Indians with whom the Southeast Asians dealt with were from Kalinga.

Before the expression of term Southeast Asia became common usage, the region was often described as 'Farther' or 'Greater India'. It is so described because Southeast Asia was closely allied to India culturally and commercially. Ancient Indians also referred to this region as *Suvarnabhumi* (the land of gold) or *Suvarnadvipa* (the island of gold). However, the scholars are of different view points regarding the territorial identification of the term *Suvarnadvipa.* Some scholars interpreted the term to mean only Indonesia or Sumatra while some others mainly applied it to Burma. It is very well accepted that *Suvarnadvipa* refers broadly to Java, Sumatra and Indonesia. *Suvarnabhumi* denotes Burma. Arab writer Alberuni testifies that Indians called the whole Southeast region *Suvarndib (Suvarnadvipa)* and the Hellenistic geographers knew the area as the 'Golden Chersonese' and the Chinese on the other hand called it 'Kin-Lin' (Kin means gold). Although the exact region meant by the term is not clear, it is probable that the name was applied to the whole Indo-chinese Peninsula and the Malay Archipelago[98].

It is not known precisely when contact began between India and Southeast Asia. The historical records, archaeological remains, accounts of the travellers are inadequate and insufficient to draw any conclusion. The excavations at Kuliana, Kuchai and Baidyapur in Mayurbhanj district of Orissa yielded Neolithic tools similar to shouldered adzes of Java, Bali and Sumatra. Some scholars believe that Orissa's maritime contact with Southeast Asia would have began from Neolithic period. However the cultural contact through Northeast land route cannot be ruled out[99]. The Buddhist Jataka stories tell us many stories of the enterprising merchants and princes, sailing to Southeast Asian countries for trade.

The Chinese Annals of the former Han Dynasty, gives the itinerary of a sea journey starting from the coast of Tonkin (Tenan) and ending on the Indian coast during the period of Emperor Wu (140-80 BC). Bagchi suggests that regular sailing from the Gangetic valley to Tonkin was taking place in the second and first centuries BC[100] and it also implies India's contact by sea with Southeast Asia. A. Lamb is of the opinion that by the beginning of the Christian era the civilisation of India had began to spread across the Bay of Bengal into both island and mainland Southeast Asia by the fifth century AD. Indianised states, that is to say states organised along the traditional lines of Indian political theory and following the Buddhist or Hindu religions had established themselves in many regions of Burma, Thailand, Indochina, Malaysia and Indonesia. Some of these states were in time to grow into great empires dominating the zone between metropolitan India and the Chinese Southern border, which have been described as 'Farther India' or 'Greater India'[101]. Gradually the pioneer sailors from Kalinga and south India penetrated into Southeast Asia and started the process of Indianization to the Southeast Asian countries. The people of India from different castes like Brahman, Vaishya, Kshatriya of different provinces some way or other were connected with the main process of Indianization of Southeast Asia[102]. Thus as a result there are close links between Kalinga and Southeast Asian countries.

Africa and Arabia

Archaeological evidences indicate the contact of Kalinga with Arabs and African countries. The Khalkatapatna excavations revealed thin variety of egg white glazed and thick chocolate glazed pottery which confirms the contact between Arabian countries with Orissa[103]. The representation of a giraffe, a strange African animal in the sculpture of Konark temple (Pl. IV), shows that Kalinga had trade and commercial relations with Eastern Africa. The sculpture is a fairly accurate representation of a giraffe and the sculptor therefore seems to have actually seen a giraffe or at least a fairly life like drawing of the one. It is hardly believable that the sculptor would have travelled to Africa. This means that a giraffe was actually brought alive by sea from East Africa to Orissa. Probably the Ganga monarch Narasimha I AD 1238-1264 heard of the existence of this strange animal from Arab traders who carried on most of the trade with Africa and commissioned them to fetch him a specimen. The sculptural panel of the Konark temple shows the king being represented with a giraffe. The problem of bringing a tall animal as giraffe (which normally lives on the green leaves of trees) on such a long sea voyage in a small boat must have been a considerably troublesome job, importantly, the sailors and traders succeeded in their mission. Similarly a Chinese admiral named Cheng Ho who visited East Africa is known to have brought back a live giraffe to the Ming court in the 15th century. It could not have been impossible to bring a giraffe to Orissa in the 13th century[104].

Bali

Bali was one of the important Indian settlements in ancient times. The Chinese accounts mention that Bali was a rich and civilised kingdom ruled by Indians who professed Buddhism. A section of Brahmanas of Bali themselves as called the Brahmana

Boudha Kalinga seems to have migrated from Kalinga. ·The river Mahendratanaya, of Bali which derives its name from the Orissan river is held high esteem. The cult of Lakshmi, associated with *dhanya* (grain) and *tandula* (rice) venerated in Bali was also the contribution the people of Kalinga. A type of temple structure is known as *Meru* in Bali[105] had its origin in Orissan temple architecture. The archaeological and literary evidence mentioned above should leave no doubt as to the close maritime contact between Kalinga and Malaya Archipelago.

Borneo

Borneo is situated to the east of Sumatra. The Hindu colonisation in eastern Borneo is recorded in the Sanskrit inscriptions found at Muara Kaman on the bank of the river Mahakam, which was a sea port during the ancient times. These inscriptions were datable to 400 AD. It is said that the Hindu colonies were established in Borneo by the end of the fourth century AD[106] if not earlier. The inscriptions also testify to the great predominance of the Brahmanas and the Hindu culture in Borneo.

Burma

Geographically Burma is close to India. Since ancient times the Indians established colonies in Pegu, Arakan and Srikshetra of Burma. Burma was colonised by Kalinga, who were pioneers in the maritime trade on the East coast even before the Christian era[107]. The rule of the Kalingas centered around at least at three places viz (i) Kala, (ii) the valley of the Arkan river and (iii) Pegu of Burma[108]. G. Coedes has observed that in lower Burma there were colonies of Indians who had come from Kalinga[109]. The discovery of coins and medals with Hindu symbols in Pegu shows close interaction between Kalinga and Burma from the very ancient times[110]. The Burmese scripture *Buddhagat* mentions a steady commercial contact between Burma and Kalinga[111] which is further attested by ancient Kalingan settlements of Srikshetra near Prome.

The maritime contacts between Kalinga and Burma and the steady flow of immigrants led to the import of Brahmanical elements from Kalinga to Burma[112]. The ancient name attributed to old Prome is Srikshetra often mentioned in the Mon records as Sikset or Srikset, and by the Chinese pilgrim as Che-li-ta-lo. Srikshetra is the holy land of Puri on the ancient Kalinga coast. The name Srikshetra given to old Prome may be apccryphal, but attribution itself is significant, however late it may be. The old name for Pegu is Ussa which is but a form of Odra or Orissa. Further Manikapatna also provided the indication of trade contacts with Burma. The excavations revealed Martuan ware (brown glaze) which is named after a place in Burma[113].

Ceylon

The contact of Kalinga with Ceylon commenced from about 5th century BC if not earlier[114]. The *Mahavamsa* mentions the first king of Ceylon, Vijaya, was the son of King Simhabahu of Simhapura. His grandmother was the daughter of the king of Kalinga, whose name was Susima[115]. It is thus evident that Ceylon had strong political links with Kalinga from very early times. Political and matrimonial relations between Kalinga and Ceylon were supplemented by religious and cultural links. Emperor Asoka sent his son Mahendra to Ceylon for propagating Buddhism[116]. The king of Ceylon, Devanampiya Tissa (247-207 BC) received Asoka's mission with great respect and deeply impressed by the new faith, embraced Buddhism[117]. Later on Asoka sent his daughter Sanghamitra to Ceylon with the Bodhi tree, under which Gautama attained enlightenment. During the reign of Agrabodhi II (AD 592-602), the Kalingan king and his queen visited Ceylon to listen to the discourses of the Buddhist monk Jyothihpala[118]. It is known from the Polonnaruva inscription that Vijayabahu II (AD 1185-87) stayed for many years in Kalinga and went back to Ceylon on the orders of the Ceylonese king Parakramabahu. The *Chulavamsa* mentions that king Vijayabahu of Simhala (AD 1054-1109) married a Kalinga princess named Triloksundari. A later Ceylonese ruler Nishankamalla (AD 1189-1198) was the son of the Kalingan king Jaya Gopa. The Kalinga prince Magha sailed from Kalinga to Ceylon in AD 1214 with an army of 24,000 soldiers to occupy the throne of Ceylon[119].

Champa

The Hindu colony of Champa named after the capital of Anga country in the lower Ganga valley included South Annam and

Cochin with Amaravati as its capital and was founded probably in the second century AD[120]. The contact of Kalinga with Champa is known from the Chinese records which say that in the year AD 137 about 10,000 Ku-liens, attacked their southernmost district, destroyed the Chinese forts and ravaged the whole country[121]. These Ku-liens, whom the Chinese called the Kula people of Burma according to Gerini, were the people from Kalinga. The term 'Kula' nowadays employed in Burma to designate foreigners in general and natives of India, the Dravidians in particular[122]. H.B.Sarkar has also specifically identified the 'Kula' people of Burma with the Kalinga people who had migrated from Kalinga in large numbers either by land or by sea route to Burma and to further lower regions of Indochina, sometime during the first century AD or still earlier[123].

China

The cultural interaction of India with China began in the early centuries of the Christian era. In the words of Kakasu Okakura, the mariners of the Bay of Bengal coast established their colonies in Ceylon, Java, Sumatra and China[124]. Tamralipti was the place of disembarkment for travellers from China to India by sea and it was here that I-tsing and other Chinese pilgrims landed in AD 673 and started their return journey to China via south India. Hiuen Tsang was also to return to China along the same route but he accidentally took a northern land route to China[125]. According to Chinese sources a celebrated scholar of Orissa named Subhakara Simha paid a visit to the court of the Chinese emperor Hussan Tsung and translated a Buddhist text *Maha Varirochana Sutra* into Chinese in the first half of the 8th century AD. In China it was believed that the son of the king of 'Ho-ling' (Kalinga) embarked for China from one of the ports of Orissa perhaps from Palur, in AD 715 and arrived in China in AD 716[126]. In AD 795 the king of Wu-Chu (Orissa) sent the Sanskrit text of the Mahayanist treatise called Ta-fang-kuang-fo- hua-yen-ching copied in his own hand with his autograph, to the Chinese emperor Te-tsong as a gift, through the Buddhist monk named Prajna, who had settled in the monastery of the king of Wu-Chu[127]. The king of Orissa as referred to above, is identified with the Bhaumakara king Subhakaradeva and he has been described in the Chinese sources as 'the fortunate monarch who does what is pure, the lion'. Whatever may be the identification, the incident, indubitably, proves the fact that in the 8th century AD Kalinga had close maritime relation with China.

The Chinese writer Wang-Ta-Yuan (14th century) says that 'because of the cheapness of living in 'Wu-Chu', nine out of ten persons going there for trade did not like to return home'. It was also in the late fourth century AD that the Chinese pilgrim Fa-hien and others found their way back to India for the purpose of visiting Buddhist shrines and assembling the Pali scriptures. The Chinese silk garments (China-msuka) was quite popular in Orissa and the discovery of celadon ware from the excavations at Palur, Manikapatna and the Chinese coin and pottery at Khalkatapatna indicate that there was close maritime contacts with China.

Funan

The oldest Indianised state of Indo-Chinese Peninsula was Kambuja or Cambodia which the Chinese called 'Funan' occupying the lower valley of the Mekong roughly corresponding to modern Cambodia and South Vietnam[128]. The discovery of Indian and Dongson style objects suggest that there was very early Indian contact with Funan. It is often suggested that civilisation in Funan began with the arrival of Indian traders[129]. The Mysore Inscription of second century AD records the grant of land to a Siva shrine of the Brahmins of the Kaundinya Gotra[130]. B.R.Chatterjee thinks that the Kaundinyas might have migrated from Mysore to Indochina. On the other hand Sarkar has proposed that the Kaundinyas might have migrated to Funan from Amaravati in view of the occurrence of Amaravati style of sculpture at Dong Duong[131]. The Kaundinya Brahmins who still live near the Mahendra mountain range of Orissa which is very close to the sea might have migrated from Kalinga. Mount Mahendra which was considered as *Kula parvat* (Phenon Kulen) and used as the abode of the family deity of Kaundinya Brahmins before the reign of Jayavarman II could have been the mount Motan of Chinese record of the fifth century AD. The very fact that the river Mekong which flows through the kingdom of Funan was called the 'Mahanadi' which is also the main river of Orissa and supports the view that the Kaundinya migrated from Orissa[132]. Mekong was also called 'Maganga' in some places[133].

Java

The island of Java or Java Dvipa, an important commercial centre in the Malaya Archipelago appears to have been colonised by Indians in the first century AD[134]. Legends and local traditions of Java mention that 20,000 families were sent to Java by the prince of Kling and these families became prosperous[135]. The term *Kling* is probably derived from Kalinga. The people of Kalinga, had a leading role in developing Java economically[136]. There was also a Hindu kingdom in central Java, and the Chinese source of Tang period namely the Ho-ling refers to Kalinga. The kingdom of Ho-ling (Kalinga) had a politically significant population[137]. Buddhist images of Java simulate those of Ratnagiri. The *Kala Makara* motif probably migrated from Orissa to Java. The *Makara* heads and the *Kirtimukhas* are fairly common motifs of Orissan art and sculpture. It is possible that some of the Orissan artists migrated to Java along with the merchants and missionaries[138] who reproduced the Orissan art traditions in Java and other places.

Buddhism also forged a cultural link between Orissa and Java. The archaeological excavations at the Buddhist sites of Lalitagiri, Udayagiri and Ratnagiri reveal the cultural intercourse of Orissa with Java and others places of Southeast Asia. Similarities are found in the Buddha and Boddhisattavas images of Java, Borobudur, Indonesia and Orissa in their massiveness and facial expressions[139]. A band of Hindu navigators sailed in AD 75 from Kalinga to Java and set up a colony, built towns and cities and developed trade with the mother country. The Hindu settlement of Sumatra was almost entirely from the East coast of India, that too from Bengal, Orissa and Masulipatnam which had a large share in colonising both Java and Cambodia[140]. Both the History of the Tang Dynasty and the New History of the Tang Dynasty[141] mention Java as Ga-ling, the Chinese name for Kalinga. The Hindu settlers at the time of the Tang Dynasty (AD 618-906) were from Orissa in overwhelming numbers[142].

Rome

The discovery of Rouletted ware from Sisupalgarh, Palur and Tamralipti[143] (Tamluk) signifies the probability of the Roman contact. Besides pottery, iron objects and clay bullae resembling

Silenus's head imitated from those of Roman coin, a unique gold coin depicting Kushana design of a standing king and a Brahmi legend of 3rd century AD on the obverse and Roman bust with legend on the reverse[144] have been found. The recent excavation at Manikapatna revealed two sherds of Indian Rouletted ware and fragment of an amphora from early historical period[145]. Beglar noticed Roman coins, the sherds of Rouletted ware, clay bullae, gold medallion, Kushana coins at Bamanghati in Mayurbhanj district. A fine piece of amphora found from Karanji village, not very far from Jayarampur, on the border of Orissa and West Bengal is said to be now in a private collection[146]. Roman coins have also been discovered in the district of Visakhapatnam in Andhra Pradesh and in Bilaspur district of Madhya Pradesh. These finds testify the close trade relations between Kalinga and Roman world[147]. Further, the demand for Indian muslin in Greek and Roman courts and the presence of Graco-Roman merchants in the Indian ports indicate extensive trade contacts[148]. Roman gold coins have also been found in Mysore, Hyderabad and in the South Indian coastal regions which corroborate the fact that East coast of India had close contact with the Roman Empire[149].

Siam

Siam, the present Thailand came in contact with the Indian subcontinent since early times. The influence of Indian culture in Siam may be traced from the first two centuries of the Christian era. The excavations at Pong Tuk and Phra Pathom in Siam have brought to light the remains of a temple sanctuary, buildings, and a small statue of standing Buddha which shows the Indian influence on Siam's art and culture. The maritime contact of Kalinga with Siam had an indirect influence on the ancient art of Siam. Among the recent finds from the cemetery site Don Ta Phet in west central Thailand include semi-precious stone and glass beads, etched carnelian beads and the so called Knobbed ware[150] which are clearly of Indian origin and closely resemble the finds from Sisupalgarh, Dhauli, Jaugada. I.C. Glover the excavator of Don Ta Phet at Thailand gives credit to Buddhist missionaries for such transaction between Orissa and Thailand[151]. The post Gupta Buddhist art of Orissa especially of Lalitagiri had a profound influence on the Buddha images of Siam[152]. The *Lingas* found in Thailand indicate the prevalence of Saivism in Siam. Further, the *Loykrathong* or *Loy Brah Prahdip* festival (the ceremony of floating of paper boats with lamp) performed in Thailand in the month of December recall similar ritual of floating boats in Orissa on the *Kartika Purnima* day (November-December). This is an indicator of ancient maritime connection between Siam and Kalinga.

Sumatra

The earliest Indianized kingdom in Indonesia was Sri-Vijaya with its capital at Palembang in Sumatra[153]. It was probably Indians who were the first to visit Sumatra and adjoining areas. The Chinese called Shih-li-fo-shih (San-to-tsi-kan-te-li or briefly, Fuche). Sumatra founded in fourth century AD and rose to great power during the close of seventh century AD[154]. I-tsing informs that it was a centre of Buddhist learning. The king of Sri-Vijaya possessed trading ships sailing between Sri-Vijaya and India. India had close maritime contact with Sumatra among which Kalinga played a central role for colonisation.

The above account shows that Kalingan ports viz Tamralipti, Manikapatna, Palur, Che-li-ta-lo, Kalingapatnam, Pithunda, etc substantially contributed to the cultural expansion of India in general and Kalinga in particular. The countries more specifically accommodated the cultural influence of India. The Kalingan art and architecture also manifested the accommodation of foreign influence.

References

1. Nandargikar, G.R., (ed. & tr.) 1897 *Raghuvamsa*, Bombay, Vol. VI, 54.
2. Sastri, T.G., (ed.) 1920-25 *Aryamanjusrimulakalpa*, 3 Vols. Trivandrum, 168.
3. Panigrahi, K.C., 1981 *History of Orissa*, Cuttack, 468.
4. McCrindle, J.W., 1985 *Ancient India as Described by Ptolemy*, (reprint), Delhi, 69-72
5. Devi, G., 1992 "Tamralipti: The Port Town of Ancient Orissa", *Orissa Review*, Vol. XLIX (4): 50-52.
6. Prasad, P.C., 1977 *Foreign Trade and Commerce in Ancient India*, Delhi, 255.
7. Cany, J.F., 1964 *Southeast Asia: Its Historical Development*, New York.

8. Das, B.S., 1978 *Studies in Economic History of Orissa from Ancient Times to 1833*, Calcutta, 40.
9. Ṣila, Tripati, & S. R. Rao, 1994 "Tamralipti: The Ancient Port of India", *Studies in History and Culture*, Journal of the Post Graduate Dept. of History, Vol. II (1): 33-39.
10. Banerjee, R.D., 1930 *History of Orissa*, Calcutta, Vol. I, 94.
11. *Vinaya Pitaka*, Vol. III. 338.
12. *Mahavamsa*, XI, 20-23, XIX, 5-6, X, 38-39.
13. Mishra, A.N., 1981 "Overseas Trade and Maritime Activities of Ancient Orissa", *Orissa Historical Research Journal*, Vol. XXVII (1-4): 77-87.
14. Behera, K.S., 1977 "Maritime Trade in Ancient Orissa", *Sidelights on History and Culture of Orissa*, (ed.) M.N. Das, Cuttack, 115-121.
15. Takakasu-Itsing, Ch.X, Quoated in Sahu, N.K., 1958 *Buddhism in Orissa*, Cuttack, 142.
16. *Indian Archaeology - A Review*, 1954-55 Archaeological Survey of India, New Delhi, 19-20.
17. *The Imperial Gazetter of India*, (Singhbhum to Trashi-Chod-Zong), 1908, Vol. XXIII, Oxford, at Clarendon Press, (New Edition): 216-218.
18. Patnaik, A.P., 1993 "Smurti O Bismurtira Katoti Chinnasutra", *Sagar O Sahitya* (Oriya) (ed.) K.S.Behera, Cuttack, 92.
19. *Ibid.* 93.
20. *Indian Archaeology 1984-85 - A Review*, Archaeological Survey of India, Delhi, 56-60.
21. Sinha, B.K., 1992 "Khalkattapatna: A Small Port on the Coast of Orissa", *New Trends in Indian Art and Archaeology*, (eds.) B.U.Nayak and N.C.Ghosh, New Delhi, 423-428.
22. Majumdar, R.C., (ed.) *History and Culture of Indian People*, Vol. VI, Bombay, 658.
23. Watters, T., 1973 *On Yuan Chwang's travel in India* (eds.) T.W.Rhys Davis and S.W.Bushell, Vol. II, Delhi, 190-194.
24. *Ibid.* 194.
25. Behera, K.S., 1992 "Glimpses of the Maritime Activities of Kalinga", *Orissa Review*, Vol. XLIX (4): 1-5.
26. Ganguly, D.K., 1975 *Historical Geography of Ancient Orissa*, Calcutta, 75.
27. Sahu, N.K., 1964 *Utkal University History of Orissa*, Vol. I, Bhubaneswar, 142.
28. Banerji, R.D., 1930 *History of Orissa*, Vol. I, Calcutta, 138.
29. Cunningham, A., 1963 *The Ancient Geography of India*, Varanasi, 430.
30. Misra, B. 1937 "Folklore and Puranic Tradition about Origin of God Jagannath", *Indian Historical Quarterly*, Vol. XIII, (4): 607.

31. Ganguly, D.K., 1975 *op. cit.*, 68.
32. Watters, T.,1973 *op. cit.*, 194.
33. Choudhary, S., 1977 "Lost and Forgotten Places of Orissa", *Sidelights on History and Culture of Orissa*, (ed.) M.N. Das, Cuttack, 65-76.
34. Watters, T., *op. cit.*, 189-200.
35. Ray, H.P., 1993 *Trade and Diplomacy in India-China Relations: A study of Bengal during the fifteenth Century*, New Delhi, 60-61.
36. Behera, K.S., 1994 "Xuan Zang and Cultural Communication Between China and Orissa in Eastern India", paper submitted to *the International symposium on Xuan Zang studies at Yanshi and Xian, China*, 16-20 April 1994.
37. Ray, H.P., 1994 "Orissa and Orissa Trade in Chinese Historical Records", *Journal of Indian Ocean Studies*, Vol. II, (1): 36-46.
38. Raut, L.N., 1988 *Socio-Economic life in Medieval Orissa*, Calcutta, 176.
39. Nigam, J.S., 1993 "A Brief Note on the Excavation at Manikapatna", Bhubaneswar, (Unpublished).
40. Pradhan, D., 1991 "Manikapatna: Ancient Port City on Chilka", *Kalingas, The Brave, Souvenir*, Bhubaneswar, 8-10.
41. Behera, K.S., 1994 "Maritime Contacts of Orissa: The Archaeological Perspectives", Paper presented in the International seminar on Techno-Archaeological Perspectives of Seafaring in the Indian Ocean, NISTADS, 28th February to 3rd March 1994, New Delhi.
42. Singh, J., 1982 *Prachin Utkal* (Oriya), Bhubaneswar, Vol. II, 137-51.
43. Mookerji, R.K., 1912 *Indian Shipping*, Bombay, 256.
44. Bhatt, K.S., 1993 "Chilka Anchalare Matyajibi Mananankar Jivandhara" *Sagar O Sahitya,* (Oriya), (ed.) K.S.Behera, Cuttack, 222-242.
45. Patnaik, P., 1993 "Odisara Loka Kathare Samudra Yatra" *Sagar O Sahitya*, (Oriya), (ed.) K.S.Behera, Cuttack, 66-84.
46. Watters, T., 1973 *op. cit.*, 197.
47. *Ibid.*
48. Choudhary, S., 1977 *op. cit.*, 65-76.
49. Gerini, G.E., 1974 *Researches on Ptolemy's Geography of Eastern Asia*, Delhi, 835.
50. Mukherjee, B.N., 1981 "The Relevance of the Periplous Tes Exo Thalasses to the History of Orissa", *Journal of the Orissa Research Society*, Vol. I: 8-9.
51. Majumdar, R.C., 1986 *Suvarnadvipa, Ancient Indian Colonies in the Far East,* (reprint), Delhi, 175.
52. Warmington, E.H., 1974 *The Commerce Between Roman Empire and India*, Delhi, 322.
53. Choudhary, S., 1977 "Lost and Forgotten Places of Orissa", *Sidelights on History and Culture of Orissa*, (ed.) M.N. Das, Cuttack, 65-76.

54. Behera, K.S., 1977 *op. cit.*, 115-121.

55. Law, B.C., (ed.) 1925 *Dathavamsa*, Lahore.

56. *Indian Archaeology 1984-85 - A Review*, Archaeological Survey of India, Delhi, 56-60.

57. Exploration carried out as part of present study.

58. Sree Padma, B., 1991 "Kalingapatnam Port Through the Ages", *Recent Advances in Marine Archaeology*, (ed.) S.R. Rao, Goa, 73-74.

59. Cunningham, A., 1963 *op. cit.*, 435.

60. Ramamurti, G.V., 1979 Nadagam plates of Vajrahasta, *Epigraphia Indica*, Vol. IV, (reprint) 183-193.

61. Fleet, J.F., 1984 Ganga Grant of Indravarma, *Indian Antiquary*, Vol. XIII, (reprint), 119-124.

62. Majumdar, R.C., 1984 Narasingapalli plates of Hastivarman, *Epigraphia Indica*, Vol. XXIII, (reprint), 62-67.

63. Melmoth, W., (tr.) 1945 *Pliny's Natural History*, Vol. II, London, 20-21.

64. Raghuvamsa, 6th Canto, 5th Verse.

65. Singh, M.R., 1972 *Geographical Data in the Early Puranas*, Calcutta, 27.

66. Rao, R.S., 1971-72 "The Historical Geography of Kalinga", *Journal of the Andhra Historical Research Society*, Vol. XXXII, No. (I-IV): 2.

67. Sree Padma, B., 1991 "Kalingapatnam Port Through the Ages", *Recent Advances in Marine Archaeology*, (ed.) S.R.Rao, Goa, 73-74.

68. *Ibid.*

69. Rao, S.R., 1978 *Progress and Prospects of Marine Archaeology in India*, Goa, 67-68.

70. Ghoshal, R.K., 1985 Jirjingi plates of Ganga Indravarman, *Epigraphica Indica*, Vol. XXV, (reprint), 281- 288.

71. Law, B.C., 1967 *Historical Geography of Ancient India*, Paris, 177.

72. Sitapati, G.V., 1926 Korni Plates of Anantavarman Chodaganga Deva, *Journal of Andhra Historical Research Society*, Vol. I: 40-48 and 106-124.

73. Law, B.C., (ed.) 1925 *Dathavamsa*, Lahore, Ch. VII.

74. Melmoth, W., (tr.) 1945, Pliny's *Natural History*, Vol. II, London, 21.

75. Geiger, W., (ed. & tr.) 1908 *Mahavamsa*, Pali Text Society, London.

76. Law, B.C., 1967 *Historical Geography of Ancient India*, Paris, 402.

77. *Ibid.*

78. Mookerji, R., 1912 *A History of Indian Shipping*, Bombay, 8.

79. Cowell, E.B., 1895-1907 *The Jatakas*, Vol. III, No. 301, Cambridge, 1-5.

80. Bhagwat, N.K., (ed.) 1936-42 *Digha Nikaya*, Pali Text Society, Vol. II. Bombay, 235.

81. Law, B.C., (ed.) 1925 *Dathavamsa*, Lahore.

82. *Uttaradhyayanasutra*, Vol. XVIII, 85-86.

83. Das, D.N., 1977 *The Early History of Kalinga*, Calcutta, 250.

84. Personal Communication with the Director of the Department of Archaeology, Government of Andhra Pradesh, Hyderabad.

85. Subrahmanyam, R., 1964 *Salihundam*, A Buddhist Site in Andhra Pradesh, Dept. of Archaeology, Government of Andhra Pradesh, Archaeological Series No.17, Hyderabad, 21-22.

86. *Ibid.* 34-45.

87. Krishnasastry, V.V. et al., 1992 *Thotlakonda* (A Buddhist Site in Andhra Pradesh), Dept. of Archaeology and Museums, Series No. 68, Hyderabad, 1-98.

88. *Ibid.*

89. Subrahmanyam, B., 1991 *Excavations at Gopalapatnam*, State Administrative Reports, Dept. of Archaeology and Museums, 1990-1991, Hyderabad.

90. Das, B.S., 1978 *Economic History of Orissa*, Calcutta, 38.

91. Levi, S., 1926 "Pithunda, Pithuda, Pitundra", *Indian Antiquary*, Vol. LV: 145-47.

92. Sarma, I.K., 1990 "Ancient Andhra Ports, Religious Centres and Seafaring", *Journal of Marine Archaeology*, Vol. I: 19-23.

93. Behera, K.S., 1977 *op. cit.*, 115-121.

94. Sahu, N.K., 1977 "Historical Geography ", *Sidelights on History and Culture of Orissa*, (ed.) M.N.Das, Cuttack, 30-43.

95. Patnaik, A.P., 1992 "Kalinga's Link with Countries of Southeast Asia", *Orissa Review*, Bhubaneswar, Vol. XLIX (4): 25-28.

96. Majumdar, R.C., *op. cit.*, 7.

97. Banerjee, R.D., 1930-31 *History of Orissa*, 2 Vols, Calcutta.

98. Singhal, D.P., 1972 *India and World Civilisation*, Vol. II, Calcutta, 121.

99. Behera, K.S., 1994 "Maritime Contacts of Orissa: Literary and Archaeological evidence", *Utkal Historical Research Journal*, Vol. V: 55-70.

100. Sastri, K.A.N., (ed.) 1957 *A Comprehensive History of India,* Vol. II, Bombay, 772.

101. Lamb, A., 1975 "Indian influences in Ancient Southeast Asia", *A Cultural History of India,* (ed.) A.L. Basham, Oxford, 442-454.

102. Coedes, G., 1971 *The Indianized States of Southeast Asia,* Honolulu, 50-63.

103. Sinha, B.K., 1992 *op. cit.*, 423-428.

104. Behera, K.S., 1977 *op. cit.,* 115-121.

105. Behera, K.S., 1992 *op. cit.*, 1-5.

106. Majumdar, R.C., (ed.) 1970 *The Classical Age,* Bharatiya Vidya Bhavan, Bombay, 658.

107. Patnaik, A.P., 1992 *op. cit.*, 25-28.
108. Gerini, G.E., 1974 *op. cit.*, 34.
109. Coedes, G., 1971 *op. cit.*, 63.
110. Phyre, A.P., 1833 *History of Burma*, London, 31.
111. Mookerji, R., 1912 *op. cit.*, 256.
112. Ray, N.R., 1932 *Brahmanical Gods in Burma*, Calcutta, 84-85.
113. Nigam, J.S., *op. cit.*,
114. Behera, K.S., 1992 "Glimpses of the Maritime Activities of Kalinga", *Orissa Review*, Vol. XLIX (4): 1-5.
115. Das, M.N., 1977 "Kalinga and Simhala: A study in Ancient Relations", *Sidelights on History and Culture of Orissa*, (ed.) M.N. Das, Cuttack, 122-131.
116. Singhal, D.P., 1972 *op. cit.*, 100-101.
117. *Ibid.*
118. Das, M.N., 1977 op. cit, 122-131.
119. *Ibid.*
120. Luniya, B.N., 1994 *Evolution of Indian Culture*, Agra, 242-43.
121. Majumdar, R.C., 1944 *Ancient Indian Colonies in the Far East*, Calcutta, Vol. I, 34.
122. Gerini, G.E., 1974 *op. cit.*, 103.
123. Sarkar, H.B., 1934 *Indian influence on the Literature of Java and Bali*, Calcutta, 109.
124. Mookerji, R., 1912 *op. cit.*, 256.
125. Watters, T., 1973 *op. cit.*, 190.
126. Behera, K.S., 1977 *op. cit.*, 115-121.
127. Watters, T., 1973 *op. cit.*, 196.
128. Singhal, D.P., 1972 *op. cit.*, 121.
129. *Ibid.*
130. Gopal, B.R., 1985 *Corpus of Kadamba Inscriptions*, Kadamba Institute of Cultural Studies, Vol. I, Sirsi, 5-7.
131. Sarkar, H.B., 1934 "The Homeland of Kaundinya of Funan and Tradition about his Marriage", *Journal of Institute of Asian Studies*, Madras, 25.
132. Gerini, G.E., 1974 *op. cit.*, 136.
133. Majumdar, R.C., 1986 *Suvarnadvipa, Ancient Indian Colonies in the Far East*, Vol. I, (reprint) Delhi, 175.
134. Luniya, B.N., 1994 *op. cit.*, 231-253.
135. Majumdar, R.C., 1986 *op. cit.*, 210.
136. Behera, K.S., 1978 *op. cit.*, 115-21.
137. Majumdar, R.C., 1986 *op. cit.*, 22.

138. Behera, K.S., 1977 *op. cit.*, 115-21.

139. Ghosh, D.P., 1983 "Influence of Indian Art on the Art of Southeast Asia", *The Aspects of Indian Art and Culture*, S.K.Saraswati Commemorative Volume, Calcutta.

140. Mookerji, R., 1912 *op. cit.*, 103-04.

141. Ji Xianlin, et al., (eds.) 1985 *Da Tang Xiyu Ji Jiaozhu, Tang Xuan Zang Bianji Yuanzhu* (Xuan Zang and Bianji's Journey to the Western Region during the Tang dynasty, Annotated), Beijing.

142. Groeneveldt, W.P., 1960 *Historical Notes on Indonesia and Malaya Compiled from Chinese Sources*, (reprint) Jakarta, 15.

143. Behera, K.S., 1977 *op. cit.*, 115-121.

144. Lal, B.B., 1949 "Sisupalgarh, An Early Historical fort in Eastern India", *Ancient India, No. 5,* Archaeological Survey of India, Delhi, 62-105.

145. Nigam, J.S., *op. cit.*

146. Acharya, P., 1969 *Studies in Orissan History, Archaeology and Archives*, Cuttack, 533.

147. Behera, K.S., 1977 *op. cit.*, 115-121.

148. Tawney, C.H. Jr., *Kathasaritsagara*, 11-45.

149. Marshal!, J., 1951 *Taxila*, Vol. II, Cambridge, 620.

150. Brandtner, M., 1988-89 "Archaeological Explorations around Bhubaneswar", *MANAV, Journal of Anthropological Society of Orissa*, Vol. III: 231-250.

151. Glover, I.C., 1990 "Early Trade Between India and Southeast Asia: A Link in the Development of Ancient World Trading System", *Occasional Paper No.16*, The University of Hull, London, 1-45.

152. Behera, K.S., 1992 *op. cit.*, 1-5.

153. Singhal, D.P., 1972 *op. cit.*, 139.

154. Majumdar, R.C., (ed.) 1970 *The Classical Age*, Bharatiya Vidya Bhavan, Bombay, 655.

3

Trade Routes and Commerce

It is evident from literary as well as archaeological sources that important routes existed for internal trade and commerce. So far, much work has been done on the trade routes of India but serious attempts have not been made for the study of the trade routes and communication pattern of ancient Kalinga. Economically Kalinga seems to have been sound and prosperous since ancient times. The trade and commercial relation of Kalinga with foreign countries made the life pattern active. The intra and inter regional cultural flow which marched through these routes found its manifestation in regional art, architecture and sculpture. The geographical location of Kalinga helped her in rising to great heights in respect of trade and communication pattern from the Pre-Buddhist period. Orissa served as a bridge between the transoceanic and inland trade routes which provided migration of people, and cultural contacts along with trade and commerce.

The recorded history of Kalinga begins in 261 BC. The two special rock edicts of Asoka[1] and the findings from Jaugada[2] and Sisupalgarh[3] excavations provide ample material on the life pattern, civic administration and socio-economic life of the people. Dhauli and Jaugada have been identified respectively with Tosali and Somapa of Asokan inscriptions. These two metropolises were the key centres of trade and royal activity. Further the excavated materials from Sisupalgarh, Jaugada and Manmunda and the existing monuments such as Asokan Edicts at Dhauli and Jaugada indicate the existence of people of various professions such as artisans, craftsmen, masons and traders, suggesting an urbanised state and society.

During this period, though agricultural economy occupied an overwhelmingly dominant position, different kinds of handicrafts gave way for development of trade. Further, the handicrafts progressively developed into small scale industries, some of which like armour manufacturing, ship-building, textile industry, mining etc were run by the State. The rural pockets existing in and around these cities were the store house of different products. These early historic sites are Asuragarh[4] (Kalahandi district), Manmunda (Phulbani district), Nehena (Kalahandi district), Ganiapallẹ (Sambalpur district), Sitabhinji (Keonjhar district), Khiching (Mayurbhanj district), Bhadrak (Balasore district), Lalitagiri and Namitigiri (Cuttack district) and Manikapatna[5] (Puri district).

Further literary sources such as the Jatakas, the *Arthasastra*, the *Samyuakta Nikaya* and the *Indica* of Megasthenese mention that Kalinga was famous for the production of rice, bajra, cotton fabrics, salt, elephants, silk, *dukula* (a kind of cloth), gems, pearls, oyster, conch, sugar, earthen pot and diamond. The information about the trade routes and roads are available from the location of coin hoards, accounts of the travellers, routes of invasion, etc. Inscriptions[6] occasionally refer to roads such as *Dharmaraja Kalinga marga, Sundarika marga, Rajapatha*, etc. It is apparent from the account of Hiuen Tsang that there was a road linking Odra, Kongoda and Kalinga. The *Vamana Purana* of 7th century AD mentions the visit of pilgrims to Viraja (Jajpur) and Purusottama (Puri). The army of Rajendra Chola passed through Orissa in AD 1022-23 as it is evident from Chola inscriptions. Anantavarman Chodaganga's inscriptions datable to 12th century AD found on the temples at Nirmaljar of Ganjam district, Puri, Alagum, Khilore, Bhubaneṣwar and Jajpur indicate the existence of a route which passed through these places.

Land Routes

The important Indian urban trade centres of India were Bharukaccha (Broach) on the West coast, Pushkalavati on the

Northwest, Sravasti, Champa (modern Bhagalpur), Pataliputra, Varanasi, Kausambi, Ayodhya, Mathura, Vidisa and Ujjain in central India and Tamralipti, Tosali (Dhauli) and Somapa (Jaugada) on the East coast[7] (Fig. 7). These trade centres were well connected with roads and communications network[8]. Mile stones were provided on the corner of the roads at regular intervals to indicate distance and direction[9]. Kalinga made herself free from the yoke of the Magadhan empire under king Kharavela (1st century BC). It is learnt from the Hathigumpha inscription that during this period socio-economic and political structure of Kalinga was well advanced[10]. Kharavela's claim of marching up to Mathura in the north, defeating the Rastrikas and the Bhojakas of the Vindhyan region and of subduing the Tamil confederacy in the south makes it apparent that Kalinganagari was well connected with the important land routes leading to north-west and south India[11]. The trade route that connected Kalinganagari the capital of Kharavela with Pataliputra and Mathura in the north was passing through Jajpur, khiching, Vaidakhia near Anandpur of Keonjhar district, Sitabhinji, Asapatvenjakia, Tentala, Bhalada, Vensusagara of Singhbhum, Telkupi Panchaet pass near Bodhagaya, Gorkhagiri and Pataliputra where this route met with all other royal routes to Mathura and Taxila[12]. The other trade route that leads on to south India starts from Kalinganagara and passes through Puri, Palur, Salihundam, Ramatirtham, Amaravati, Nagarjunakonda and Kaveripatnam[13]. This route was perhaps followed by Kharavela to reach the Kaveri valley. The explorations along this route have revealed the ruins of monastic establishments[14].

The recent archaeological explorations at Baneswarnasi, Boud, Manmunda on the lower Mahanadi valley and Sirpur, Ratnapur on the upper Mahanadi valley have yielded monastic complexes of the early medieval period which testify that there was a trade route[15]. This route was possibly used for the transportation of goods to hinterland from the coastal area as well as the forest tract and to the diamond rich areas of Orissa. Further, Tosali on the coast line had direct contact with Tamralipti on the north and Kaveripoompattinam (Kaveripatnam) on the south, thus forming a trade circuit (Fig. 8). By the second century BC the entire east coast seems to have been linked to a single coastal network which facilitated transport of tin from Magadha, iron from Kalinga as well as gold from present Karnataka. Further the sea ports of ancient Orissa, Andhra and Tamil Nadu were also linked to ports of Southeast Asia and Sri Lanka to deal with pearls, gem and semi-precious stones. However, much work has to be done in this regard particularly on Orissa coast. A systematic archaeological exploration and excavation is highly necessary to find out the historical evidences to establish this long standing hypothesis.

The references in early Sanskrit and Pali literatures indicate private ownership of land and the rise of very rich households of the land owners, i.e. the *grahapatis* in the middle Ganges valley. It was from the ranks of the *grahapatis* that the trading communities, viz *vanikas* and *sresthis* arose. Salt, metals, textiles and pottery were the standard items of trade[16]. This growing long distance trade between the Gangetic valley and the Deccan peninsula had its impact on the east coast. An important route that leads from Mathura to Vidisa, Sanchi and joins with the southern route from the Ganges plain and its eastern branch was leading to Sahajati sector, Cedi country on the Narmada and Daksina Kosala and Kalinga. Another trade route could be traced from Tosali to Vidisa as the antiquities make us believe that this route started from Asokan headquarters Tosali. It went along the river Daya through Aragada, Govindapur, Kantilo up to the Mahanadi basin. It further passed via Baramula, Boud, Manmunda then on the bank of the river Anga and reached Sirpur, Ratnapur. Finally, it terminated at Vidisa and Ujjain[17] (Fig. 9). The coastal route between Tosali to Tamralipti was very hazardous due to the rivers and robbery but it became popular in 1st century BC. This route could be traced from Tosali, then on the coastal line Lalitagiri, Darmasala, Jajpur, Soro, Jayarampur and finally connected Tamralipti[18].

The distribution of the Kushana copper coins suggest a trade route might have started from Patna to Bilaspur, Raipur through Sambalpur and Kalahandi region of ancient Orissa. The excavations at Salihundam, Ramatirtham and Samgharma have yielded the Satavahana coins. The inscription of Kodavali mentions that this entire region including Ganjam district was under the sway of the Satavahanas[19]. The Satavahanas were famous for their construction of monasteries in south eastern India which accelerated the growth of trade and guild activities. Tosali and Tamralipti were linked with Vaisali[20]. Recently the excavations at Lalitagiri by

Archaeological Survey of India revealed the remains of a foremost Buddhist centre connected with other parts of India during 3rd century AD. A number of Kushana donatory inscriptions have been found from its aspidal temple[21]. The routes connecting ancient Kalinga with other countries is known from the Allahabad Pillar Inscription of Samụdra Gupta. The Gupta army is said to have marched to Kalinga from Allahabad through Kosala. The next phase of Orissan trade continues with peasant and trading communities occupying different pockets in the river valleys from fourth century AD to sixth century AD. The royal dynasties ruled from places stretching extreme south-eastern part, i.e. Koraput to north boundaries of Orissa. The minor ancient dynasties like the Matharas, the Nalas and the Nagas spread over the whole territory. The rise of several dynasties gave new turn to Kalingan trade. The grant of land to Brahmanas and religious establishments implied large scale agrarian expansion in the regions of Tosali and Somapa of Asoka, Kalinganagara and Pithunda of Kharavela and Dantapura of Pali literature. New city centres developed under the then rulers. There are references to prosperous towns viz. Pisthapura, Simhapura, Vardhamananagara, Sunagara, etc. in the Kalingan Empire.

Contemporary records indicate that the principal trade during the period was carried on through guilds and corporations not only of the merchants, but also of the workers like weavers, potters, oilmen and stone cutters[22]. Textile was known to be the principal industry of Kalinga and among other articles of trade mention may be made of spices, coconuts, indigo, incense, ivory materials and drugs. A few epigraphical sources of (post Gupta period) allude to the traders of the potter and braziers. The Midnapore plates of Somadatta and Subhakirtti indicate that the entire village belonged to the makers of pottery[23]. The villages which Madhavaraja donated to one Prajapatisvamin of Vatsasa *gotra,* seems to have belonged to potters[24]. The name of a bronze smith *(Kamsyakara)* Sri Samanta Svayambhu identically appears in a record implies that the bronze smith peacefully plied his trade in Kalinga[25].

The Nalas (5th-6th century AD) ruled over the Bastar and Koraput regions which was part of the ancient Atavika territory. The Trikalinga trade route i.e. from Kalinga to Kosala, as well as to central and northern India passed through their kingdom and rivers like the Indravati and the Godavari were connected with Vengi and other territories in the south. The prosperity of trade of the Nalas was testified by the circulation of gold coins by the the Nala rulers[26]. The Mana dynasty, contemporary to the Nalas, were ruling over the territory laying to the north of the Mathura kingdom beyond the river Mahanadi. A hoard of 147 coins of this dynasty has been discovered from village Nanduru and Gandibedha in Balasore district. According to S.N.Rajaguru, palaeographically they are datable to fifth century AD[27]. The Mana family is said to have been originally a merchant family. Subsequently the dynasty migrated to Chota Nagpur region of Bihar. As the ruling dynasty itself was merchant class, it is needless to mention that there were brisk trade relations with other regions during fifth-sixth century AD. Further, the excavations at the Buddhist sites of Latitagiri and Ratnagiri reveal the constructional activities of the people of Kalinga between first and sixth-seventh century AD. Though the patrons of *Sri Chandraditya Samagra Arya Bhikshu Sangha* and *Ratnagiri Vihara Arya Bhikshu Sangha,* are new evidences but these establishments received large chunk of donations from the merchants, pilgrims and monks. Probably this was the custom of that period as evidenced from western Indian cave monasteries. These two Buddhist establishments had close relations with the Buddhist epicentres of Vaisali, Sravasti, Rajagriha, Nalanda, Saranath, Tamralipti, Nagarjunakonda and Dhanyakataka. Thus the monks, scholars, pilgrims as well as merchants of this period visited all these centres which is evidenced from sculptures and inscriptions[28].

Tamralipti formed the eastern starting point of the northern route *Uttarapatha*, connecting it with the leading cities of northern India up to Pushkalavati (Charasadda) in the extreme northwest. The goods and merchandise of Pushkalavati, Taxila, Sakala (Sialkot), Mathura, Pataliputra and Champa were brought through this land route to Tamralipti for their export to Ceylon, Southeast Asia and China. It also formed the eastern starting point of the east-west trade route i.e. *Purvaparantapatha* between Tamralipti and Bharukaccha connecting the cities of northeast India with those of Malwa and Gujarat. Articles of trade were brought from eastern India through the northern route to Kausambi and from here they were brought by the *Sarthavahas* to Bharukaccha (Broach) via Vidisa (Besnagar), Ujjayani (Ujjain) and Dasapura (Mandasaur) for exporting to western Asia and the Mediterranean world. The *Brhatkathaslokasangraha* mentions that traders of the northern and east-west regions as well as foreigners *(Vaidesikan)* used to go to Tamralipti carrying cooking utensils in old leather bags[29]. The route linking coastal Orissa with Western Orissa passed along the course of the Mahanadi river. The *Ratnavali*, a work on drama of the 7th century AD suggests a route from Kalinga coast up to Kausambi passing through South Kosala. The Somavamsi rulers first occupied South Kosala and in due course extended their power over the coastal region. The *Skanda Purana* mentions that king Indradyumna of Avanti, passed through Charchika (present Banki), Cuttack, Ekamra (Bhubaneswar) and finally reached Purusottama Ksetra (Puri). Another route passed from Cuttack to Bihar through Keonjhar and Mayurbhanj district. This is suggested on the basis of the discovery of imitated Kushana coins at Dharmasala, Sitabhinji, Bhanjakia. In AD 1380 Sultan Feroz Shah Tughluq started from Bihar and reached Cuttack by passing through Mayurbhanj and Keonjhar districts[30].

The references to Purusottama (Puri) in inscriptions from Bihar (as for instance Govindapur inscription) and Madhya Pradesh (Maihar inscription) would suggest pilgrim routes to Puri. It is known from Orissan inscriptions that many Brahmanas immigrated to Orissa from Madhyadesh, Sravasti, Tirabhukti, Radha, Varendra *mandala*, etc which suggest the existence of interstate routes. Obviously such ancient routes facilitated internal and inter-regional trade. It is seen that the coast of Kalinga, its ports and market towns were humming with trade and cultural activity and inter linked with land as well as sea routes starting from North-west region to the plains of the Ganges. The merchandise from the Gangetic valley and Madhya Bharat reached the Krishna and the Kaveri valley through Kalinga. The long Southeast coast with convenient anchorages had not only been a transmitter of brisk overseas trade but also of religion and culture.

Water Routes

The transport system of ancient India has been grouped under two divisions viz land and water. Water route was more important and preferable than land route. Fallen tree trunks in the river were their guideline for water communication. Further, man had conquered water at a much earlier date than has been supposed hitherto. Transportation by water is cheap. It also carries a huge volume of commerce since river or sea is a readymade highway, free to all water transportations. It is not burdened with three types of expenses viz construction, maintenance and supervision of the route. The people used the water routes from earliest times, and the existence of water route is known from the Harappan seals[31]. Ancient literatures like the *Rig Veda* and the *Atharva Veda*, epics like the *Ramayana*, the *Mahabharata*, the *Indica* of Megasthenes and the *Arthasastra* of Kautilya etc throw a flood of light on the sea routes and sea-borne communication of different types. Boats were used for the water borne trade. Boat motifs have been noticed on walls of Jagannath temple Puri, Konark and Bhubaneswar. The lexicon *Trikandasesha* of Purushottama[32], describe various kinds of boats namely *bhelaka, variratha, nauh, tarikah, plavah, tarandhuh, vahanah, tarandah* and *varavatah*. The Pulindas used a kind of boat[33] named *Padaraka*. One Bhaumakara inscription[34] refers to the grant of right over landing places on the bank of the river *ghattas* and ferry places *naditirasthana* to the beneficiaries, suggests the use of boats on a considerable scale and therefore emphasises the importance of river traffic. The chief routes of internal trade were probably the waterways of the state. The rivers Baitarani, Brahmani, Mahanadi, Godavari, Rushikulya, Vamsadhara and their tributaries served as arteries of commerce. In addition to the ports, the water routes played a leading role in the maritime activities of ancient Kalinga. The growth of ports, cities, towns, trade centres, marts, domestic and foreign trade and the economy of the country were greatly influenced by the water routes.

Water routes were divided into three divisions viz *Nadipatha* (river route), *Kulya* (artificial water way or canal route) and *Varipatha* (sea route). *Varipatha* has been classified into further two groups such as *Kulapatha* (coastal route) and *Samyanapatha* (overseas route). The people of Kalinga made use of both *Kulapatha*, the coastal route and *Samyanapatha*, the overseas route. *Kulapatha* was the most busy route because of lesser risk. It was an outer commercial chain which linked all the ports of the coast line. For example, the *Mahodadhi Kulapatha* was connected with Southeast Asia, Persia, Mesopotamia, Arabia, Egypt, Phonesia, Asia Minor, Greece, Rome and other countries. *Samyanapatha* was an overseas route with foreign countries across the sea. In commercial communication, India held a privileged place due to location and long coast line[35]. The East coast played a remarkable role through this route and had relations with foreign countries from different ports of the Bay of Bengal, Indian Ocean, the Arabian Sea, Persian Gulf, Red Sea and the Mediterranean sea and had relations with Ceylon Java, Sumatra, Bali, Borneo, China and Japan in the East and Roman Empire and Africa in the West.

River Routes

The navigable rivers of coastal India helped to a great extent the progress of internal as well as international commerce. It was preferred to sail down from Benaras to Tamralipti on way to sea despite the caravan route. The *Rig Veda* mentions ninety navigable rivers for river traffic. The important river routes of the coast were the Ganga-Mahodadhi (Bay of Bengal) route, the Brahmaputra-Mahodadhi route and the Mahanadi-Mahodadhi route. Some of these rivers were navigable throughout the year. The trade centres on the bank of the Ganges had direct contact with *Suvarnabhumi,* Southeast Asia, China and eastern ports of India. The prince of *Mahajanaka Jataka* sailed from Champa to Tamralipti through the lower course of the Ganges[36]. Ptolemy has described the river Mahanadi as Manada[37] and mentioned Sambalpur as Sambalaka a riverine port town. Further he has also mentioned one more port named Dosarene[38]. Dosarene has been identified with parts of coastal Orissa[39]. The archaeological explorations have revealed the remains of the ancient culture at this region. Perhaps in ancient times Tosara was the capital and trade centre of Kosala. The Tel river has been mentioned in the Buddhist Jataka stories.

The river Mahanadi was the main communication and trade system for Kosala country. There were a number of trade centres in the upper Mahanadi valley. Presently Sirpur, Rajim, Sourinarayana towns of Madhya Pradesh and Padmapur, Sambalpur, Sonepur, Charada, Boud, Kantilo, Cuttack and Ali of Orissa, on the bank of the Mahanadi are located on the ancient trade route. Cargo was transported from Sonepur to Tosara through the river Tel. Even during the Maratha period the traders of Puri used to go to Sambalpur from Cuttack by boat in the river Mahanadi. During other seasons (when water column was at a lower level) traders followed the land route and used to carry commodities by bullock cart, horse and ass. These traders were known as *Banjara*. This word has been derived from *vanijya* (business). The river Vamsadhara was navigable during the rains over some 100 km and its mouth constituted a kind of dock with a depth of 4.0 m. It was easily reached because the bar was submerged beneath a maximum water depth of 4.50 m. During the monsoon a large number of ships sought refuge there. At the entrance to the river the roadstead is protected by a rocky point projecting 800 m into the sea, permitting the trans-shipment of cargoes at all seasons[40]. The Rushikulya river, accessible to smaller crafts during the rainy season over 50 km, formed at its opening a port which was having a water depth of 2 or 3 m over the bar. It could receive boats of 200 to 300 tonnage, and was also a shipyard[41]. The distribution of Painted Grey Ware (PGW) and Northern Black Polished (NBP) ware in the sites along the rivers of Ghaghara, Ganga and Yamuna clearly suggests the use of riverine routes for the ancient trade channels. Further the movement of country boats towards Kausambi, Champa and Tamralipti along the Ganga and the Yamuna mentioned in the Buddhist literature[42], confirm the ancient riverine routes.

Sea Routes

The ancient kingdom of Kalinga on the East coast of India extending from the mouth of Ganges to the Godavari had taken the lead in maritime activities at least sixth centuries before the birth of Christ. The ancient sailors and sea-faring merchants of Kalinga did not leave anything in the form of inscriptions on their maritime activities. However, on the basis of the prevailing Orissan local traditions the ancient seafaring activities could be deciphered. To cite an example, on the day of *Kartika Purnima* (Full Moon day of October-November) coastal people celebrate the ritual i.e. the sailing of miniature boats made out of banana stem etc. in the memory of their old voyages. Further, the literatures and sculptural friezes on the temples of Bhubaneswar, Puri and Konark are faithful representations of the sea-faring activities. In those days, sea voyages were full of danger. Sailors depended upon the Sun, Moon and Stars for direction and ships could set sail with the help of trade winds. Apart from storm, cyclone and bad weather, there was the danger of hidden rocks, sea animals and piracy.

To get rid of the piracy problem Asoka had issued a copper plate edict known as *Marine Edict* for the Naga rulers, which was however, contemptuously set at naught by those for whom it was meant[43]. The adventurous tradesmen tossed their cargo in the waves of the sea in times of dangers and promise their Gods to make a donation if ever He brought them safely out of this peril. The Buddhist Goddess Tara is the protectress. Numerous images of Tara have been found in Orissa. In an image, found at Ratnagiri, a scene of shipwreck is carved in the relief[44]. In spite of such travails the sailors of Kalinga travelled on the sea for the sake of sea borne trade. The mariners used to set sail for Southeast and Southwest countries when the Northeast trade wind began to blow and return before monsoon.

In ancient times, long distance trade was not possible without halting at intermediate places for want of water and food. Sailors voyaging from Tamralipti, Palur and Kalingapatnam to foreign countries used Nicobar Islands as halting station. I-Tsing mentioned that Nicobar Islands was a month's sail from Tamralipti, and China from Sri-Vijaya was twenty days sail[45]. The Arthasastra is the only state craft that provides a detailed account of the maritime history of India in 3rd century BC. The text clearly mentions the rules and regulations of the ports, traders, trade systems, tax patterns and other aspects pertaining to sea trade[46]. These rules seem to have been in operation at the ports of Kalinga as it was under the dominion of Magadhan empire. It has already been suggested that during the ancient times numerous ports developed and flourished on the coast of Kalinga for overseas and inland trade. The sailors and traders followed different sea routes from these ports to Ceylon, China, Malay Archipelago, Japan, Rome, Greece etc. This led to diffusion of Indian trade, commerce, political system, and cultural life to those countries from the Kalingan coast in particular and India in general. Various reliable evidences are available regarding the sea routes followed by the Indians on the east coast. It seems that the Indian ships from different ports of east coast used the Coromandal coast to keep contact between themselves. Gradually by extending the length of their journey they crossed this coast and established relations with the outside countries through sea voyages. From Tamralipti there was regular sailing of vessels which either proceeded along the coast of Bengal and Burma, or crossed the Bay of Bengal and made a direct voyage to the Malaya Peninsula and then to the East Indies and Indo-China and beyond it. There were other similar ports and embarkation points like Palur, Poompuhar, Arikamedu, Sopatma, Masulipatnam from which ships sailed across the Bay of Bengal to the coasts of the Southeast Asia and the Far East. Ships used to go to Java directly then to Ceylon and other ports on the eastern coast of India. Further, these ships took a course to the north east from Java to reach Canton. This was the route followed by the merchants who traded with the West and the East[47]. There was a regular coastal voyage from the mouth of the Ganges along the eastern coast of India to Ceylon. People from all ports of India came by land or river route to the nearest sea port and then made a coastal voyage to Tamralipti, Palur or to one of the harbours near Masulipatnam, whence ships made a direct voyage to the Far East across the Bay of Bengal[48]. Hall mentions that the relations of India with Southeast Asia probably goes back to prehistoric period[49]. Traders from both sides must have visited others ports. Majumdar draws attention to the voyages between India and *Suvarnabhumi* as reflected in the Jataka stories. Clifford points out, 'The sea route to China via the straits of Malacca was no longer unknown to the mariners to the East'[50]. The merchants of India followed the sea route along the coast of the Bay and discovered a port on the Malaya Peninsula whence they could proceed over land to Siam and Cambodia. They were soon in a position to sail round the Peninsula and go up to Tankin. This sea route at first terminated at Tankin (Kiao-Che) which was the principal port of China on this side and all ships coming from India and the island from the South Sea used to unload there. Subsequently the port shifted from Canton which was under Chinese territory. Further emphasising on this, Bagchi[51] suggests that regular sailing from the Gangetic valley to Tankin was taking place in the second and first centuries BC. His theory is based on the authority of the Annals of the former Han dynasty, which gives the itinerary of a sea journey starting from the coast of Tankan (Te-nan) and ending on the Indian coast, belonging to the period of Emperor Wu (140-80 BC)[52]. The *Mahaniddesa* tells us that ships from Tamralipti and Paloura called at Sada, anchoring enroute at Gumpa. The most important port of call in this route was Takkola from where ships sailed to Siam, Cambodia and Annam[53]. From Takkola the vessels reached Yavadiwpa and Champa. Beyond Champa, the route to China was direct. I-Tsing (AD 633-713) the Chinese traveller recounting his itinerary says that from Canton he arrived at Palembang. Onwards his route lay via Malaya, on the river Jambi, Kedah, on west coast of the Malaya Peninsula, Nicobar Islands and finally he finished his journey at Tamralipti[54]. The ships of Kalinga bound for Southeast Asian countries were passing via Andaman and Nicobar Islands (Fig. 10). In those days long and distant voyages could not have been performed by trading vessels without intermediate halts for food and water. The Nicobar Islands were no doubt used as halting stations by the ancient mariners voyaging from the different Indian ports viz Tamralipti, Palur, Kalingapatnam and Masulipatnam. Similar courses were evidently taken by Arab navigators as early as the 9th century AD when Muslim influence began to spread in Southeast Asian countries[55].

Apart from direct voyages, the merchants of Orissa sailed along with the sailors from Tamil Nadu and Kerala to Southeast Asian countries, Rome and Arab countries. The mariners took their voyage to Malaya Peninsula through straits of Malacca to Sumatra, Java, Bali, Celebes, Borneo through the Sunda straits to Champa and Kambuja[56] from east coast of India (Fig. 11). The stages in the voyages in the eastern seas mentioned by I-Tsing is that, from Tamralipti a month's sail to Nicobar Islands and from Sri-Vijaya and twenty days sail from China. The sailors and merchants of Kalinga had landed at various places including Srikshetra in Burma, Takkola, Kokkonagara, Kataha Kadharam in Malaya Peninsula, Sri-Vijaya in Sumatra, Purva Kalinga in Java, Tonking in Cambodia and Kwang-fu in China[57]. Voyages to Southeast Asian countries from the ports of Kalinga was regular. Kalinga had her colonies in Burma, Sumatra, Thailand, Champa, Malaya Peninsula and beyond. Subsequently the political as well as cultural ties strengthened the relations[58]. The religious preachers travelled in merchant vessels to preach Buddhism in Southeast Asian countries. The journey to the Malaya Peninsula was made from the port of Palur[59]. The legends narrate that two thousand families migrated to Java along with the prince of Kalinga. The Jaha inscription of Java AD 480 mentions the Kling (Kalinga) people and its contact with Java. The Buddha images of Ratnagiri recall the Buddha figures of Java[60]. The contact with Java was so close that it has been reflected in the later period art history of Orissa.[61] The *Periplus of the Erythraean Sea* describes the trade relation of Orissa with Roman empire. The excavation findings at Tamralipti[62] and Sisupalgarh[63] of 3rd century AD also throws light on this aspect. The discovery of Roman coins in Mayurbhanj and coastal Andhra strongly suggests the trade relations with Roman empire[64]. The evidence from the archaeological finds like Rouletted ware, glass and Roman coins from different sites of Orissa may not necessarily indicate direct contact, rather their occurrence in the port-towns and towns close to the coast may point to an indirect contact between Kalinga and the Roman empire through the intermediaries, say the merchants of south India who probably took the *Kulapatha* (coastal route) from the ports of Coromandal coast to those of the east coast. The different stages of the coastal routes between India and China (Fig. 12) touching the east coast trade colonies are indicated in the *Mahaniddesa*, the Geography of Ptolemy, the *Brhatkathaslokasangraha,* the *Kathasaritsagara*, and the *Brihatkathamanjari*[65]. It is a known fact that the sea route to China followed by ancient merchants passed through Ceylon and Java. Fa-hien[66] returned from India to China through this route in the early 5th century AD. Fa-hien has recorded the dangers of the sea voyage in the small wooden boats during his travel. To quote from his account, he "took passage in a large merchant man onboard of which there were more than 200 men and to which was attached by a rope a smaller vessel, as a provision against damage or injury to the large one from the perils of navigation. With a favourable wind they proceeded eastward for 3 days, and then they encountered a great wind. The vessel sprang a leak and water came in. The merchants wished to go to the smaller vessel, but the men onboard it, fearing that too many would come, cut the connecting rope. The merchants were greatly alarmed feeling their risk of instant death. Afraid of that the vessel would fill, they took their bulky goods and threw them into the water. In this way the tempest continued day and night, till on the 13th day the ship was carried to the side of an island, where on the ebbing of the tide, the place of the leak was discovered, and it was stopped, on which the voyage was resumed". "The merchants were full of terror, not knowing where they were going. The sea was deep and bottomless and there was no place where they could tell East and West and the ship again went forward in the right direction. If she had come on any hidden rock, there would have been no way of escape. After proceeding in this way for more than 90 days they arrived at a country called Javadvipa (Java)"[67]. However in spite of such inevitable and unpredictable danger and peril associated with sea voyage, the maritime activity of the people of Kalinga continued to flourish with undaunted zeal and vigor.

Internal Trade

The progress of life and society of a country depends upon the extent of the facility of communications. The sailors and merchants of Kalinga were competent in their professional life. If the foreign evidence seems to indicate commercial activities of the people, the inscriptions of Orissa give information about Kalinga's economic condition. The growth of towns that specialised in crafts strengthened the commercial activities. Towns depended upon neighbouring villages for their basic essentials and traders therefore played an important role in linking the city with the countryside. Trade and commerce at regional and inter regional level were facilitated with the circulation of Punch Marked Coins, Kushana copper coins and imitation Kushana coins. Kushana gold coins discovered in Orissa were not the currency of Orissa but mostly used as ornaments. Kushaṇa copper coins coming to Orissa by way of trade, remained there in circulation. Later on these were imitated for use in commercial transactions[68]. While the silver Punch Marked Coins were in circulation up to AD 300 the imitation Kushana coins (also called Puri-Kushana coins) continued from about 2nd to 4th-5th century AD. This is suggested by the evidence of stratigraphy at Sisupalgarh[69] and legend *tanka*, which is datable to 4th-5th century AD on the basis of palaeography. In internal trade, fairs and weekly markets (*hatta*) proved to be an important mechanism for commercial transactions. Such markets used to be held near a temple. An inscription of the Bhaumakara period mentions market (*hatta*), which is quite significant[70]. The articles involved in internal trade covered many household articles of daily use. The manufacture of textiles appears to have been carried out in Orissa since ancient times. During the time of Kautilya, Kalinga was one of the main centres of textile production besides Bengal, Kamarupa, Magadha, Madura, Aparanta, Kasi, Vasta and Mahisa.

Kalinga figures along with other places like Nagapattana, Anilavada (Anhilwara) in Gujarat, Mulasthana (Multan) and Vanga[71]. This shows that Kalinga produced clothes of high quality. The Nagas of Kalinga had earned a reputation in the art of weaving which is evident from the fact that the word Kalinga in the Tamil language denote cloth. Regarding the quality of cloth of Kalinga, Mitra[72] remarks that, "in neatness, elegance and richness of design and execution, it is in no way inferior to the finest production of the Benares loom of the present days".

The Nagari plates[73] of the Ganga king Anangabhima III AD 1230 mentions the grant of a township situated in Puranagrama and Jayanagaragrama, which may actually be represented by the present village of Nagari, literally meaning a township which is about 11 miles from Cuttack[74]. This township was inhabited by a number of artisans and merchants such as perfumers (*gandhika*), workers or dealers in conch shells (*sankhika*), splitters of wood (*patakara*), goldsmiths (*svarnakara*), braziers (*kamsyikah*), sellers of betel leaf (*tambulika*), dealers in sugar (*gudika*), weavers (*tantuvaya*), potters (*kumbhakara*) and the fisherman (*kaivarttah*). This important epigarphical source clearly indicates the fragrant substances, conch shells, wood, ornaments, bronze goods, betel leaves, sugar, cloth, earthen vessels and fish as some of the articles of internal trade. Further, commodities of everyday use such as food grain, vegetable, milk, oil, fruits, etc were chiefly sold in village markets for local consumption. Kalinga also exported wild elephants, which was much praised by the neighbouring provinces, as told by the Chinese pilgrim[75]. Diamond was another valuable commodity of sale in Kalinga[76]. It is quite clear that Kalinga had trade relations with the neighbouring states of the Palas, Senas, Tummanas, Kalachuris, Cholas, Eastern Chalukyas etc. In the earlier period Kalinga maintained commercial links with Magadha and Madhyadesa[77].

A copper plate grant of the Bhanja king Nettabhanja[78] assigned to the 8th century AD informs that Angulaka (identical with Angul of the present day) was made prosperous by the merchant's community. They sold commodities of all descriptions on a large scale. Hiuen Tsang gives a picture of towns and their business transactions. Referring to Kong-u-To (Kongoda), he mentioned that, "within its limits there are several small towns which border on the mountains and are built contiguous to the sea. The cities themselves are strong and high. This country bordering on the sea, abounds in many rare and valuable articles. People use cowries and pearls in commercial transactions. The forests of Orissa abounded in good timber. The country produced large dark coloured elephants which were capable of long journeys. People harness to their conveyance and make long journeys"[79]. An inscription of the Ganga king Anantavarman[80] son of Devendravarman, of 11th century AD informs that bullocks, buffaloes and asses were also used for conveyance. Pack horses seems to have been used for transport, especially in the hilly area. Since bullocks were used in carrying merchandise from one place to another, it may be assumed that carts were also engaged for the purpose of transport. The Buddhist literature clearly refers to the fact that the Utkalas were coming to Gaya with goods loaded in carts for trade purposes[81]. The merchants of Kalinga traded on varieties of commercial crops like cotton[82], sugar cane[83], betel leaves and nuts[84], coconuts[85]. The merchants also traded in finished products like textiles, perfumes, etc. The walls of the medieval temples of Orissa like Lingaraj, Jagannath and Konark are full of images, whose dress and costume indicate finest of textures[86]. Later on Abul Fazal has referred to the production of very good quality cotton and silk fabric in Orissa[87]. Salt was an item of trade. The Ganga and the Gajapati rulers appointed Salt tax collector *Lavana Kara adhikari*, who used to collect tax from salt traders. The early Muslim expeditions into Orissa were mainly motivated by the desire to obtain elephants. The *Tabaqat-i-Nasiri* states that the Bahamani ruler Feroz Shah took away along with him a number of elephants from Orissa. The sculptures on gateways of Parasurameswara and Lakshamaneswar temple depict the capture of elephants from the forest. Anàntavarman Chodaganga Deva in one of his inscriptions had adopted the title of *Nava-Navati-Sahasra-Kunjaradhiswara* (Master of 99,000 elephants). It is believed that because of abundance of elephants in Orissa, the Suryavamsi rulers assumed the title of Gajapati or the 'Lord of Elephant'.

Foreign Trade

A very few literary, inscriptional sources, material remains and art evidences throw some light on the pattern of foreign trade of Kalinga. It is evident that coastal Orissa was somewhat indirectly connected with the Western world. Goods from Kalinga used to be transhipped to southern and western India through coastal voyages taking advantage of the changing cycle of monsoons and then to the Roman world. Between 2nd and 4th century AD Kalinga had direct maritime trade contact with Southeast Asian countries[88]. The importance given to sea trade with Southeast Asia was partly the result of the extension of the inland and interregional trade and commerce. It was predominantly the outcome of the rising demand in the West for spices. It is likely that the Kalingan 'middle man' merchants took advantage of this situation and involved themselves in the spices trade especially the trade in cloves. The people of Kalinga maintained commercial intercourse with Bali, Java, Sumatra, Borneo, Malayan Peninsula. Majumdar refers, "there is a story preserved in the chronicles of Jaya that the Hindus from Kalinga coast colonised the Island. Similar traditions of colonisation from Kalinga are preserved in many other Islands"[89]. There was a Hindu kingdom in central Java which the Chinese called Ho-ling or Kalinga[90]. Kalinga had also trade relations with Valabhi, Patala and the Persian coast during the reign period of Kharavela[91]. Kalinga had also commercial intercourse with Burma in ancient times. According to Ray, Lower Burma is the land of a people who were and still are called 'Ṭalaings'. The term used as early as in AD 1170 in the Mon records is but a derivation of 'Triligana' or Trikalinga, referring to the whole of Andhra-Kalinga zone[92].

The maritime trade was prosperous and extensive, as is indicated by the existence of a number of ports, through which Kalinga carried on her trade with the outside world. A copper Chinese coin attributable to the 8th century AD found at Sirpur during the excavation[93], leads us to infer that China was commercially linked with Kalinga. It is known that one of the Bhaumakara king had copied with his own hand the *Gunga Vyuha*, the Mahayana text, and presented it to the emperor of China. This cultural relation presupposes maritime contact. The discovery of Kharosthi terracotta objects and seals from southern Bengal prove that the merchants of Kushana or Yuezhi origin exported horses and perhaps also rice to Southeast Asia. The evidence of Kang Tai (3rd century AD) of Wu Dynasty indicates contact between India and China through the Southeast Asian kingdoms of Funan, Geying, Yepoti (Java-Sumatra), Takkola and Linyi, where a number of Brahmi-Kharosthi inscriptions and other historical remains have been discovered which prove the existence of Indian colonies. Probably the Southeast Asians, the Kalingas and their neighbours were carriers of these scripts. The *Milindapanho* proves that a network of traders existed between India and China through Takkola in the Southeast Asia[94]. The basis for China's interest in Kalinga could be to procure muslins of different varieties from Bengal and other neighbouring countries and also locally produced pearls, diamonds, topaz, carved ivory chests and intricate wood carvings. The foreigners demand for jewellery was satisfied by the delicate filigree ornaments in gold and silver made by Kalingan artists. Elephants were also among the inventory of export[95].

Thus it has been observed that the number of ports which existed in Kalinga during the period under review bear testimony to its flourishing maritime trade with different foreign countries. The agrarian and industrial products of ancient Orissa viz rice, wheat, barley, incense, timber, ivory, textiles, conch shells, stone products, iron products, diamonds, elephants were mainly exported to the foreign countries. The export of cloth is indicated by the *Manasollasa*, which mentions the Kalinga fabric in the list of its varieties for the royal use. Kalingan textile was manufactured and exported in such quantities that the term Kalinga was used for cloth by the ancient Tamils. Frequent sea voyages were made to the countries outside India, on account of which the Indians came to be called Kalingas in the Malaya Peninsula in the early periods[96]. Elephants were also exported[97]. Further, the *Manasollasa* mentioned the export of rice from Kalingan ports. The diamond, gold and other jewels of Sambalpur were exported to foreign countries. Among them, diamond of Sambalpur region was very much appreciated in Persia, Greece and Rome. The products such as muslins, pearls and silk were sent to Tamralipti and other ports of western coast from Northeast regions of India for overseas shipment. The Bengali Buddhist manuscript of 11th century AD discovered in Horiuzi temple of Japan, suggests the commercial contact of Bengal/ancient Kalinga with Japan[98]. Rhinoceros horns, elephant tusks, tortoise shells, pearls and jades, copper, fruits and cloths were the items exchanged with China[99]. As regards the articles of import, the sources either epigraphic or literary are completely silent. Even Hiuen Tsang's valuable account does not help us much. However, it seems that certain metals such as silver and copper were probably imported into Kalinga from the silver mines of Ceylon, where from it was supplied to other parts of India in the Gupta period[100]. Some species like cloves, spikenard, etc were especially mentioned as the native products of Java and Sumatra. These seems to have been imported into Kalinga. The silk of China, which was very famous might have been supplied to Kalinga. The other main imports to Kalingan ports were cardamon, chilly, clove, betel nut from Southeast Asia and woolen cloth from China and muslin from ancient Bangladesh. The *Brihadkalpasùtrabhashya* informs that Nepal, Sindh and Tamralipti were famous as good cloth manufacturing centres. The *Manasamangal* a Bengali text mentions a large number of items including horses and spices imported to Tamralipti[101].

Currency

In the early centuries of Christian era, cowries, punch marked coins, Kushana and Puri-Kushana coins were used as the medium of exchange. References are not available regarding the coins issued by the various dynasties of Kalinga viz Sailodbhavas, Bhaumakaras and Somavamsis during later period. It seems that during these period cowry currency were in circulation. Hiuen Tsang who travelled through Kongoda (Puri-Ganjam region) in 7th century AD, observed that the people use cowry[102] and pearls in commercial transaction. The copper plate grant of Subhakara II of Bhaumakara dynasty refers to cowry as medium of exchange[103]. The Alagum inscriptions dated AD 1140 of Chodaganga Deva refers to cowry currency[104]. The Ganga and the Gajapati period inscriptions mention the continuance of cowry currency[105]. The *Mahabharata* of Sarala Das refers to the prevalence of cowry currency. The *Madala Panji* has also referred to cowry currency along with other currencies[106]. The cowry currency continued to exist in Orissa up to colonial period. The inscribed Puri-Kushana coins of copper with the legend *tanka*, circulated in Orissa for several centuries. Silver coins were also circulated but there is no actual specimen, except punch marked coins of the earlier period. The gold coins of the Nala[107], the Sarbhapuriyas and gold *fanam* of the Ganga have been brought to light. This suggests the circulation of metal coinage in Kalinga during the period under discussion.

In the inscriptions ranging from the 6th to the 13th century several coin names are mentioned which suggest the prevalence of metallic currency. They include *aripindaka churnika pana, purana, nishka, dinara, Rupya, Sobhana rupya, Ruake, Vendi tanka, Sasukani tanka*, etc. The inscriptions of the Imperial Gangas especially of Chodaganga and his successors frequently mention the *mada* or *madha*[108] which was apparently the most important medium of exchange. It was applied to the coins in the general sense of the term like that of modern *Tanka*[109]. The inscriptions also mention varieties of *madas* such as *ganda mada, gandaniska, mallamada, matsya mada, chamara mada, ganda hasti mada, Kullitunga mada, Surabhi mada*, etc[110]. The *mada* probably denoted a coin as the phrase *suvarna mada panchaika* suggests. The use of words like *ganda-niska* suggests the existence of gold coins. The *aripindaka churnika satam ekam* formed the annual rent of a village. Similarly *rupya* often denoted a silver coin. An inscription mentions the revenue of a village as *rupya kha-chatur vimsati*. The other Ganga gold coins very thin and small in size were popularly known as *fanam*. These Ganga *fanam* gold coins have been found in different parts of Orissa. They are also known as the Gajapati *pagodas* and have been found from different parts of south India. They have been so named because of the representation of a caparisioned elephant on the obverse. The Orissan copper coins were particularly suitable for support of local trade and commerce. Precisely speaking, the history of Kalinga is replete with maritime activities as known from the foregoing account. The ancient trade routes passing through Kalinga brought form, obviously, material prosperity by way of production and surplus distribution and exchange of commodities, monetization of society, spread of settlements and culture.

References

1. Hultzsch, E., 1969 *Corpus Inscriptionum Indicarum*, Vol. 1, Archaeological Survey of India, (reprint), Delhi, 66-70.
2. *Indian Archaeology—A Review*, 1956-57 Archaeological Survey of India, Delhi, 30-31.
3. Lal, B.B., 1984 "Excavations at Sisupalgarh", *Ancient India*; No. 5, Archaeological Survey of India, (reprint), Delhi, 62-105.
4. Behera, S.C., 1982 *Interium Excavation Reports*, Sambalpur University, Sambalpur.

5. Nigam, J.S., 1993 *A Brief Note on the Excavations at Manikapatna*, (Unpublished), Bhubaneswar.
6. Rajaguru, S.N., 1960 *Inscriptions of Orissa*, Vol. II, Bhubaneswar, 29-33, 318-322.
7. Ghosh, A., 1973 *The City in Early Historical India*, Simla, 94.
8. Thapar, R., 1974 *History of India*, Vol. I, New Delhi, 106.
9. Ray Chaudhari, H.C., 1950 *Political History of Ancient India*, Calcutta, 233-34.
10. Jayaswal, K.P., 1983 "The Hathigumpha Inscription of Kharavela", *Epigraphia Indica,* (reprint) New Delhi, Vol. XX, 71- 89.
11. *Ibid.*
12. Das, A., 1965 "Asanapata", *Orissa Historical Research Journal*, Vol. XIII, (2): 1-8.
13. Sila, Tripati., & Patnaik, S.K., 1996, "Trade Routes and Communication Pattern of Ancient Orissa". *GAURAVAM, Recent Researches in Indology*, (Prof. B.K.Gururaja Rao Felicitation Volume), (eds.) K.V.Ramesh, et. al., New Delhi, 396-404.
14. Ray, A., 1983 *Life and Art of Early Andhradesa*, New Delhi, 35.
15. Patnaik, S.K., 1991 "Routes in ancient Orissa", *The Journal of Orissan History,* Vol. XI: 13-20.
16. Agarawal, V.S., 1953 *India as Known to Panini*, Lucknow, 240.
17. Mahapatro, K.N., 1975 *Tosalira Itihasa* (Oriya), Cuttack, 25.
18. Acharya, P., 1955 "Ancient Routes in Orissa", *Orissa Historical Research Journal,* Vol. IV, (3&4): 43-50.
19. Margabandhu, C., 1985 *Archaeology of the Satavahana - Kshtrapa Times*, Delhi, 58.
20. Chandra, M., 1977 *Trade and Trade Routes in Ancient India*, Delhi, 238.
21. Personal Communication with Dr.G.C.Chauley, Archaeological survey of India, Bhubaneswar.
22. Sahu, N.K., 1964 *Utkal University History of Orissa*, Vol. I, Bhubaneswar, 497.
23. Majumdar, R.C., 1945 Two Midnapore Plates, *Journal of Royal Asiatic Society of Bengal*, Vol. XI, (1): 7-9.
24. Laskar, G.M., 1904 The Khurda Copper Plate Grant of Madhava, King of Kalinga, *Journal of Royal Asiatic Society of Bengal*, Vol. LXXIII, (3): 282-86.
25. Das, D.N., 1977 *The Early History of Kalinga*, Calcutta, 268.
26. Sahu, N.K., 1964 *op. cit.*, 510.
27. Rajaguru, S.N., 1956-57 "Visvanatha Mishra a Smriti-writer of Orissa", *Orissa Historical Research Journal*, Vol. V, (3&4): 157-59.
28. Inscription donated by the residents of Vardhamana and Agottosila

of 3rd century A.D., have found near Apsidal temple of Lalitagiri. This place was visited by the people of different places.

29. Roy, U.N., 1991 "The Brihatkatha Sloka - Samgraha on Maritime Activities in the Gupta age", *Recent Advances in Marine Archaeology*, (ed.) S.R.Rao, NIO, Goa, 29-33.
30. Haque, M.A., 1967 "Route of Feroz Shah's invasion of Orissa - 1380 AD", *Orissa Historical.Research Journal*, Vol. XV (3&4): 66-68.
31. Konishi, M.A., 1985 "Notes on the Harappan Boat During the 3rd-2nd Millennia B.C.", *Manjusha, Recent Researches in Archaeology, Dr. S.R.Rao 60th Birthday Felicitation Volume,* (ed.) Satyavrat Shastri, Bangalore, 145-53.
32. Sah, A.P., 1976 *Life in Mediaeval Orissa 600-1200 AD*, Varanasi, 102.
33. Mahapatra, K.N., 1953-54 "Purusottama Deva, the lexicographer", *Orissa Historical Research Journal*, Vol. II (3&4): 64-80.
34. Subuddhi, U., 1978 *The Bhaumakaras of Orissa*, Calcutta, 103-117.
35. Prasad, P.C., 1977 *Foreign Trade and Commerce in Ancient India*, New Delhi, 135.
36. Malalasekera, G.P., 1937 *Dictionary of Pali Proper Names*, Vol. I, London, 482.
37. McCrindle, J.W., 1985 *Ancient India as Described by Ptolemy*, (reprint), Delhi, 71.
38. *Ibid.* 172.
39. Mukherjee, B.N., 1982 "Desarene-Dasarna-Coastal Orissa (?)", *The Journal of Orissan History*, Vol. III, (1): 1-3.
40. Maltby, T.J., 1918 *The Ganjam District Manual*, (reprint), Madras, 43-44.
41. Deloche, J., 1994 *Transport and Communication in India*, (Vol. II water transport), New Delhi, 112.
42. Lahiri, N., 1992 *The Archaeology of Indian Trade Routes*, Delhi, 268-399.
43. Mookerji, R., 1912 *A History of Indian Shipping*, Bombay, 114-115.
44. Fabri, C.L., 1974 *History of the Art of Orissa*, Delhi, 28.
45. Syamchaudhuri, N.K., 1977 *Social Structure of Car Nicobar Islanders*, Calcutta, 11-15.
46. Kangle, R.P., 1963 *The Kautilya's Arthasastra*, Bombay, 128-165.
47. Prasad, P.C., 1977 *op. cit.*, 154.
48. Majumdar, R.C., 1944 *Hindu Colonies in the Far East*, Calcutta, 13.
49. Hall, D.G.H., 1958 *A History of Southeast Asia*, 2nd edition, London, 12-13.
50. Majumdar, R.C., 1986 *Suvarnadvipa*, Vol. I, (reprint), Delhi, 5.

51. Bagchi, P.C., 1944 *India and China*, Calcutta, 27.
52. Bagchi, P.C., 1957 "Cultural and Colonial Expansion: Central Asia and the Far East", *A Comprehensive History of India*, (ed.) K.A.N. Sastri, Vol. II, Bombay, 772.
53. Srivastava, B., 1968 *Trade and Commerce in Ancient India*, Varanasi, 109-110.
54. Sastri, K.A.N., 1939 *Foreign Notices of South India*, Madras, 108.
55. Syamchaudhari, N.K., 1977 *op. cit.*, 11-15.
56. Kanchan, R.K., 1990 *Hindu Kingdoms of Southeast Asia*, Delhi, 372.
57. Mukherjee, R.K., 1956 *Ancient India*, Allhabad, 517.
58. Kanchan, R.K., 1990 *op. cit.*, 372.
59. Chakrabarti, H., 1966 *Trade and Commerce of Ancient India*, Calcutta, 144.
60. Misra, P.P., 1981 "The Contact Between Orissa and Southeast Asia in Ancient Times", *The Journal of the Orissan History*, Vol. I, (2): 10-17.
61. Ghosh, D.P., 1933 "Relation Between the Buddha Images of Orissa and Java", *Modern Reviews*, Vol. LIV, Calcutta, 500-504.
62. *Indian Archaeology — A Review 1954-55*, Archaeological Survey of India, New Delhi, 19-20.
63. Lal, B.B., 1984 *op. cit.*, 62-105.
64. Behera, K.S., 1977 "Maritime Trade in Ancient Orissa", *Sidelights on History and Culture of Orissa*, (ed.) M.N.Das, Cuttack, 115-121.
65. Srivastava, B., 1968 *op. cit.*, 108-110.
66. Majumdar, R.C., 1963 *Hindu Colonies in the Far East*, Calcutta, 12.
67. Majumdar, R.C., 1963 *op. cit.*, 12-13.
68. Tripathy, S., 1986 *Early and Medieval Coins and Currency System of Orissa*, Calcutta, 35-57.
69. Lal, B.B., 1984 *op. cit.*, 62-105.
70. Subuddhi, U., 1985 "Inland Trade of Orissa in the Early Medieval Period (650-1200 A.D.)", *Journal of the Orissa Research Society*, No. 3: 21-24.
71. Mazumdar, B.C., 1984 *Orissa in the Making*, Patna, 46.
72. Mitra, R.L., 1961 *Antiquities of Orissa*, Vol. I, (reprint), Calcutta, 80.
73. Sircar, D.C., 1985 Nagari plates of Anagabhima - III, *Epigraphia Indica*, Vol. XXVIII, (reprint), New Delhi, 235-258.
74. *Ibid.* 248.
75. Beal, S., 1906 *Si-Yu-Ki- Buddhist Records of the Western World*, Vol. II, London, 207.
76. Mazumdar, B.C., 1984 *op. cit.*, 78.
77. Misra, B., 1933 *Dynasties of Medieval Orissa*, Calcutta, 80- 81.

78. Sircar, D.C., 1985 Russellkonda plates of Nettabhanja, *Epigraphia Indica*, Vol. XXVIII, (reprint), New Delhi, 258-263.

79. Beal, S., 1906 *op. cit.*, 207.

80. Hultzsch, E., 1918-19 *Madras Epigraphist's Report No. 9.*

81. Kashyap, J. 1960 *Anguttara Nikaya,* Vol. I, Devanagari Pali Series, Nalanda, 26.

82. Sircar, D.C., and Sarma, K.H.V., 1987 Veligalani Grant of Kapilesvara, *Epigraphia Indica,* Vol. XXXIII, (reprint), New Delhi, 275-292.

83. Sircar, D.C., 1985 Kendupatna Plates of Narasimha - II, *Epigraphia Indica,* Vol. XXVIII, (reprint), New Delhi, 185-195.

84. Sircar, D.C., 1955 Bhubaneswar inscriptions of Ganga Narasimha - I, *Indian Historical Quarterly*, Vol. XXXI, 81-84.

85. Sircar, D.C., 1985 Asankhali plates of Narasimha -II, *Epigraphia Indica*, Vol. XXXI, (reprint), New Delhi, 110.

86. Mitra, R.L., 1961 *Antiquities of Orissa*, Vol. I, (reprint), Calcutta, 119.

87. Sarkar, J.N., 1975 *Studies in the Economic Life in Mughal India*, New Delhi, 47.

88. Behera, K.S., 1992 "Glimpses of the Maritime Activities of Kalinga", *Orissa Review*, Vol. XLIX, (4): 1-5.

89. Majumdar, R.C., 1963 *op. cit.*, 13-14.

90. *Ibid.* 22.

91. *J.A.H.R.S.,* Vol. II, (1), 24.

92. Ray, N.R., 1932 *Brahmnical Gods in Burma*, Calcutta.

93. *O.H.R.J.,* No. 2, 104.

94. Mukherjee, B.N., 1990 "Kharoshti and Kharoshti-Brahmi inscriptions in West Bengal", *Indian Museum Bulletin* No.25, Calcutta, 34.

95. Ray, H.P., 1993 *Trade and Diplomacy in India -China Relations: A Study of Bengal during the Fifteenth Century*, New Delhi.

96. O'Malley, L.S.S., et al., 1933 *Cuttack Gazetteer*, Patna, 21.

97. Beal, S., 1906 *op. cit.*, 207.

98. Mookerji, R., 1912 *op. cit.*, 256.

99. Ray, H.P., 1990-91 "The Identity of Huangzhi: An Ancient Indian kingdom in intimate contact with Han China", *Indian Historical Review*, Vol. XVII, (1-2): 1-34.

100. Maity, S.K., 1957 *Economic life of Northern India in the Gupta period*, Calcutta, 132.

101. Dikshit, K.N., & Pandeya, R.C., 1978 "Ancient maritime contact of West Bengal - Literary & Archaeological evidences", *L.N.Mishra Commemoration Volume*, (ed.) U.Thakur, Bodhgaya, 232-237.

102. Beal, S., 1906 *op. cit.*, 207.

103. Misra, B., 1933 *op. cit.*, 15-24.

104. Sircar, D.C., 1987 Alagum inscription of Anantavarman, *Epigraphia Indica*, Vol. XXIX, (reprint), New Delhi, 44-48.

105. Mohanty, A.B., (ed.) 1940 *Gadya-Padyadarsa*, Prachi Samiti, (Oriya), Cuttack, 48.

106. Tripathy, S., 1986, *op. cit.*, 176.

107. Rajaguru, S.N., 1957 "Pandia Pathar Copper plate inscription of Maharajadhiraja Bhimasena of Nala dynasty", *Orissa Historical Research Journal*, Vol. VI (2&3): 97-102.

108. Tripathy, S., 1986 *Early and Medieval Coins and Currency System of Orissa*, Calcutta, 132-195.

109. Tripathy, S., 1986 *op. cit.*, 42-179.

110. *Ibid.*

4

Ship-Building and Navigation

Indian Background

In India limited archaeological evidences are found to study the history and development of ship-building. Limited work has been done in this field. To trace the history of ship-building and navigation of Kalinga, the local traditions as well as the existing literary works have been consulted.

The ship motifs have been noticed on seals and sealings of Harappan culture[1], Ajanta Paintings[2], Sanchi stupa, Bharhut stupa (Pl. V a-b) Kanheri caves, Essar caves, Aurangabad caves (Pl. VI), Konark temple, Jagannath temple, other temples of Bhubaneswar, Borobudur in Java (Pl. VII a-b), Satavahana coins, clay tablets of Chandraketugarh and Bangarh[3]. Besides, the description of different ships is available in the *Rig Veda*, the *Ramayana*, the *Mahabharata*, the Jaina and the Buddhist literatures. The different types of Indian ships, their shape and measurements have been described in the literature. Similarly description of ships used by the marine traders of Kalinga are found in the contemporary Oriya and Bengali writings.

It is to be noted that the terms pertaining to various parts of the ship, officials and their work differed from region to region depending upon the language and environment. It may also be a fact that some particular types of ships, out of the many described in Indian literatures, were probably used by a particular section of regional sailors depending upon the suitability of the ports and their particular merchandise. Further, boats used in the rivers for internal transport and commerce differed from the ships used for overseas trade and inter coastal trade.

Ship-building, ships and shipping are three important and motivating elements for the development of maritime activities of the east coast during ancient times. The shipbuilders had a good knowledge of material as well as the varieties and properties of wood and the mechanical science of ship-building in ancient times. There were mainly two groups of vessels viz river going and sea going. Each again had various types depending on dimension, capacity and height. The river going vessels were mostly oval at the bottom, smaller in size, required lesser depth of water for movement and fast moving. The sea going vessels were bigger in size, sharp cutting from both sides, strongly built to make technically suited to operation in high tides and against strong winds. But strictly speaking the technical details of ship-building from construction stage to navigation stage are few and far between. Moreover, whatever details are available have not been analysed properly. This statement possibly hints that both *dirgha* and *unnata* types were special types of ships and the latter were more suited for sea going purpose. It is quite natural to presume that the river going vessels were mostly oval at the bottom, since they required lesser depth of water for fast movement in a comparatively less disturbed water. These are also corroborated from available depiction. Its shape was designed in such a way that upthrust owing to the weight of the displaced water was very large, and it is equal to the weight of the ship and its content. The centre of gravity can easily be disturbed for uneven distribution of weights. It is due to this reason, the passengers or goods are arranged on this type in an even fashion.

The sea going vessels were larger in size and sharp cutting. The measurement was achieved possibly from many years of experience in the sea. For a floating body remaining in equilibrium position, the centre of gravity should coincide with the centre of buoyancy or upthrust. In such cases no resultant couple acts on the body and the body remains in equilibrium. When the floating body is tilted, the centre of buoyancy gets displaced. The resultant movement of the couple formed by the buoyant force acting upward and the weight of the ship acting downward try to bring the floating body back to its original position. Ships are so designed that the centre of gravity is as low as possible and the centre of buoyancy acts vertically below the centre of gravity. If the centre of buoyancy remains above that centre of gravity, then the line of buoyancy will meet the line of centre of gravity at a considerably low point, the resultant movement of which will make the ship unstable. From large heights of ships found from the *Yuktikalpataru,* it is clear that most of them were stable sea going vessels. The vessels with low height were used for speed and in less disturbed sea conditions.

The *Rig Veda* refers to well rigged ships. Varuna and Vasistha sailed to the mid ocean in similar ships[4]. Navigation is termed in the *Atharava Veda* as *Nava-Prabhramsana*[5]. The *Rig Veda* mentions *Nava* as *Nau. Nava*[6] stands for big boats or ships. *Nau*[7] stands for a simple boat for crossing rivers. It was simple in construction pliable only by oars[8]. The *Astadhyayi*[9] makes a clear distinction between coastal island cargoes (*Dvaipya*) and mid ocean island cargoes (*dvaipa* or *dvaipaka*). The epics like the *Ramayana* and the *Mahabharata* also throw welcome light on the navigation, ships etc. In the *Ramayana* big boats or ships used to carry life vessels. It refers to mercantile as *Mahanava*[10]. The *Amarkosa* contains various items of naval terminology, such as *nau bandhana* (anchorage or mooring), *naukarana* (helm or steering) and *naukaranadhara* (helmsman)[11].

Kautilya has classified the boats and ships under four groups according to use and need viz. *Potavanika* (commercial), *Svanava* (private), *Rajanava* (Royal ship) and *Himsrika* (warship). *Potavanika* or commercial fleet again divided into *Samyati nava* (for merchandise) and *Pravahana* (for passengers). It is also mentioned in the commentary on the *Uttaradhyayanasutratika* that the sea going merchants or passengers cross the ocean in *Pravahana. Samyati nava* was an ocean going commercial vessel used especially for merchandise but in the time of emergency the military supplies were also carried. It had to pay tolls at the harbours which it touched[12]. *Svanava* or private boats were also called ferry boats belonging to private persons and were allowed to cross the rivers at all times and places[13]. These boats were also called *Svataranavi*[14].

Rajanava[15] or royal boat was of two types namely *Swastika* and *Sankhamuktagrahina. Swastika*[16] was manned by trustworthy sailors and for the safety of the king tagged on to another boat. The king never used a vessel that had once been weather beaten[17]. As a precautionary measure the soldiers were also stationed on the bank or shore when king boarded a vessel. *Sankhamuktagrahina*[18] was also a royal boat used for pearl fishing in various parts of the ocean. It was also let out to private individuals on payment of necessary fee, *Nauhataka*[19]. *Himsrika*[20] was a warship of the naval force.

Among all the literatures on the sea borne trade and boat building technology, the surviving Sanskrit text throwing welcome light on the ship-building in India is the *Yuktikalpataru*[21], (the wishing tree of artifices). It is supposed to have been composed by the king Bhoja of Dhara (modern Dhar in Central India) in 11th century AD. King Bhoja was well versed in both literature and history. In the *Nispadayanoddesa* and *Jaghanya Jalayanani* of the *Yuktikalpataru* there are descriptions of the ship-building and their explanatory notes. There is sufficient information on viz (i) seasons suitable for ship-building, (ii) varieties of wood best suited for the construction (iii) Bhoja's injunction regarding the use of iron nails in the sea going vessel, (iv) classification of ships like river going or ordinary and sea going or special, (v) names and measurements of ordinary type of vessels (vi) two types of special ships such as *dirgha* (length) and *unnata* (height), (vii) names and measurements of *dirgha,* (viii) Bhoja's view on *dirgha* ship, (ix) names and measurements of *unnata* ship, (x) Bhoja's opinion on *unnata*, (xi) painting of ships, (xii) decoration of ship, (xiii) ships with cabins, (xiv) characteristics of royal ships and (xv) despicable water vessel *jaghanya jalayanani*.

Seasons for ship-building: The ship-building time is said to be selected on an auspicious day, hour, tithi, Moon, when the Mars is in the sixth from the Capricorn and other signs of the zodiac (*Rasis*) when the last Star of the Constellation of the Seven Stars transits from one position to another.

Construction of ships: It is needless to mention that ships in ancient India were made of wood. Due importance however was attached to selecting wood best suitable for the construction of ships[22]. In the *Vrksayurveda* (the Science of plant life) it is mentioned that four varieties of wood are there altogether. *Brahmana jati* is light and soft and can be easily joined to other wood. *Ksatriya jati* wood is light and hard and cannot be joined with other classes[23]. The soft and heavy variety is *Vaisya jati* and hard and heavy is *Sudra jati* respectively. According to the *Yuktikalpataru*, if the ship constructed of *Ksatriya* class of wood brings wealth and happiness. But ships made of other properties of wood is capable of bringing all kinds of troubles and not at all comfortable and good[24]. They soon rot in water and are liable to be split at the slightest shock and to sink down. Bhoja stated that iron should not be tied to a sea going vessel by means of a string because that iron may be attracted by magnetic rock in the sea and may cause danger[25] to the vessel.

According to Bhoja, a ship constructed with *Ksatriya jati* wood may bring wealth and happiness. It is capable to pass through troubled waters. The woods of *Ksatriya jati* were usually used for outer parts of boats and the other types for internal decoration of the boat. For repair of the outer side, usually woods of the same varieties were used. The ships made of two different types of wood bring neither good nor comfort. They do not last for long, but rot, split and sink in the water. For this reason, same type of wood was used for new construction or repairs. The planks were joined edge to edge both by wooden pegs and by carefully cut tenons sunk with the surface of the planks. The planks were fixed on wooden panels and tenons from inside with the help of wooden nails made from the same type of woods. The gaps between the planks were also filled up with hemp, string and at times cane foils soaked in a kind of gum or resins extracted from trees. Same process was also repeated to stop leakage of water in the ship. The bark of Jamun (eugineajambulana) were also used for the purpose.

Classification of ships: The *Yuktikalpataru* mentions two types of ships such as *Samanya* (ordinary) and *Visesa* (special). These ships again have been classified into various categories viz *ksudra* (diminutive), *madhyama* (moderate), *bhima* (formidable), *capala* (moving to and fro), *patala* (with covering), *bhaya* (dangerous), *dirgha* (tall), *patraputa* (doubled), *garbhara* (with inner compartments) and *manthara* (curved). *Bhima, bhaya, garbhara* were considered as inauspicious[26]. Probably because the dimensions may not be well steady and balanced on the water. All the ships except *manthara* are sea going vessels and as regards their merits, these are endurable and spacious[27]. Sea going ships fall under special class category and further classified under two heads, *Dirgha* and *Unnata*[28].

The *Yuktikalpataru* describes the furnishing and decorating system of the vessels. Metals which are used in ships are mentioned as gold, silver, copper and a compound of all these three. Four varieties of colours are suggested for four kinds of vessels, those with four masts, three masts, two masts and one mast should be coloured with white, red, yellow and blue respectively. Ships were also named after the shape of the prow. On the prow eight types of faces viz of lion, buffalo, serpent, elephant, tiger, bird, frog and man are depicted on the ship. The text further mentions three types of ships differentiated on the basis of the length and position of their cabins. Ships with cabins are of three kinds. The *Sarvamandira*, the ship having cabin extending from one end to other which is suitable for transport of the royal treasure, horses and women. The *Madhyamandira* vessels have their cabins only just in the middle part and are used in the pleasure trips by the king and suitable in the rainy season. Ships may have their cabins towards their prows in which case they will be called the *Agramandira* and it is convenient in the dry seasons without rains, for long voyages and naval warfare[29].

The ships represented at Sanchi stupa (Pl. VIII) with a prow having the figure of a winged gryphon and with a chamber extending from one end of the ship to the other comes under the category of the *Sarvamandira* vessel. In Ajanta paintings an actual specimen of the *Madhyamandira* vessel is available (Pl. IX). Another representation from Ajanta (Pl. X) shows a cabin towards the prow of the ship with twelve jars in it. It belongs to the *Agramandira* type[30]. Dhanapala describes in the *Tilakmanjari* that Somaraketu when proceeded to punish turbulent feudatories of Dvipantara is said to have entered the cabin erected in the fore part of the vessel.

Mast and Sail: Mast is an essential equipment of a sea going vessel. It was a feature of ancient Indian vessels since the Harappan times. In early historical period there are representations of ships having two masts. A three masted ship is depicted at Ajanta. The Buddhist Jatakas also refer to ships with three masts[31]. With regard to the position of mast in a vessel, single masted ship used to have it at its centre. As depicted on the ships on the Andhra coins a vessel having two masts erected spaciously to keep up the balance of the vessel. Compound masts spars stepped some feet apart but so inclined that their upper ends eventually meet. Such specimens are depicted in ships of Borobudur of Java[32]. The increase of masts suggests increase in dimensions of the ships. Mast could have been erected only on the keeled base of the ship meant for sea voyages. The *Milindapanho* refers to the function of a mast as to carry ropes, braces and sails[33]. The mast used to have been quite high, proportionate to the dimensions of the ship. A Borobudur ship depicts ladders to climb up the mast. Precisely, the kind of timbers the ancient shipwrights preferred for erecting masts is not known. However, looking to the position and function of the mast in a seagoing ship the timber used seems to have been preferably a single log, without joints, long, straight, strong, elastic and not too heavy suited to withstand the pressure of wind[34]. There is no detailed discussion about the masts and sails in the *Yuktikalpataru*. However blue for the one masted, yellow for the two masted, red for three and white for the four masted ships were the various colours recommended by the treatise. The sail was made of *avajnasika* cloth painted with various colours but identification of cloth has not been possible.

The earliest form of sail seemed to have been square or semi rectangular in form. In India square or semi rectangular sail may be assumed in the Harappan times, although there is no definite evidence for it. The three masted ship at Ajanta appears to have a semi rectangular sail. It also depicts a stay sail. No evidence so far has been noticed to indicate that lateen sail was known to early Indian navigation. L. Gopal suggests on the basis of one of the ships depicted on the Andhra coins that lateen sail was known in ancient India[35]. Lateen sails are also not found in the inland waters of India in those regions which are remote from foreign influences[36]. It appears that lateen sail was not indigenous to India. Square rig has the advantage of stability on large ships and in heavy seas; but it is important to note that with square sail, ship has to sail before the wind and cannot beat into the wind. This means that ancient voyages had necessarily to be timed, according to the seasonal wind movements. But with the development of lateen sail, ships could beat into the wind and thus took advantage of even not so favourable a wind[37]. The sail in use in the Bay of Bengal seems to have been single, square or quadrangular. With such a sail, it is not possible to run close to the wind. The boat would in effect, sail in a direction between reach and run, nearer reach than run. Sailing against wind, the wind itself used to help in keeping course. Practical experience of sailing seems to have aided the early seamen in evolving a safe route.

Rudder

It is not known whether a rudder was in use in the early days but if one was in use, it seems to have been primitive, with limited manoeuvrability. In such cases, the self-propelled boat was driven by wind and current, and the steering and turning direction was worked through the use of paddles and oars. In such a situation, the ease and reliability of steering of the boat rested on dynamic stability of the route and hence an intimate perception and understanding of the sea and skies was probably mandatory.

Parts of the Ship

In Indian sculptures, paintings, coins, etc different parts of the ships are not indicated because of flat portrayals. The keel and hull are important parts of the ship. Hull consists of joined horizontal planks. These single planks of the ship not only showed in the representation of Sanchi[38], Bharhut[39] but also painted at Ajanta. The Indian boat motifs of Borobudur suggests that the horizontal planks were joined to vertical ones which give more strength to the boat. Accounts of the Foreign travellers mention open ships[40]. The sculptured representations from Borobudur reveal some decking and fencing systems on the ships which have been carved out by the Indian migratory[41]. The Ajanta paintings[42] and Sanchi ship motifs point to the existence of cabins on ships. The *Yuktikalpataru* mentions three types of ships differentiated on the basis of cabins, length and position which are discussed earlier.

Description of Sewn Boat

In an interesting passage of the *Yuktikalpataru,* it is mentioned that sea going vessels are sewn with fibres and ropes and no iron nails are used. Because of the apprehension that the submerged magnetic rock in the sea would attract the iron nails. But the ship paintings of Ajanta probably show nails fixed in the upper portions of the ship. Al-Masudi noticed that since early medieval times, sewn ships being plied on the Indian coasts[43]. Planks seem to have been joined by ropes and coconut fibres. The ship representations at Bharhut clearly depict the stitching systems of planks. The *Tilakmanjari* mentions that the broken planks being fastened together tightly and the chief sailors duty was to examine all joints before the ship set sail. The holes were used to be caulked by wax and wool. The Jain text *Acaranga Sutra* mentions that in case of emergency the holes used to be caulked with any part of human organ, clothes, grass and clay and metal dishes[44].

SHIP-BUILDING AND NAVIGATION IN KALINGA

Boat-building Techniques

The expansion of sea trade is closely connected with the development of boat-building technology and techniques of navigation. The *Datha Dhatu Vamsa* mentions the transfer of the tooth relic from Dantapura of Kalinga to Sri Lanka in a ship. It was firmly constructed with planks sewn together with ropes, having a well rigged, lofty mast with a spacious sail and manned by skillful navigators[45]. *Bhelaka, Variratha nauh, Tarikah Plavah, Vahanah, Varavatch* and *Tarandhuh* etc are the different kinds of boats mentioned in the *Trikandasesha*[46] a text of early medieval period. It will not be out of context to discuss the boat-building technology of ancient Kalinga which probably corresponded to ancient Indian traditions. The boats are also shown on illustrated palm leaf manuscripts of different period. They give some details about the construction of flat bottom boats of Chilka lake with illustrations. A study of the boats, depicted in sculpture and manuscripts, indicate the existence of both carvel and clinker construction. The specimens from the *Bhogamandapa* of the Puri temple and the detached sculpture representing a royal barge (Pl. XI) from the Indian Museum, Calcutta, reveal the practice of reversed clinker technique. Its continuance till date is proved by a drawing of *Patua* made by B. Solvyris in the early part of the 19th century and *Patia* boat types, which are found in the northern coast of Orissa from the river Dhamra to the river Suvarnarekha. The survival of clinker construction, both ordinary and reversed type, is significant as clinker constructions of boats is not available in southern and western coast of India. Of course such types are found in present West Bengal and Bangladesh.

Boat drawings have been found on the art and sculptures of Orissa. The sculptural frieze collected from the vicinity of the Brahmeswar temple of Bhubaneswar depicts boats carrying elephants. Another slab containing an image of *Mahisasura Mardini* lying under a baniyan tree near the Brahmeswar temple is interesting as having representation of a boat below the pedestal of the Goddess. The drawing of elephants being carried out in a boat has been carved on a rock, is kept in Bhubaneswar museum[47]. At Konark on the parapet of the *Jagmohan* the *Martanda Bhairava* is shown as dancing on boat. An interesting sculpture of Orissa, supposed to have been collected from Konark and now preserved in the Indian Museum, Calcutta depicts a boat being rowed by four persons. A royal personage sits inside the boat. On the *Bhogamandapa* of famous Jagannath temple of Puri there is a magnificent representation of a boat in chlorite stone[48]. These sculptures are indicative of the fact that association of the people of Kalinga with the boat was quite intimate. Secondly they depict the ability of the Orissan boats to carry elephants and that the Orissan vessels were propelled by oarsmen. Thirdly, a ship voyage from Kalinga for overseas trade was associated with the worship of Goddess Durga or Chandi.

There are references to the boat and their construction technique in Oriya literary sources of the later period, viz the *Prastabasindhu* of Dinakrushna Das describes the construction of boat and their carrying capacity. The *Labanyabati* of Kabisamrat Upendra Bhanja describes the boat, its arrival at Ceylon and offering of welcome ceremony by ladies to the boat. The *Prem Sudhanidhi* describes the varieties of boats meant for pleasure and amusement[49]. The Jayadev museum of Bhubaneswar has collected 400 palmleaf manuscripts in which only 4 manuscripts contain the drawings of boat. These drawings are (Pl. XII a-b) in the *Ushavilasha* of Sisushankar. Siva, Parvati, Usha, Chitralekha and sailors have been depicted on the boat. A close observation of the boats do indicate the differences. The prows of the boats are in different shapes. Among eight boats, prows of six boats are similar, seventh one is of the face of a bird and the eight one is of an elephant. The construction of five boats are similar but rest three are different to each other[50]. Out of eight boats four boats were sailed by women which is highly significant. The description of boats has been mentioned in the text according to the Sastras. In the *Paika Kheda*, Kanhei Champatiray mentions different names for boats such as *Gandia, Chotamukhi, Surachaturi, Rajpura, Lanjua, Khaigaja, Ganga Prasad, Nandia, Khudupa* which were different from the *Yuktikalpataru*. The length and width of some of the boats have been given in hands as the unit of measurement[51].

Use of Timber for Construction of Boats

India has a rich maritime heritage dating back to the Harappan culture. All along its coastline there were various kinds of rafts, dug-outs, keel-less boats and plank-built sea going vessels which were used in maritime activities. Rafts, dug-outs and small boats are often built with a single timber species, locally available. Larger plank-built sea going vessels make use of a variety of timber in a single boat for various considerations. The native vessels use tropical hard wood which is available in the nearby forest. A careful choice of specific timber variety for a particular boat component is made by comparing and weighing the merits of different timbers for specific boat part. Of the different boat components, the keel and keelson, the stem and stem posts, the lower ribs, the side planks, which remain permanently below the water level. The cross beams, the masts and spars are the most exact ones in terms of the timber quality specifications. Upper level side planks remain above water the level. The inner decks, cabins and platforms permit a much greater degree of flexibility in the use of timber. The sophistication, finish and appearance of the vessel depended upon the craftsmen.

Keel is the vital key timber of a vessel and it gives strength and stability. It is the backbone of a vessel and is the single massive timber of the boat. In small or medium vessels the length of keel would be 5 m or less. Keel timber is a single log, but there are traditions of larger sea going vessels with keel length of 30 to 40 m having been built on Indian shores. More often, in case of such a long keel, two or three same type of timber pieces of comparable dimensions are used by joining the planks together. The keel planks are joined by inter fingering tongues and fastened with wooden pegs.

Stem is the next important timber of the boat. This timber as compared to keel is long and slender, fixed at a high angle to enable to cut through water. Stem as vulnerable segment makes angular curve through which it is perfectly fitted into the fore of the keel. It has to resist the water pressure, and should not split, crack or bend. The required curvature at keel end is fixed with the stem by knee joints. Some times wooden pegs and wedges were used for further fastening. *Babul* (acacia sp.), *khair* or *khaeer* (acaciacatechu), *harra*, *sissoo* (dalburgia sissoo), *shiwan* (gmelina arborea) are used as stem and stern timber, because, they are readily available in local jungles and provide logs at various desired angular curves. In Indian boat-building traditions once keel and keelson is laid on the keel, the bottom-most three planks and on either side of the hull, planks are carefully fitted with the keel, by pegging and riveting. Then the skeleton is built by adding the ribs at the hull base from the stem to stern end. Then the plank frame is built upwards by adding ribs. The ribs inside the boat, have to be sturdy and load bearing. Rib timber is never straight, it is always 'U' shaped or sharply angular.

Planking: Side planking is done row by row upwards, each row from end to end. Side fitting of planks is done by inter fingering and row to row by perfect *Vadhera* jointing. Side planks are carvel (flush fit) joined or clinker fitted (with overlap of plank). Individual timber planks are sawn, planed to a good finish. Further the side planks which remain submerged underwater should be durable and free from insects and wood borers. The traditional timber built vessels were mostly sewn or stitched. Only in Bengal coast, and a Southeast Asian nailed tradition boats were used. Sewing holes are bored with hand drills and the sewing coir taken through them for fastening. A combination of pegging of wooden wedges and stitches enhance the over all strength of the stitched boat, imparting it a quality of resilience that helps withstand if the vessel is grounded, crashed or wrecked[52].

Traditional Boats

There are references to a good number of traditional boats or vessels in the contemporary literary sources of Kalinga. The following are the different kinds of boats which were used in maritime activities.

Bhela: In Oriya literature *Bhela* provided the indirect mea ing of one ordinary variety of boat. Different types of *bhelas* v ere found in Orissa which were made out of banana trees, bamboo, pith and logs of light wood. *Bhela* is used generally in coastal, shallow, and confined water. *Bhelas* were made out of light logs tied together. The logs were tied in such a way that if the sea water gets inside *bhela*, water automatically get released through the gaps of the logs. The sea water did not do any damage to *bhela*. The middle log of *bhela* fixed in lowerside and all other logs are usually fixed slightly above the middle log. This gave little slope to the craft from fore and aftside. Hence the fore and aftside which remains a bit high help to cut waves smoothly. It was rowed by oars and never sank because of its light weight. Similar type of crafts were also used in Tamil Nadu coast.

Pota (dug-out): *Pota*, was used in sea trade. The life period of pota is more because it is directly scooped out from the log. *Kathua, Nauka, Sapeidanga* and *Dengi* are the various local names for *pota*. The shape of *pota* looks like a long tub which is used to feed the animals. *Pota* is suitable for use in calm and shallow water. The lower portion of *pota* looks like a half circle. Generally *pota* is used more in Anusupa and Chilka lake region.

Nauka: *Nauka* is a craft without keel, stem, stern, rib and cabin. The maximum length, width and depth is 14.30 m, 2 m and 50 to 60 cm. The thickness of the plank is 1 and 1/4 inches. The dimension of different parts of *nauka* is in accordance with the length of the lowermost plank. All the joints are made of iron and wooden nails but not by sewing. Nails are used at every 5 to 6 inches and in some cases of joints at 3 inches. Local builders use the hand, finger and feet as the unit of measurement. The horizontal planks of *nauka* are arch shaped. The process of shaping is very easy and simple. The part of the plank to be bent is heated for certain time and care is taken to see that the plank does not burn. After a few minutes, when the plank beeomes hot the plank used to be bent to the needed shape with the wooden posts and metal bars. The plank then becomes ready for planking.

The method of planking is very simple. Planks are laid edge to edge and in some cases they are overlapping. Cotton is also used to make the *nauka* watertight during nailing. The planks on either side of *nauka* are held together from outside. The lowermost plank of *nauka* is called *tali* and two lower side planks are called as *dasi*. *Dasi* is overleaped by *tali* on both sides. Both ends of *tali* and *dasi* are baked and bent upwards for 5 hands in each side. Baking is known as *seka*. *Bedha* is the lower and *bahuti* is the upper side plank of *nauka*. *Dasi* and *bedha* are jointed by *khera*, which is a small narrow plank. Six horizontal planks are known as *polanda* fixed in *bahuti* to provide additional strength. Wooden nails provided to *polandas* on outer side of *bahuti* are known as *khila*. Planks put on the top of *nauka* all around is known as *chapundi*, which is meant for walking. A triangular big plank put on the frontside is known as *muhala*, meant for sitting. The foreside is known as *agamanga* and aft is as *pachhamanga*. Both tapered ends of *nauka* is called *jata*[53].

Padhua and Kosaladanga: *Padhua* and *Kosaladanga* type of crafts were also used in ancient Orissa for trade. Perhaps in ancient times the people of Kosala (upper valley of the river Mahanadi) were using this craft therefore named it as *Kosaladanga*. Even now these crafts are used in the rivers Mahanadi, Brahmani and Baitarani. During later period masts were provided on the craft and then the craft was called as *sulupa*. In the *Samar Taranga,* Brajnath Badajena[54] has mentioned this craft as *solapa*. The planks of *padhua* or *Kosaladanga* were joined by stitching. In England similar type of stitching was called as carvel built. In ancient times, *Kosaladanga* was joined by small wooden pegs. It was known as fish joinery. Coir ropes and palm leaf ropes were sometimes used for stitching. Long shafts or bamboos were provided for further strengthening on both sides of *padhua* and *Kosaladanga*. These shafts were known as *pakhi*. In southern Orissa these crafts were used for cargo transportation. In shallow water bamboo and shafts and in deep water oars were used for riding the craft.

Chapa: Big boats were known as *chapa*. These were used for cargo transportation and for sea journey. Similar type of boats were also used in the *Chandan Yatra* festival of Orissa in the month of *Baisakha*. The *Madala Panji* describes that Lord Jagannath was taken to Chilka in similar boat to keep away from the attack of Muslims. This boat is known as *Duaidulia* in northern Orissa. In ancient times sail and mast were not used in *Duaidulia*.

But the construction of *Chapa* provides an indirect evidence of boat-building technology of Orissa. The lower part of boat looks like English letter 'U'. Then the wooden ribs *pankhi* were joined with intervals on both sides of lowerpart of the boat. Stitchings were made to join planks. These type of crafts were known as *Masula* boat in Tamil Nadu Coast.

The Ceylonese Buddhist text *Datha Dhatu Vamsa* gives an interesting picture of the ship carrying Dantakumara and his wife from Tamralipti with the sacred tooth relic of Buddha, bound for Ceylon. It was said to have been firmly constructed with planks sewn together with ropes, having a well rigged, lofty mast, with a spacious sail. It was commanded by skillful navigators. This was the ship of Guhasiva, the king of Kalinga. He was a contemporary of Mahasena, the king of Simhala. It seems that Dantakumara had sailed during 4th-3rd century BC. Some scholars have suggested that these crafts were not suitable for long open sea sailing and could be used only for coastal trade. Perhaps this type of boat was used for trade with Ceylon, Burma, Java, Bali, Sumatra, Malaya and China. Both nailed and stitched boats were used by the local people for ocean trade. The nails were known as *godichala* and *duiamunda gujia* (both end pointed). Dinakrushna Das describes the nailed craft in the *Prastabasindhu* and Bansidas in the *Manasmangala* also mentioned use of nail in boats. Nails were also protected from the sea water corrosion by soldering them. Sometimes the metal sheets were also provided to the bottom of the boats[55]. Lac, coir, gum and jute were used to fill up holes of the boat. Mast is made out of very strong log. Masted boat sailed with big square sail and mast used to be at the centre. Even today the sailed boats of northern Orissa are having one mast which are similar to *Khudupa, Khaigaja* and *Ganga Prasad* described in the *Paika Kheda*. In later period two masted boats were used. These two masted boats were similar to *Sulupa*. This was known as *Akadulia* in north Orissa. Even two masted boats of Orissa were similar to the *dhow* of Arab and *brigantine* of Europe. In course of time three masted boats came into existence which were known as *duaidulia* and *gorap* in northern Orissa. Birupakhya Kar describes these boats as *grab* in his work the *Prachina Utkalara Nau Vanijya*[56]. These boats were very deep and suitable for carrying huge quantity of cargo. Depth was made more by providing additional planks on the sides of the boat. Similar type of boats were known as *barkantain* in Western countries. Jagabandhu Singh describes in the *Prachina Utkala* that three masted boats were generally red in colour[57].

Masts were made out of teak, sesam and other strong wood. The sitting place of captain positioned near the mast was known as *chapadar*. Kabi Kankan refers to it as *chaighar* (chati) and *patatan* (deck). During British period this was known as cabin. Senapati mentions in the *Fakir Mohan Granthavali* that the rope between *chapadar* and mast as *nabara daudi*. The rope which used for unloading the cargo was known as *pagada*. The flagpost of the boat was known as *bahutia kunda*[58]. Sails were known as *pala* and *ajhala*. It helps to sail the boat speedily. Sails were of rectangular, square and triangular in shape. Senapati mentions the sails such as *karaju, kalomi, jivi, sabar, tavar, jaria* and *pala*. Sails were made out of cloth, bamboo, sack and canvas. Boats of north Orissa used to have 6 to 12 sails. Gopal Chandra Praharaj (*Utkal Kahani,* 1907, Cuttack) describes the *tabara* at the upper, *gabhi* at the middle, *jivi* at front side of the boat. *Tabara* and *gabhi* were the rectangular and square in shape. The front portion of the boat *manga* used to have different types of faces of animals such as sawn, vulture, elephants, lion, horse, crocodile which were attached to the foreside of the boat later on. The *Manasmangala* describes prows were like snacks, tiger, buffalo etc. Captain *mangala* use to sit near *manga*[59]. Anchor is known as *nangara* in Sanskrit. The *Milindapanho* refers to anchors. Anchor holds the ship fast and brings it to stand still. The *Tilakmanjari* refers to ships halted by its heavy anchors made of rocks[60]. The boats of Orissa used to carry a number of anchors. Chintamani Mohanty describes that the boats of Chilka lake used to have perforated stone anchors[61]. Senapati mentions that 14 to 15 quintal weight stone anchors were made at Balasore in ancient times[62].

NAVIGATION

The Indian Ocean has been the scene of varied activities of ancient explorers and maritime traders from the very beginning of recorded history. The experienced seafarers had much information about the sea pertaining to weather, winds, currents, waves and tides. Their observations were often correct and they succeeded in presenting a general picture of the physical conditions of the Bay of Bengal. Historically, the subject is of considerable interest. The principal sources which preserve these early concepts are of Indian origin. The Indian sources are derived mainly from Sanskrit, Pali and Tamil literatures, and archaeological excavations, numismatics and paintings.

Coastal Navigation: Small coastal vessels were put to sea only when conditions were favourable. Hence, these vessels cast anchor at night and in dangerous circumstances. They were beached or sought refuge in the mouth of a river. If they were not aware of the features of the coast line or land marks, they did not set sail nearer to the coast line. They were often threatened by the hidden reefs, sandbars and pirates. The ship's crew were dependent upon the captain's sense of orientation and knowledge of the coastline which enabled him to determine the boat's position in relation to a number of fixed points such as topographic features and identifiable land marks. These were often noted on old maps of India's coast. Buildings having conspicuous features served also as orientation points for example, the Konark and Puri temples on Orissa coast[63].

Open Sea Navigation: Sailing within territorial area was possible through direct observation, without any instruments. But open sea navigation without the supporting orientation of landmarks, necessitated the use of specific procedures and instruments. It is likely that sailors in ancient period possessed precise astronomical knowledge and they navigated with an approximation in relation to the Sun's azimuth or the stars according to time and season. The position of ship was estimated with its average speed on the basis of experience and velocity of wind or the prevailing conditions of the sea. Tamed birds were kept on deck as land finders to indicate the coast. Ancient texts emphasise the skill of the pilots, their nautical experiences to know the conditions, of the sea and the changes in the behaviour of wind and water. It seems that in ancient times there was significant progress in nautical science[64].

Ancient Knowledge of Currents: In the early Vedic texts no reference is found on the reversal of surface wind and the ocean currents as against that documented in the present time. But the *Satapatha Brahmana*, of later Vedic period, gives some ideas about the circulation of ocean water, the text mentions, 'The ocean flows round this world on all sides'. Eggeling's commentary for turning to the right (or south) is form east to south, etc following the course of the Sun[65]. An examination of the above passage reveals that it referred to the Southwest monsoon which lasts from May to September. During this period the general flow is easterly towards south. *Aryasura* in the Jatakamala of 4th century AD differentiates waves from currents and terms the latter as *salila*. It is interesting that they were aware that there are three physical phenomena in the ocean, viz the tides, the currents and the waves[66]. By observing fishes, colour of water, species of ground, birds, rocks etc the mariners knew how to ascertain rightly the part of the sea. The sailors threw a handful of sand or shell and feathers into the calm sea. Drifting of feathers on surface and sinking of sand or shell in the sea provide an estimate of the rate of current on the basis of which they anchored the vessel off the coast[67]. Many early practices are still surviving in the eastern coast of India.

Present Climatological Current Pattern

The information on the wind drift currents in the Indian Ocean is well documented by Cutler and Swallow[68]. Figure (13 A- F) shows the monthly distribution of ship drift current vectors.

In January, an equatorward current is present along the east coast of India and the equtorial current is directed westward from the Sumatra coast. The coastal current along the east coast reverse swiftly to northward while the equatorial current still continues towards west. This circulation pattern prevails up to March-April. However, the westward equatorial flow weakens and absent in April. The circulation is clockwise in the Bay of Bengal during March-April. A weak eastward flowing current is developed near the equator east of 80° E. The northward flowing coastal current along the east coast of India still persists up to May and the eastward current in the eastern equatorial Indian Ocean is strengthening.

At the beginning of Southwest monsoon period, the northward coastal current along the east coast of India is weakened while the eastward flowing monsoon current is widened and intensified (Fig. 13 C). As the Southwest monsoon intensifies, the coastal current once again is directed northward along the east coast of India and a strong eastward flowing monsoon current is intensified in the southern Bay of Bengal (Fig. 13 D, 13 E top). As the Southwest monsoon withdraws from the Bay of Bengal, the coastal currents along east coast of India swiftly reverse equatorward from October and persist up to December (Fig. 13 D bottom, 13 E). Along the east coast of India Equatorward coastal current prevails from September to December. The Poleward coastal current prevails from February to August. In the Southern Bay, the currents are Westward from November to March and are Eastward from April to October.

Ancient Knowledge of Wind

The extensive maritime activities during the Mauryan rule, as outlined in Kautilya's the *Arthasastra*[69] could not have been possible without adequate knowledge on part of the seafarers of that time, in harnessing the wind by sails. The Buddhist Jatakas[70] and the *Jain Canonical*[71] literature refer to ships moving by force of wind *Pavanabalasamahaya*. The masts of ship depicted on the Andhra coins testify the use of wind in oceanic navigation during the early centuries of the Christian era. As ships could set sail only with a favourable wind, ancient voyages had necessarily to be timed according to seasons. For the Bay of Bengal, the force of the wind is a predominant factor. The seasonally reversing winds are almost consistent during the monsoon periods. However, a number of weather disturbances occur during the pre-monsoon, monsoon and post-monsoon periods. The problem of the studies related to the circulation is whether the large scale mean wind field remains as the factor controlling the circulation or the local dynamics control and affect the whole system during such weather disturbances[72].

Present Climatological Wind Pattern

The general progress of the wind system over the Bay of Bengal on a climatological basis is shown in Figure 14 A-B. In the month of January the wind field shows the presence of Northeast monsoon winds (blowing from the Northeast direction) prevailing all over the Bay, more so in the central and southern Bay. These

Northeast winds are also known as Northeast Trade winds. During February, winds turn clockwise over the northern part of the Bay. In the northeastern part, the northerlies are present. Generally the magnitudes of the wind speed are weak all over the Bay[73]. During March, the development of the anticyclonic wind field over the Bay of Bengal, particularly in the central region with weak winds is quite conspicuous. During April, the winds are relatively strong in the Northwestern Bay. Elsewhere in the Bay the winds are weak. In the month of May, the wind system is almost southwesterly indicating the 'burst' of the Southwest monsoon. In the northern most region the southerly wind system prevails with weak intensity. In the southern Bay, the Southwest monsoon winds become fully established.

During June southwesterly winds prevail all over the Bay of Bengal. Higher wind speed prevails in the central Bay and the direction of the wind field is consistent throughout the months of July and August with the maximum wind speeds (9m/sec) occurring during July. During the monsoon period the central Bay is subjected to maximum wind force and the magnitudes reduce towards the land bounded regions. September also shows southwesterly winds almost all over the Bay. However, the Southwest monsoon withdrawal takes place from the North Bay with its magnitudes decreasing considerably[74]. The wind system is quite irregular and becomes weak in magnitude by October. This forms the transition period between Southwest monsoon and Northeast monsoon. The Northeast trade winds set in by November through the eastern half of the Bay. The southern Bay is under the presence of a cyclonic wind field whereas the northern and western parts experience northeasterly winds. The northeasterly winds with high magnitudes establish all over the Bay during December.

Sailing seasons: The seafarers had a fair amount of knowledge of the monsoons. The wet monsoon of the Northern Hemisphere summer permitted ships of the Greek and Arab traders to infiltrate into the Arabian sea and the Bay of Bengal, and return during the periods of dry monsoon of the Northern Hemisphere winter reconciling the favourable winds for their homeward journey. It was the reversing currents associated with the monsoon winds of the northern Indian Ocean that favoured most of this traffic. As the ports of Kalinga were exposed to the Bay of Bengal, climatic conditions in the Bay were crucial in determining sailing in and out of these ports. Sailing were carried out on north and south along the coast and eastwards across the Bay. A vast knowledge was acquired by generations of sailing by communities of mariners, pilots and merchants.

The people of Kalinga took a route along the coast line and went up to Sri Lanka after which with the help of equatorial current proceeded towards Java. Hiuen Tsang took this route for his return journey to China. The timing of the journey was also related to the route. The merchants first went to Sri Lanka then to other countries. While returning through the same route they had to consider two factors, viz the direction of the wind and the movement of the water for their journey. During June - September, the Southwest monsoon wind blowing from Southwest naturally helped a ship to return from Sri Lanka and southern India to Kalinga. Similarly, during November-February, the Northeast monsoon winds blowing from Northeast helped the ships to sail from Kalinga to Sri Lanka for the overseas trade. This can be corroborated with the regional festivals like the *Taapoi* or the *Khudurukuni Osha* and the *Kartika Purnima* which are observed by the people of Orissa even today. The *Kartika Purnima* is celebrated on the full moon day of Kartika in the month of November to wish good luck to the merchants. On this day sailors commenced their journey. The ships of Kalinga left Tamil Nadu from April to mid-September for ports on the eastern and north-eastern parts of the Bay—Malacca, Kedah, Pegu and Ceylon. Ships returning from above ports arrived in Madras from the end of February to June. Similarly, the *Khudurukuni Osha* is celebrated by unmarried girls in September who used to wait for their brothers to return back with wealth. The social and religious festivals as well as scientific data corroborate that the Kalinga merchants probably commenced their journey between November and February and returned back between June and September. Just as the Arabs had a thorough knowledge of the winds and currents of the Arabian Sea, Kalingan and Dravidian sailors of the east coast of India had expert knowledge of the Bay of Bengal.

To cap it all, from the above discussion it appears that the boat and ship-building tradition prevailed in ancient times and Kalinga had her own distinct style. The boat motifs of Kalinga on coins, sculpture, texts and palm leaf manuscripts of Orissa testify to this fact. Further, the knowledge of sailing, wind, current, seasonal monsoons, etc helped the Kalingan mariners to nurture a rich maritime heritage for centuries together.

References

1. Konishi, M.A., 1985 "Notes on Harappan Boat During the 3rd - 2nd Millennia B.C.", *Manjusha, Recent Researches in Archaeology, Dr. S.R.Rao 60th Birthday Felicitation Volume,* (ed.) Satyavrat Shastri, Bangalore, 145-153.
2. Schlingloff, D., 1988 *Studies in the Ajanta Paintings*, Delhi, 195-218.
3. Sarma, I.K., 1991 "Rare evidences on Maritime Trade on the Bengal Coast of India", *Recent Advances in Marine Archaeology* (ed.), S.R.Rao, NIO, Goa, 38-40.
4. *Rig Veda*, Vol. VII, 88.3.
5. *Arthava Veda*, Vol. XIX.39.8.
6. *Rig Veda*, I.46.7.
7. *Ibid.* I.131.2.
8. Majumdar, R.C., (ed.) 1971 *Vedic Age*, Bharatiya Vidhya Bhavan, Bombay, 532.
9. *Astadhayi*, Vol. IV.3.10; VI.3.58.
10. *Ramayana*, Vol. V.57.21.
11. Sastri, T.G., (ed.) 1914-17 *Amarakosa,* Trivandrum.
12. Kangle, R.P., 1986 *The Kautilya Arthasastra*, Part-II, Delhi, 162-165.
13. Geiger, W., (tr.) 1912 *Mahavamsa*, London, 51.
14. Prasad, P.C., 1977 *Foreign trade and Commerce in Ancient India*, New Delhi, 130.
15. Geiger, W., (tr.) 1912 *Mahavamsa*, London, 28.4.
16. *Ramayana*, Vol. II, 89. 12.
17. Shamasastry, R., 1967 *Kautilya's Arthasastra*, Mysore, 142.
18. *Ibid.*
19. Prasad, P.C., 1977 *op. cit.*, 130.
20. Shamasastry, R., 1967 *Kautilya's Arthasastra*, Mysore, 143.
21. Sastri, I.C., (ed.) 1917 *Yuktikalpataru*, Calcutta, 223-230.
22. Gopal, L., 1962 "Art of Shipbuilding and Navigation in Ancient India", *Journal of Indian History*, Vol. XL: 313-328.
23. Mookerji, R., 1912 *A History of Indian Shipping*, Bombay, 256.
24. Chaudhary, M., 1976 "Shipbuilding in the Yuktikalpataru and Samaranganasutradhara", *Indian Journal of History Science*, Vol. II, (2): 137-147.

25. *Ibid*.
26. Devi, S.M., 1978 *Economic Condition of Ancient India*, Delhi, 148-210.
27. Mookerji, R., 1912 *op. cit.*, 256.
28. Chaudhary, M., 1976 *op. cit.*, 137- 147.
29. Gopal, L., 1962 *op. cit.*, 313-328.
30. Griffth, J., 1896 *The Paintings in the Buddhist Cave Temples of Ajanta*, London, 17.
31. Cowell, E.B., (tr.) 1895-1907 *The Jatakas*, 6 Vols, Cambridge.
32. Hornell, J., 1920 "The Origin and Ethnological Significance of Indian Boat designs", *Memoirs of the Asiatic Society of Bengal*, Vol. VII, (3): 139-287.
33. Davids, Rhys., 1894 *The Questions of King Milinda*, Vol. II, 300.
34. Hourani, G.F., 1975 *Arab Seafaring in the Indian Ocean in Ancient and Early Medieval Times*, New York, 100.
35. Gopal, L., 1962 *op. cit.*, 313-328.
36. Hourani, G.F., 1975 *op. cit.*, 101.
37. Van Buk, G.W., 1960 "*Pre-Islamic South Arabian Shipping in the Indian Ocean*", *Journal of the American Oriental Society*, Vol. LXXX: 137-138.
38. Marshall, J., 1940 *A Guide to Sanchi*, Calcutta, Vol. II, pl. LI.
39. Barua, B.M., 1934 *Bharhut*, Book I & II, Calcutta.
40. Hourani, G.F., 1975 *op. cit.*, 98.
41. Mookerji, R., 1912 *op. cit.*, 256.
42. Griffth, J., 1896 *op. cit.*, 7.
43. Hourani, G.F., 1975. *op. cit.*, 96.
44. Gopal, L., 1962 *op. cit.*, 313-328.
45. Das M.N., 1977 "Kalinga and Simhala - A study in Ancient Relations", *Sidelights on History and Culture of Orissa*, (ed.) M.N.Das, Cuttack, 122-131.
46. Sah, A.P., 1976 *Life in Medieval Orissa*, Varanasi, 107.
47. Bisoy, K.K., 1993 "Odissara Talapatra Pothi re Nauka Chitra", *Sagar O Sahitya* (Oriya) (ed.) K.S.Behera, Cuttack, 176- 181.
48. Behera, K.S., 1977 "Maritime Trade in Ancient Orissa", *Sidelights on History and Culture of Orissa*, (ed.) M.N.Das, Cuttack, 115-121.
49. Samal, B.C., (ed.) 1992 *Prem Sudhanidhi*, (Oriya), 1st edition, Cuttack, 9.
50. Orissa State Museums Catalogue No. Ext.1, Ext. 25, Ext. 318, Ext. 319.
51. Das, R.N., 1993 "Odissare Aranab Pota Nirmanre Parampara", *Sagar O Sahitya* (Oriya), (ed.), K.S. Behera, Cuttack, 234-256.
52. Arunachalam, B., 1997 "Timber Traditions in Indian Boat Technology", *Ship-building. Navigation in the Indian Ocean Region AD 1400-1800*, (ed.) K.S. Mathew, Delhi, 12-19.

53. Raut, L.N., & Sila, Tripati., 1993 "Traditional Boat-building Centres around Chilika Lake of Orissa", *Journal of Marine Archaeology*, Vol. IV: 51-55.

54. Das, R.N., 1993 *op. cit.*, 234-256.

55. *Ibid.*

56. Kar, B., 1973 *Prachin Utkalara Nau Vanijya*, (Oriya), Cuttack, 307.

57. Singh, J., 1982 *Prachin Utkal* (Oriya), Vol. II, Bhubaneswar, 137-151.

58. Sila, Tripati., 1997, "Ports and Maritime Activities of Orissa (16th-19th century A.D.)", *Ship-building and Navigation in the Indian Ocean Region, AD 1400-1800*, (ed.) K.S.Mathew, New Delhi, 155-164.

59. Devi, S.M., 1978 *op. cit.*, 148-210.

60. Gopal, L., 1962 *op. cit.*, 313-328.

61. Dash, R.N., 1996 "Boatbuilding in Orissa", *Maritime Activities and Trade in Orissa*, Orissa State Archives, Bhubaneswar, 13-21.

62. Senapati, F.M., 1963 *Fakir Mohan Granthavali,* Vol. II, 2nd Edition, Cuttack, 715.

63. Horsburgh, J., 1836 *India Directory*, Vol. I, London, 513.

64. Mookerji, R., 1912 *op. cit.*, 72.

65. Enggeling, J., (tr.) 1882-1900 *Satapatha Brahmana*, 5 Vols, Sacred Books of the East, Vols. XII, XXVI, Oxford, 301.

66. Tripathy, M.P., 1969 *Development of Geographic Knowledge in Ancient India*, Varanasi, 152.

67. Edye, J., 1833 "Description of the Various Classes of Vessels constructed and employed by the Natives of the coasts of Coromandel, Malabar and the Island of Ceylon for their Coasting Navigation", *Journal of Royal Asiatic Society*, London, Vol. I: 13.

68. Cutler, A.N., and Swallow, J.C., 1984 *Surface currents of the Indian Ocean* (to 25°S, 100°E): Compiled from historical data archived by the Metrological Office, Bracknell, UK, Report 187, Institute of Oceanographic Sciences, Wormley, England, 36 charts, 8 pp.

69. Shamsastry, R., 1967 *Kautilya's Arthasastra*, Mysore, 142 -145.

70. Mehta, R.N., 1939 *Pre-Buddhist India*, Bombay, 230-231.

71. Jain, J.C., 1947 *Life in Ancient India as Depicted in the Jain Canons*, Bombay, 118.

72. Leemaa, A., and Bunker, A.F., 1978 "Updated Charts of the mean annual wind stress, Convergence in the Ekman layer and Sverdrup transport in the North Atlantic", *Journal of Marine Research,* Vol. XXXVI: 311-322.

73. Hastenrath, S., and Lamb, P.J., 1979 *Climatic Atlas of the Indian Ocean*: Part-I. Surface Climate and Atmospheric circulation, The University of Winconsin Press, USA, Washington DC, 97 charts.

74. 1953 *Bay of Bengal Pilot*, 8th edition, London 40-49 & Horsburgh, J., 1836 *India Directory*, Vol. I, London, 606-609.

5

Causes of Decline

History provides information on India's contact with overseas countries since third millennium BC. The peninsular India played a key role in the maritime history of the Indian Ocean. The available antiquities of the transocean route of India is datable to Harappan culture, i.e. 3000 BC. The long coastline of India had a number of flourishing ports which in different geographical locations and during different periods of history.

A number of ports existed along the coast of Kalinga, stretching from the mouth of the Ganges to the estuaries of the Godavari. Kalinga had close commercial, cultural, social and political relations with all the Southeast Asian countries as well as the Roman world. The archaeological excavations findings at Tamralipti, Manikapatna, Palur, Kalingapatnam, Dantapura, and Khalkatapatna, the accounts of Ptolemy, Hiuen Tsang, and other literary and inscriptional evidences corroborate this fact. The ports of Kalinga flourished during different periods ranging between earliest period to early medieval period. In the absence of references to the ports of ancient Kalinga in the inscriptional and literary sources of the Gajapati period, it may be suggested that the ancient ports referred to above were no more in operation around 14th and 15th century AD. Even during later medieval period in the Factory Records, Correspondences as well as travel accounts references to the ancient ports of Kalinga are not found. But it is known the European traders set up their trade centres in the northern part of Orissa during 16th and 17th centuries AD. However reference to Manikapatna as a port is available from earliest period up to the 18th century AD. On the basis of archaeological data and existing literary sources, it is difficult to catalogue chronologically the operation of individual ports of Kalinga. However, the rise of the ports and their maritime activities are confirmed beyond doubt. The location of Palur, Dantapur, Pithunda, Kalingapatnam etc ports has been identified earlier on the basis of archaeological findings. The excavations at these port sites show the period of maritime activity and its operation but it is not possible to suggest the actual cause of decline of the individual ports. The question which arises now is, by what time and under what circumstances the ports of Kalinga declined.

Generally scholars hold the opinion that the rise of feudalism in India around 8th century AD became responsible for the decline of oceanic trade and commerce. In the context of the history of Orissa, it is believed that during this period Orissa/Kalinga presented a different picture. During historical period, Orissa had minor kingdoms viz Matharas, Sailodbhavas, Bhaumakaras and Somavamsis. In early medieval period Kalinga became a major kingdom extending between the river Ganges to the mouth of Godavari under the Imperial Gangas. Orissa undoubtedly witnessed unification, stability and prosperity during the Ganga rule in Orissa. This is indicative of continuation of ancient, it is not documented in the contemporary sources.

It is often held that the occupation of some portion of Kalingan territories by Chola emperors contributed to the decline of Kalingan sea borne commerce and ports. But the excavation findings at Khalkatapatna, Manikapatna and Palur proved that Kalinga had maritime connections with Ceylon, China and Southeast Asian countries during 12th to 14th century AD. From the stand point of material prosperity of the Kalingan empire, the Ganga rule attains the pinnacle of glory. The gigantic temple construction activities and expansion of cultivable land, systemisation of administration, military conquests etc are suggestive of material prosperity. Under such circumstances, it is difficult to think of a complete decline of ports and maritime activities of Kalinga during this period. It is therefore conjectured that ports and port towns continued to exist in Kalinga and contributed to the material prosperity of the Kingdom. The actual decline of ancient ports of Kalinga probably belong to the succeeding period. The causes of decline were essentially natural.

By the 16th century AD with the coming of European factories a chain of ports viz Pipili, Hijli, Balasore, Hariharapur, etc developed on the northern coast of Orissa. The ancient ports of Kalinga which flourished essentially in the southern coast of Kalinga did not attract attention. This shows that ports viz Palur, Kalingapatnam, Dantapur, Che-li-ta-lo, Pithunda, etc declined completely. The following are the probable natural causes for the decline of ancient ports of Kalinga.

The Orissa coast is characterised by long sandy beaches with high and wide backshore. Natural factors like tectonic movement, coastal sedimentation, development of sand dunes in the navigational channels, change of river course, flood, cyclone, sea level fluctuations, etc played a crucial role for taking away the erstwhile commercial advantages of ancient Kalingan ports and port towns. Tectonic activity could bring out major changes on the coast line. Evidences are present on the Orissa coast along with the Indian coast. Ptolemy, the geographer of AD 150 stated that Konarkanagar (Konark) was a port. Perhaps he had referred to the same Konark which was subsequently lost its importance due to tectonic movement. It is evident that in the middle of thirteen century AD Konark temple was constructed on the sea shore. Presently the sea is 4.8 km away from the temple sight. This is due to tectonic activity[1].

A survey of coastal belt of India shows that Orissa coast is having more rivers than other coasts. On the confluence points of the rivers there emerged a number of ports and port towns enabling the people to carry on sea borne trade and commerce. As is known the riverine character transforms the shape of land. This change has been perceptible as an abrupt geographical phenomena, beyond human control to resist its course. The riverine character of the Chandrabhaga, the Kushabhadra and the Rupanarayana took away the port installations of the ports viz Konark, Khalkatapatna and Tamralipti. The silting of rivers and the shifting of sandbanks are the regular phenomena of the coastal processes. Rivers which admit large ocean going vessels within a short span of time become difficult for use due to siltation. This shallowing of entrance points caused decline of some ports and rise of others, or shifting of the location of ports along the coast to take advantage of changing entry channels. Shifting of port from one place to another neighbouring suitable place become necessary depending on the changing circumstances. The coast line is constantly affected by the physical processes which are the net results of prevailing coastal currents, causing sedimentation in a particular pattern. The important factors for coastal processes is the long shore sediment transport which is mainly due to the wave characteristics and near shore topography. The beach sediment transport has regional variation due to the geological and physiographic factors.

The studies on sediment transportation carried out along the coast line of Orissa show that the direction of annual net transport is towards north east. During Southwest monsoon due to strong wind activity the rate of sediment transport become much higher[2]. It is possible that these processes might have swallowed some of the port cities like Palur in course of time. Based on data obtained for 10 years on sedimentological studies at Konark and Puri it was concluded that the amount of sediment input is higher at Konark coastal region than at Puri coast[3]. On the basis of the above studies it seems that Khalkatapatna got silted up due to sedimentation. Similarly most of the ports of ancient Kalinga could have silted up. References are there recording the existence of a number of ports around Chilka lake during the period of our study (i.e., from earliest times to the thirteenth century AD). The decline of the ports in and around Chilka lake could be due to sedimentation.

During monsoon the tropical rivers of Orissa transport enormous quantity of sediment to the Bay of Bengal. The river Mahanadi discharges several tons of sediment load into the sea. The formation of a large sand spit near the mouth of Chilka could have led to the origin of this brackish water lake. Geomorphology of the region suggests that the earlier coast line was irregular, and the formation of spits at the Chilka lake mouth resulted in the straightening of the coast. The existence of rocky islands and hills on the Northwest bank of the lake suggests a case of local submergence as compared to the local emergence in the Northeast region of the lake.

The longshore sediment transport takes place towards north during March to October and south during November to January.

Further, the annual longshore transport rate is observed to increase northward along the east coast of India[4]. The Chilka lake is situated almost on the northern end of the Bay of Bengal and the waves approaching from north are limited. The data on daily littoral current observation shows that the longshore sediment transport is northward throughout the year along the shorefront of the Chilka lake. The major rivers such as the Krishna, the Godavari and the Mahanadi, supply a large quantity of sediment in this region. The fresh water discharge during the Southwest monsoon flushes out the part of the sediment deposited in the inlet mouth. The migration rate of the inlet mouth is higher during the Southwest monsoon period. In fair weather season, the inlet mouth gets silted up since the tidal prism becomes very low[5].

The siltation process of the spit and ridge started[6] during the last sea level rise i.e., before 3750 ± 200 years BP. The lake became unsuitable for the ships to get inside and so the navigational importance of the ports declined. The marine activities slowly disappeared and the seagoing and the ship-building industries in the surrounding region gradually vanished. The traditional builders changed their technology to the construction of flat bottom boats called *Nauka* for local transport and fishing[7].

Perhaps of all territories in India, Orissa suffered over centuries due to change in the river courses. The river cycle leading to bifurcation of natural courses arose out of the change of speed owing to the load of soil carried by the rivers. The coastal zone of Orissa is marked by sand dunes. These dunes have been blown inland by the force of wind. The inner limit of the coastal dunes may be set by some topographic obstruction and prevent the rivers falling directly into the sea. The diversion of river course made the port unoperational and this would have been the case perhaps with Palur port. Recent explorations at Palur revealed pottery and other antiquities which are extensively scattered in the sand dunes[8], and deserves a systematic excavation. The studies carried out on the Mahanadi delta suggest that five million cubic metres of coarse sediment is deposited in the mouth of the Mahanadi river. Hence the reworking of the sediment by waves, elongated spits and barriers at the northern side of the Mahanadi river mouth enclosing a large body called Hakitola Bay[9]. Hakitola Bay near Paradip served as a berthing place of ships but due to barriers and spits, it is non-functional today.

The river Prachi was among the oldest rivers of Orissa, known to the Greeks and described in classical literature. The recent excavations on the banks of Prachi revealed early historical habitational remains such as sculptures, pottery, coins and inscriptions. Such a great river vanished from the land surface of Orissa by changing its course. Archaeological evidence suggest that the Prachi disappeared by 16th century[10]. In ancient times Konark was a port on the bank of the river Chandrabhaga. The river was navigable in the interior and builders of the Konark Temple used to carry huge stone pieces from long distances on massive crafts on the river. Subsequently the river changed the course. Presently Chandrabhaga river flows away from Konark. Among the big rivers of Orissa the Mahanadi, the Brahmani, the Baitarani, the Budhabalanga, the Suvarnarekha, the Rushikulya all have been changing their courses.

On the basis of studies, conclusion has been drawn that the rise of sea level is 60 to 90 m in the last 11,000 years on the west coast of India[11]. It is obvious that the coastal Orissa might have also been effected due to similar transgression on east coast. The systematic study of sea level on east coast is required to ascertain the facts. The recent explorations on coastal Andhra have brought to notice the evidences of Palaeolithic cultures at places like Barua, Bhimunipatnam, Rishikonda and similar evidences also have been found in Tamil Nadu coast[12]. This may be attributed to the sea level changes. Since no exploration is known to have been carried out on coastal Orissa, it can be inferred that being in the same coastal belt, possibilities of palaeolithic culture may have existed along the Orissa coast. Evidently the Bay of Bengal is prone to cyclones and storms since time immemorial. Such natural calamities undoubtedly affected the continued flourishment of individual ports for centuries together. The ports of Kalinga were no exception to this. The above discussion shows that the decline of ancient Kalingan ports were mainly due to natural factors. At different points of time different factors contributed to the shifting or decline of the ports.

References

1. Ahmed, E., 1972 *Coastal geomorphology of India*, New Delhi, 222.
2. Chandramohan, P., & *et al.*, 1989 Sediment transport along the Indian Coast, *Technical Report No.-6/89*, NIO, Goa, 1-34.

3. Chauhan, O. S., & et al., 1988 "Variations in Mean Grain size as Indicator of beach sediment movement at Puri and Konarak beaches Orissa, India", *Journal of Coastal Research*, Vol. IV, (1): 27-33.
4. Saxena, P. S, & et al., 1976 "Design and behaviour of sandtraps in regions of high littoral drift", *Proceedings of 15th Conference of Coastal Engineering*, ASCE, Vol. II 1377-1393.
5. Anand, N. M., & Chandramohan, P., 1992 Studies on waves and longshore sediment transport along the coast line of Chilka Lake, NIO, Goa, 1-4.
6. Venkatarathnam, K., 1970 "Formation of the Barrier spit and other sand ridges near Chilka lake on the east coast of India", *Marine Geology*, Vol. IX, (2): 101-116.
7. Raut, L. N., & Sila, Tripati., 1993 "Traditional boat-building centres around Chilika Lake of Orissa", *Journal of Marine Archaeology*, Vol. IV: 51-55.
8. *Indian Archaeology—A Review*, 1984-85, Archaeological Survey of India, New Delhi, 56-61.
9. Rao, K. N., 1988 "Development of Spits and Barriers at the Delta" *Monograph on short course on Modern Deltas*, Andhra University, Visakhapatnam, 35-38.
10. Ray, P. K., (ed.) 1975 *Prachi Valley*, Archaeological survey Report, Bhubaneswar, 43-45.
11. Nair, R. R., 1974 "Holocene sea-levels on western continental shelf of India" *Proceedings Indian Academy Science*, Vol. LXXIX, (5): 197-203.
12. Subrahmanyam, B. R., & Sireesha, E. J., 1990 "Fossil Beaches and Palaeolithic evidences in Coastal Andhra" *Journal of Marine Archaeology*, Vol. I: 24-38.

Conclusion

An indepth study of the maritime heritage of our country shows that the sailors, merchants and traders of Kalinga during the period under review contributed substantially to the mainstream of Indian overseas trade and expansion of maritime culture. This was possible owing to her flourishing ports and the enterprise of the Kalingas. Further, it was the people of Kalinga who had tremendous impact on the culture and economy of other countries and they played a leading role in overseas activities not only for economic progress but for missionary, political and cultural interactions.

Since the beginning of the recorded history of Kalinga, it is known that Kalinga had a continuous maritime history from 3rd century BC onwards. Prior to this, archaeological exploration and excavation findings show Kalinga had contact with Southeast Asian countries, since the Neolithic period. The other archaeological and art objects also directly and indirectly give detailed information of Kalingan contact with Southeast Asian countries and the Roman world. Historical sources indicate that emperor Asoka attacked Kalinga only with the intension to get the facilities of the sea ports of Kalinga. In course of time for propagation of Buddhism he sent his son Mahendra and daughter Sanghamitra to Ceylon from Tamralipti port, which flourished during that time. In later period, the Chola rulers attacked Kalinga with the intension to occupy and to control the sea ports of Kalinga.

The exploration and excavation at various coastal sites of Kalinga helped to identify unknown ports. Simultaneously some new port sites came to light viz the Manikapatna, Khalkatapatna, Bavikonda and Thotlakonda etc. These were not known earlier. The excavations also revealed the operation period of individual ports and trade and cultural contacts with other overseas countries. The longstanding confusion regarding the location of Dantapura and Palur, Pithunda and Kalingapatnam have been resolved. The ports of Kalinga helped to spread the Indian culture on the soil of Java, Bali, Burma, China, Champa, Africa and the Roman world. In course of time, the people of Kalinga set up their colonies in Southeast Asian countries. Kalinga had significant influence on the art and architecture of Southeast Asian countries. The Borobudur stupa and the Khemer temples of Cambodia are the outstanding examples of the Kalingan influence on Southeast Asian monuments. Their ground plans, the subject matter and sculptural decoration on the temples are similar to Kalingan style. There are a large number of Javanese monuments with vestibules, diminishing storeys and turrets closely resembling those on Indian temples. Some favourite motifs of the Orissan temples, such as *Makara Torana* and *Kirtimukhas* are also found in the decorative art of Javanese temples. However, the most notable Javanese monuments found at Borobudur, which still excite the wonder and admiration of the world, are unique in conception.

There was brisk intercourse between Kalinga and Burma as known from coins and medals with Hindu symbols found in Pegu. In Thalon, i.e. the ancient Rammandesa, the land par excellence of the Tailangas, Indian elements were imported from Kalinga. Existence of Buddhism in Ceylon can be attributed to the maritime intercourse of Kalinga with Ceylon, the relation which dates back to the Proto-historic times. Above all, the Bhaumakara rulers of Orissa propagated Buddhism in China and Southeast Asian countries. The Bhaumakara king sent a Buddhist text to the emperor of China which shows the contact of Kalinga with China. Similarly during the Somavamsis and the Ganga period, Hindu religion came into dominance and huge temples were constructed in Kalinga as well as in Southeast Asian countries.

The trade routes and commerce of Kalinga shows that a number of inland trade routes existed, which linked Kalinga with other parts of India. The rulers of Kalinga used these land routes for warfare. As discussed, Kalinga also had direct sea route connections with Java, Bali, Burma, China Champa, Ceylon etc via Andaman and Nicobar Islands and Ceylon. Along with the sailors of Kalinga, the religious leaders and royal family members used to go to foreign countries through these routes. The surplus agrarian and industrial products of Kalinga were exported to Southeast Asian countries. The jewels, elephants, textiles of Kalinga were highly appreciated in foreign countries. Kalinga used to import silver and spices to home land through these routes.

Sources do not supply sufficient data whether the trade and commerce were under any state policy. Probably trade and commerce were not under any state policy till Colonial expansion. Due to the lack of information of trade and commerce under the state policy system, it could be presumed that trade and commerce of the state was under private enterprise. The traders used to give taxes to the royal treasure. The trade and commerce made Kalinga rich and prosperous. The construction of temples in and around the kingdoms show the progress of life and society in every aspect. The boat motifs and sculptures on the wall of the temples are the silent witnesses to its prosperity due to maritime activities.

Since the ancient times the people of Kalinga used cowry as medium of exchange. It was continued till the colonial period. It could be presumed that the entire trade and commercial organisation was based on barter system. Subsequently, silver and gold coins came into existence. The Kushana, the Nala, and the Ganga rulers issued gold coins during their time.

The mariners of Kalinga had good knowledge of building traditional boats and ships, suitable for the environmental conditions of the Bay of Bengal. The traditional boat-building techniques of Kalinga were similar to the descriptions of boat-building techniques described in the *Yuktikalpataru*. Besides boat-building, the mariners had sound knowledge on the masts, sails, anchor, repairing and decoration of the boats of Kalinga. They used different kinds of boats for their coastal and transoceanic trade, which were different in construction pattern. They were aware of the use of suitable kind of wood for different parts of the craft. The traditional boats and ships of Kalinga were viz *Bhela, Chapa, Nauka, Padhua/ Kosaladanga* etc.

The Kalingan sailors possessed sound knowledge of navigation. They were aware of the current pattern, wind direction and depth in different parts of the Bay of Bengal. The sailors used to set sail to Southeast Asian countries for oceanic trade when the wind used to blow from NE direction and favourable current pattern (i.e. from October-November to January-February). During Southwest monsoon the wind and current used to flow towards North and the sailors used to return home from Southeast Asian countries. The same also used to help the sailors of Kalinga to sail to Burma. The usefulness of wind and current pattern to the sailors have been scientifically proved. Even the sailors of Kalinga were aware of the shore landmarks for coastal navigation. The use of sun, moon and stars were known to the sailors of Kalinga for open sea navigation.

As has been seen Tamralipti, Manikapatna, Che-li-ta-lo, Palur, Khalkatapatna, Dantapura, Kalingapatnam, Pithunda etc were the important ports of ancient Kalinga. They flourished during different periods. However, the ancient ports declined completely around 14th century AD. Neither the literary, inscriptional references nor the archaeological finds speak about the actual causes of decline. The decline of these ports therefore seems mainly due to natural factors like tectonic activities, change of river pattern, sea level variation, sediment transportation, natural hazards etc. The ports of ancient Kalinga rose and fell with the march of time. However, the maritime traditions are preserved in the legends and cultural institutions of present day Orissa. The *Taapoi* festival and the *Bali Yatra*, observance of the *Khudurukuni Osha* and the *Kartika Purnima* festival are commemorative traditions of ancient Kalingan maritime heritage.

Bibliography

Primary Sources

Archaeological Reports

Ancient India, Archaeological Survey of India.

Indian Archaeology — A Review, Archaeological Survey of India.

Memoirs of the Archaeological Survey of India.

Inscriptions

Barua, B.M., 1946 *Asoka and his Inscriptions*, Calcutta.

– –, 1929 *Old Brahmi Inscriptions in the Udayagiri and Khandagiri Caves*, Calcutta.

Basak, R.G., (ed.) 1877 *Corpus Inscriptionum Indicarum* (Old Series), Vol. I.

Epigraphia Indica, Archaeological Survey of India.

Fleet, J.F., 1888 (ed.) *Gupta Inscriptions*, Corpus Inscriptionum Indicarum, Vol. III, Calcutta.

Hultzsch, E., 1890-1929 *South Indian Inscriptions*, 3 Vols, Archaeological Survey of India, New Imperial Series, Madras.

– –, 1969 *Corpus Inscriptionum Indicarum*, Vol. I, Archaeological Survey of India, (reprint), Delhi.

Mirashi, V.V., 1955 "Inscriptions of the Kalachuri - Chedi Era", *Corpus Inscriptionum Indicarum* , Vol. IV, Part - I & II, Ootacamund.

Rajaguru, S.N., 1958-66 *Inscriptions of Orissa*, Vol. I - IV, Bhubaneswar.

Sewell, R., et al., (ed.) 1932 *Historical Inscriptions of Southern India*, Madras.

Sircar, D.C., 1942 (ed.) Select Inscriptions Bearing on Indian History and Civilization, Vol. I, (From 6th century BC to 6th century AD), Calcutta.

Sanskrit Texts

Agni Purana, (tr.) Dutt, M.N., Calcutta, 1903.

Amarakosa, (ed.) Sastri, T. G., Trivandrum, 1914-1917.

Arthasastra, Shamasastri, R., Mysore, 1967.

Aryamanjusrimulakalpa, (ed.) Sastri, T.G., Trivandrum, 1920.

Atharva Veda, (tr.) Whitney, W.D., Cambridge, 1905.

Brahmananda Purana, Published by Venkateswara Press, Bombay, 1913.

Brihatkathakosa, (ed.) Upadyye, A.N., Bombay, 1943.

Brihatkathamanjari, (ed.) Sivadatta and Parab, N.S.P., Bombay, 1931.

Brhatkathaslokasangraha, (ed. & tr.) Poddar, R.P., Varanasi, 1986.

Brihatsamhita, (ed.) Sastri, S., & Bhat, M.R., Bangalore, 1974.

Buddhacarita, (tr.) Johnston, E.H., Calcutta, 1936.

Chulavamsa, (ed. & tr.) Geiger, W., and Rickmers, R., London, 1930.

Dasakumaracharita, (ed.) Kale, M.R., Bombay, 1917.

Dathavamsa, (ed. & tr.) Law, B.C., Lahore, 1925.

Digha Nikaya, (ed.) Rhys Davids, T.W., London, 1890-1911.

Dipavamsa, (ed. & tr.) Oldenberg, H., London, 1879.

Divyavadana, (ed.) Cowell, E.B., & Neil, R.A., Cambridge, 1886.

Harivamsa, (ed.) Kinjawadekar, R., Poona, 1936.

Harsacarita, (tr.) Cowell and Thomas, Royal Asiatic Society, London, 1897.

Jataka Stories, (tr.) Cowell, E.B., Cambridge University Press, London, 1895.

Kathasaritsagara, (tr.) Tawney, C.H., Calcutta, 1880-87.

Mahabharata, (ed.) Kinjawadekar, R., Poona, 1929-33.

Mahabharata, (ed.) Sukthankar, V.S., *et al.,* Poona, 1927-56.

Mahavamsa, (tr.) Geiger, W., London, 1912.

Manasollasa, (ed.) Shrigondekar, G.K., 2 Vols, Baroda, 1925.

Manusamhita, (tr.) Buhler, G., Varanasi, 1935.

Manusmrti, (ed.) Jha, G., Asiatic Society of Bengal, Calcutta, 1932-39.

Markendeya Purana, (ed. & tr.) Pargiter, F.E., 1904.

Milindapanho or *The Questions of King Milinda*, (tr.) Rhys Davids, T.W., New York, 1965.

Ramayana, (relevant Volumes as referred) (ed.) Raghuvira, Lahore, 1938.

Raghuvamsa, (ed. & tr.) Nandargikar, G.R., Bombay, 1897.

Rig Veda, (tr.) Max Muller, F., Oxford, 1891-97.

Samaranganasutradhara, (ed.) Sastri, T.G., Baroda, 1925.

Satapatha Brahmana, (ed.) Weber, A., London, 1885.

Tilakamanjarikatha, (ed.) Parab, N.S.P., Bombay, 1903.

Trikandasesha of Purushottama, (ed.) Seelakhandha, C.A., Bombay, 1916.

Uttaradhyayanasutra, (ed.) Charpentier, J., Uppasala, 1922.

Valmiki Ramayana, (tr.) Griffth, R.T.H., 1915, Varanasi.

Vinaya Pitaka, (tr.) Rhys Davids, T. W., Oxford, 1881-85.

Vrihat Samhita, Varaha Mihira (ed.) Kern, H., Calcutta, 1965.

Yuktikalpataru, (ed.) Sastri, I.C., Calcutta, 1917.

Chinese, Greek and Persian Texts

Akbarnamah, (tr.) Beveridge, H., Calcutta, 1939.

Alberuni's India, (tr.) Sochau, E.C., London, 1914.

Ancient India as Described by Ptolemy, McCrindle, J.W., (ed.) Delhi, 1985.

Ancient India as Described in Classical Literature, McCrindle, J.W., Westminster, 1901.

Ancient India as Described by Megasthenes and Arrian, McCrindle, J.W., Calcutta, 1877.

Beal, S., 1884 *Buddhist Records of the Western World,* 2 Vols., London.

– –, 1906 *Si-Yu-Ki or Buddhist Records of the Western World,* (tr.) From the Chinese Accounts of Hiuen Tsang 629 A.D., New Delhi.

Fa-Hien's Record of Buddhists Kingdoms, Legge: Oxford, 1886.

India as Described by Ktesias, McCrindle, J.W., Calcutta, 1832.

Megasthenes Accounts, (tr.) Twany, C.H., London, 1936.

Pliny's Natural History, (tr.) Melmoth, W., Vol. II, London, 1945.

The Geography of Strabo, (tr.) Hamilton, H.C., and Falconer, W., London, 1892-93, 3 Volumes.

The Periplus of the Erythraean Sea, (tr.) Schoff, W.H., New Delhi, 1974.

Articles

Acharya, P., 1955 "Ancient Routes in Orissa", *Orissa Historical Research Journal*, Vol. IV, (3-4), Bhubaneswar.

Ardika, I.W., & Wellwood P., 1991 "Sembiran: the beginning of Indian contact with Bali", *Antiquity*, Vol. LXV, (247), Cambridge.

Agarawal, V.S., 1941 "Trade and Commerce from Panini's Astadhyayi", *Journal of the United Provinces Historical Society*, Vol. XIV, Lucknow.

Ahmad, N., 1972 "Attribution and Typology of the Satavahana Coins", *Coinage of the Satavahanas and Coins from Excavations*, (ed.) A.M. Shastri, Nagpur.

Aquique, M., 1975 "Ship-building Industry in Ancient India", *Journal of the Bihar Research Society*, Vol. LXI, Patna.

Arunachalam, B., 1985 "The haven finding Art in Indian Navigational Traditions and its application in Indian navigational Cartography", *Indica*, Vol. XII, (5), Bombay.

– –, 1993 "The Route of the Bali Yatra—A Scientific Appraisal", *Journal of Indian Ocean Studies*, Vol. I, (2), New Delhi.

– –, 1995 "Indigenous Indian Sea-charts and Navigation", *Orissa Historical Research Journal,* Vol. XXXX, (1-4), Bhubaneswar.

Bag, A.K., 1988 "Ships and Ship-building Technology in Ancient and Medieval India", *Marine Archaeology of Indian Ocean Countries*, (ed.) S.R. Rao, NIO, Goa.

Bajpai, K.D., 1997 "Contribution of Kalinga to Indian Culture", *Facets of Indian Civilisation, Recent Perspectives, Essays in Honor of Prof. B.B.Lal*, (eds.) J.P. Joshi, *et al.*, New Delhi.

Bajpai, S.G., 1989 "Mathura: Trade Routes, Commerce and Communication Patterns during Post-Mathura period to End of Kushana period", *Mathura, The Cultural Heritage*, (ed.) D.M. Srinivasan, Delhi.

Basa, K.K., 1994 "Problems and Prospectives in Archaeology of Orissa, India", Occasional Paper No. 4, Utkal University, Bhubaneswar.

Basham, A.L., 1949 "Notes on Seafaring in Ancient India", *Art and Letters*, Vol. XXII, London.

Behera, D., 1987 "Orissa's Overseas Relations", *Orissa Review*, Vol. XLIII, (2), Bhubaneswar.

Behera, K.S., 1977 "Maritime Trade in Ancient Orissa", *Sidelights on History and Culture of Orissa*, (ed.) M.N. Das, Cuttack.

– –, 1991 "Trade and Patterns of Commerce in Orissa (700-1200 AD)", *Utkal Historical Research Journal*, Vol. II, Bhubaneswar.

– –, 1992 "Glimpses of the Maritime Activities of Kalinga", *Orissa Review,* Vol. XLIX, (4), Bhubaneswar.

– –, 1993 "Ancient Orissa/Kalinga and Indonesia: The Maritime Contacts", *Utkal Historical Research Journal*, Vol. IV, Bhubaneswar.

– –, 1994 "Maritime contacts of Orissa—Literary and Archaeological evidence", *Utkal Historical Research Journal*, Vol. V, Bhubaneswar.

Behera, S.C., 1964 "Origin of the Mathara Dynasty of Kalinga", *Orissa Historical Research Journal*, Vol. XII, (2), Bhubansewar.

– –, 1970 "Mathara Rule in Kalinga", *Journal of Indian History*, Vol. XLVIII, Trivandrum.

Bhatt, K.S., 1993 "Chilka Anchalare Matyajibi Manankar Jivandhara", (Oriya) *Sagar O Sahitya*, (ed.) K.S.Behera, Cuttack.

Bhatt, B., 1997 "The Chilka Lake: Its Maritime Importance", *Utkal Historical Research Journal*, Vol. IX, Bhubaneswar.

Bisht, R.S., 1988 "Some Glimpses of Mercantile and Marine Activities of the Rg Vedic Aryans", *Marine Archaeology of Indian Ocean Countries*, (ed.) S.R. Rao, NIO, Goa.

Bisoy, K.K., 1993 "Odissara Talapatra Pothire Nauka Chitra", *Sagar O Sahitya*, (Oriya), (ed.) K.S. Behera, Cuttack.

Blue, L., 1996 "The Potential Identification of Early water Transport in Coastal Orissa", *Utkal Historical Research Journal*, Vol. VII, Bhubaneswar.

Blue, L., *et al.*, 1997 "The Patia Fishing Boat of Orissa: A Case Study in Ethnoarchaeology", *South Asian Studies*, Vol. XIII, New Delhi.

Bopearachchi, O., 1996 "Seafaring in the Indian Ocean: Archaeological Evidence from Sri Lanka", *Tradition and Archaeology*, (eds.) H.P. Ray and J.F. Salles, New Delhi.

Brandtner, M., 1988-89 "Archaeological Explorations Around Bhubaneswar", *Manav, Journal of Anthropological Society of Orissa*, Vol. III, Bhubaneswar.

Bronson, B., & Dales, G.F., 1973 "Excavations at Chansem, Thailand, 1968-69: a preliminary report", *Asian Perspectives*, Vol. XV, Honolulu, USA.

Casson, L., 1980 "Rome's Trade with the East: The Sea Voyage to Africa and India", *Transactions of the American Philological Association*, Vol. CX, New Haven, USA.

Chakravarty, P.C., 1930 "Naval warfare in Ancient India", *Indian Historical Quarterly*, Vol. VI, Calcutta.

Chakravarty, S., 1997 "Some Aspects of Navigation in Ancient India", *Facets of Indian Civilisation, Recent Perspectives, Essays in Honor of Prof. B.B. Lal*, (eds.) J.P. Joshi *et al.*, New Delhi.

Chandra, L., 1980 "Oddiyana—A New Interpretations", *International Journal of Dravidian Linguistic*, Vol. VIII, Trivandrum.

Chaudhuri, K.K., 1990 "South India's contact with China: A study in the Earliest phase from Chinese sources", *Researches in Indian History, Archaeology, Art, and Religion, U. Thakur Felicitation Volume,* (eds.) G. Kuppuram and K. Kumudamani, New Delhi.

Chaudhary, M., 1976 "Ship-building in the Yuktikalpataru and Samaranganasutradhara", *Indian Journal of History of Science*, Vol. II, (2), New Delhi.

– –, 1986 "Ship-building in Ancient and Medieval India", *The Cultural Heritage of India,* Vol. VI, The Ramakrishna Mission Institute of Culture, Calcutta.

Choudhary, S., 1977 "Lost and Forgotten Places of Orissa", *Sidelights on History and Culture of Orissa,* (ed.) M.N. Das, Cuttack.

Chauhan, O.S., and *et al.,* 1988 "Variations in Mean Grain size as Indicator of beach sediment movement at Puri and Konarak beaches of Orissa, India", *Journal of Coastal Research*, Vol. IV, (1), Florida.

Chauhan, O.S., 1990 "Sedimentological Parameters of Beach Sediment on the East Coast of India", *Journal of Coastal Research*, Vol. VI, (3), Florida.

Cooper, Z., 1996 "Archaeological Evidence of Maritime Contacts: the Andaman Islands", *Tradition and Archaeology*, (eds.) H.P. Ray and J.F. Salles, New Delhi.

Christie, A., 1970 "The Provenance and Chronology of the early Indian Cultural influence in Southeast Asia", *R.C.Majumdar Felicitation Volume*, (ed.) H.B. Sarkar, Calcutta.

Das, A., 1965 "Asanapata", *Orissa Historical Research Journal*., Vol. XIII, (2), Bhubaneswar.

Das, A.C., 1975 "Kalinga, The Ancient Maritime Power", *Orissa Historical Research Journal*, Vols. XVI, (4) to XXII, (1), Bhubaneswar.

Das, M.N., 1977 "Ancient and Medieval Empires and Kingdoms", *Sidelights on History and Culture of Orissa*, (ed.) M.N. Das, Cuttack.

– –, 1977 "Kalinga and Simhala: A Study in Ancient Relations", *Sidelights on History and Culture of Orissa,* (ed.) M.N.Das, Cuttack.

Das, R.N., 1993 "Odissare Aranab Pota Nirmanre Parampara", *Sagar O Sahitya* (Oriya), (ed.) K.S. Behera, Cuttack.

Dash, K.C., 1996 "Apheterion of Periplous: A Study of its Location in South Orissa", *Maritime Activities and Trade in Orissa*, Orissa State Archives, Bhubaneswar.

Dash, R.N., 1996 "Boat Building in Orissa", *Maritime Activities and Trade in Orissa*, Orissa State Archives, Bhubaneswar.

Davidson, J.L., 1975 "Indian Influences on China", *A Cultural History of India*, (ed.) A.L. Basham, Oxford.

De, S.C., 1947 "The Coins of Orissa", *Journal of Kalinga Historical Research Society*, Vol. I, (4), Bolangir.

– –, 1952 "The Cowry Currency in Orissa", *Orissa Historical Research Journal*, Vol. I, (1), Bhubaneswar.

Deloche, J., 1983 "Geological Considerations in the localisation of ancient Ports of India", *Indian Economic and Social History Review*, Vol. XX, (4), New Delhi.

– –, 1991 "Boats and Ships in Bengal Terracotta Art", *Bulletin de l Ecole Franciase d Extreme - Orient*, Vol. LXXVII, Paris.

– –, 1996 "Iconographic Evidence on the Development of boat and ship structures in India (2nd cent. BC - 15th cent. AD): a new approach", *Tradition and Archaeology*, (eds.) H.P.Ray and J.F.Salles, New Delhi.

Deraniyagala, S.U., 1989 "Excavations in the Citadel of Anuradhapura-Gedige, A Preliminary Report", *Ancient Ceylon*, Vol. VI, Colombo.

Deshpande, M.N., 1981 "Trade Routes in Ancient India", *Science Today*, Feb. 1981.

Devi, G., 1992 "Tamralipti: The Port of Ancient Orissa", *Orissa Review*, Vol. XLIX, (4), Bhubaneswar.

Dikshit, K.N., & Pandeya, R.G., 1978 "Ancient Maritime Contacts of West Bengal—Literary and Archaeological Evidences", *L.N. Mishra Commemoration Volume*, (ed.) U. Thakur, Bodhagaya.

Donaldson, T.E., 1994 "Navigation and Maritime Goddesses of Orissa" *Studies in History and Culture*, Vol. II, (2), Berhampur.

Dubreil, G.J., 1930 "Buddhist Antiquities in the East Godavari District", *Journal of Andhra Historical Research Society*, Vol. V, Rajahmundry.

Edye, J., 1833 "Description of the Various Classes of Vessels constructed and employed by the Natives of the coasts of Coromandel, Malbar and the Island of Ceylon for their Coasting Navigation", *Journal of Royal Asiatic Society*, London.

Filliozar, J., 1950 "Intercourse of India with the Roman Empire during the Early Centuries of the Christian Era", *Journal of Indian History*, Vol. XXVIII, Trivandrum.

Ghosh, A., & Sarkar H., 1964-65 "Beginnings of Sculptural Art in Southeast India: A Stele from Amaravati", *Ancient India* No. XX-XXI, Archaeological Survey of India, New Delhi.

Ghosh, D.P., 1933 "Relations between the Buddha images of Orissa and Java", *Modern Reviews*, Vol. LIV, (5) Calcutta.

– –, 1983 "Influence of Indian Art on the Art of Southeast Asia", *The Aspects of Indian Art and Culture, S.K. Saraswati Commemorative* Volume, Calcutta.

Gopal, L., 1962 "Art of Ship-building and Navigation in Ancient India", *Journal of Indian History,* Vol. XL, Trivandrum.

Glover, I.C., 1990 "Early trade Between India and Southeast Asia: A Link in the Development of Ancient World Trading System", *Occasional Paper No.16*, The University of Hull, London.

– –, 1996 "Recent Archaeological Evidence from early Maritime contacts between India and Southeast Asia", *Tradition and Archaeology*, (eds.) H.P.Ray and J.F.Salles, New Delhi.

– –, 1998 "The Role of India in the Late Prehistory of Southeast Asia", *Journal of Southeast Asian Archaeology*, Vol. XVIII.

Haque, M.A., 1967 "Route of Feroz Shah's invasion of Orissa 1380 AD", *Orissa Historical Research Journal*, Vol. XV, (3-4), Bhubaneswar.

Hariharan, K.V., 1956 "Sea Dangers in Early Indian Seafaring", *Journal of Indian History*, Vol. XXXIV, Trivandrum.

– –, 1965 "Some Aspects of Ancient Indian Ship-building and

Navigation", *Journal of the University of Bombay*, Vol. XXXIV, Bombay.

Hall, K.R., 1991 "Coinage, Trade, Economy in Early South India and Southeast Asia", *Coinage, Trade, and Economy*, (ed.) A.K.Jha, Anjaneri.

Hornell, J., 1918 "The Origin and Ethnological Significance of Indian Boat Designs", *Memoirs of the Asiatic Society of Bengal*, Vol. VII, Calcutta.

– –, 1951 "Sea Trade in Early Times", *Antiquity*, Vol. XV, Cambridge.

Jain, P.S., 1975 "An Account of the Trade and Shipping in Prakrit Literature", *Contribution of Jainism to Indian Culture*, (ed.) R.C. Dwivedi, Varanasi.

Jayaswal, K.P., 1917 "Hathigumpha Inscription of the Emperor Kharavela", *Journal of the Bihar and Orissa Research Society*, Vol. III, Patna.

Joshi, M.C., 1988 "Navigational Terms in Namalinganusasanam", *Marine Archaeology of Indian Ocean Countries*, (ed.) S.R.Rao, NIO, Goa.

Joshi, J.P., 1988 "Archaeological Perspectives of Marine Activities in Ancient India", *Marine Archaeology of Indian Ocean Countries*, (ed.) S.R.Rao, NIO, Goa.

Kennedy, J., 1898 "Early Commerce with Babylon with India", *Journal of the Royal Asiatic Society*, London.

Kentley, E., 1996 "The Sewn Boats of India's East Coast", *Tradition and Archaeology*, (eds.) H.P.Ray and J.F.Salles, New Delhi.

Keswani, D.G., 1980 "Indian Cultural and Commercial influences in the Indian Ocean from Africa and Madagascar to Southeast Asia", *Historical Relations across the Indian Ocean*, Unesco, Paris.

Konishi, M.A., 1985 "Notes on Harappan Boat During the 3rd-2nd Millennia B.C.", *Manjusha, Recent Researches in Archaeology, Dr. S.R. Rao 60th Birthday Felicitation Volume*, (ed.) Satyavrat Shastri, Bangalore.

Kumar, P., & *et al.*, 1989 "Remote sensing study on the coastal process of Orissa coast", *Proceedings of Third National*

Conference on Dock & Harbour Engineering, Suratkal.

Lal, B.B., 1949 "Sisupalgarh, An early Historical Fort in Eastern India", *Ancient India* No. 5, Archaeological Survey of India, New Delhi.

– –, 1967 "Sisupalgarh", *Orissa Historical Research Journal*, Vol. XV, (1-2), Bhubaneswar.

Lamb, A., 1975 "Indian Influence in Ancient Southeast Asia", *A Cultural History of India*, (ed.) A.L. Basham, Oxford.

Law, B.C., 1955 "Cultural Life as Depicted in the Buddhist Jatakas", *Journal of Indian History*, Vol. XXXII, Trivandrum.

Litvinsky, B.A., 1970 "India and Soviet Central Asia", *India's Contribution to World Thought and Culture, Vivekananda Commemoration Volume*, (ed.) Lokesh Chandra, Madras.

Mahadevan, R., 1991 "Storm Surge Simulation Studies", *Coastal Zone Management in Tamil Nadu*, (ed.) R. Natarajan & *et al.*, Madras.

Mahapatra, N.K., 1953-54 "Purusottama Deva, the lexicographer", *Orissa Historical Research Journal*, Vol. II, (3-4), Bhubaneswar.

Mallik, B.K., 1997 "Trade and Transmission of Early South-Asia", *Utkal Historical Research Journal*, Vol. VIII, Bhubaneswar.

McCrindle, J.W., 1879 "Periplus of the Erythraean Sea", *Indian Antiquary*, Vol. VIII, London.

– –, 1884 "Ptolemy's Geography of India and Southern Asia", *Indian Antiquary*, Vol. XIII, London.

McGrail, S., 1983 "The Interpretation of Archaeological evidence for Maritime Structures", *Sea Studies*, (ed.) Paw Annis, National Maritime Museum, Greenwich.

– –, 1996 " Maritime Archaeology and Ethnography in Orissa", *Utkal Historical Research Journal*, Vol. VII, Bhubaneswar.

Mirashi, V.V., 1941 "Some seal stamps from the Central Provinces", *Journal of the Numismatic Society of India*, Vol. III, Varanaṣi.

Mishra, A.K., 1992 "Bali Yatra-1992", *Orissa Review*, Vol. XLIX, (4), Bhubaneswar.

Mishra, A.N., 1981 "Overseas Trade and Maritime Activities of Ancient Orissa", *Orissa Historical Research Journal*, Vol. XXVII, (1-4), Bhubaneswar.

Mishra, R.K., 1978 "Traditions of Temples and Shrines in Ancient Sea Ports of Kalinga", *Orissa Historical Research Journal*, Vol. XIII, (1-4), Bhubaneswar.

Mishra, V.K., 1954 "Sea and Land Routes in India as Revealed in the Buddhist Literature", *Journal of Indian History*, Vol. XXXII, Trivandrum.

Misra, B., 1937 "Folklore and Puranic tradition about Origin of God Jagannatha", *Indian Historical Quarterly*, Vol. XIII, (4), New Delhi.

Misra, P.P., 1980 "The Contact between Orissa and Southeast Asia in Ancient Times", *The Journal of Orissan History*, Vol. I, (2), Bhubaneswar.

Mohanty, K.P., 1992 "Evolution of Orissan Culture in Bali", *Orissa Review*, Vol. XLIX, (4), Bhubaneswar.

– –, 1993 "Indonesiare Odia Sanskruti", *Utkala Prasanga*, (Oriya), Vol. XLVIII, (6), Cuttack.

Mohanti, M., 1990 "Sealevel rise: Background, Global concern and implication for Orissa Coast, India", *Sea level variation and its impact on coastal Environment*, (ed.), G.V.Rajamanickam, Thanjavur.

Mohanty, S.K., 1990 "Utkalara Pradhana Bandara Dhamara O Chandabali", *Utkal Prasanga*, (Oriya), Vol. XLXII, (4), Cuttack.

Mohapatra, L.D., 1989 "The Export of Commodities used as Ballast from the Ports of Orissa (1630-1720)", *Proceedings of the XV Orissa History Congress.*

Mahapatro, K.N., 1973 "Utkalara Prachina Sahityara Samudra O Samudrayatra Varnana", *Jhankara* (Oriya), Vol. XXV, (3), Cuttack.

Mukherjee, B.N., 1981 "The Relevance of the Periplous Tes Exo Thalasses to the History of Orissa", *Journal of the Orissa Research Society*, Vol. I, Bhubaneswar.

– –, 1982 "Desarene-Dasarna-Coastal Orissa (?)", *The Journal of Orissan History*, Vol. III, (1), Bhubaneswar.

– –, 1989 "Decipherment of the Kharoshti-Brahmi Scripts", *Asiatic Society Monthly Bulletin*, XVIII, (8), Calcutta.

— —. 1989-90 "Discovery of Kharoshti Inscriptions in West Bengal", The *Quarterly Review of Historical Studies*, Vol. XXIX, (2), Calcutta.

— —. 1990 "A Kharoshthi-Brahmi seal matrix from Oc-Eo", *Asiatic Society Monthly Bulletin*, Vol. XIX, Calcutta.

Nadvi, S.S., 1937 "The Early Relations between India and Arabia", *Islamic Culture*, Vol. XI, Hyderabad.

Nair, R.R., 1974 "Holocene sea-levels on western continental shelf of India", *Proceedings Indian Academy Science*, Vol. LXXIX, (5), Bangalore.

Panda, B., 1982 "The Military and Maritime Traditions of Orissa", *Souvenir, Orissa Sahiyta Academy*, Silver Jubilee, Bhubaneswar.

Panda, B., 1996 "Maritime Orissa: As depicted in Ancient Literature", *Maritime Activities and Trade in Orissa*, Orissa State Archives, Bhubaneswar.

Panda, S.C., and Sahu, R.M., 1989 "The Migrant Kalingas in Southeast Asia," *Proceedings of the XV Orissa History Congress*.

Pandey, M.S., 1973 "Foreign Trade Routes and Ports in Ancient India", *Journal of the Bihar Research Society*, Vol. LIX, Patna.

Panikkar, N.K., & Srinivasan, T.M., 1971 "The concept of tides in Ancient India", *Indian Journal of History of Science*, Vol. VI, (2), New Delhi.

Parida, A.N., 1994 "Ports of Ancient Orissa", *Utkal Historical Research Journal*, Vol. V, Bhubaneswar.

Patnaik, A.P., 1989 and 1992 "Kalingan Link with Countries of Southeast Asia", *Orissa Review*, Vol. XLIV and XLVIII (9), Bhubaneswar.

– –, 1993 "Smurti O Bismurtira Katoti Chinnasutra", *Sagar O Sahitya*, (Oriya) (ed.) K.S.Behera, Cuttack.

Patnaik, J., 1977 "Jainism in Orissa", *Sidelights on History and Culture of Orissa*, (ed.) M.N. Das, Cuttack.

Patnaik, J.K., 1996 "Palur port through the Ages", *Studies in History and Culture*, Vol. II, (2), Berhampur.

– –, 1997 "Ancient Orissa's Maritime Contacts as Gleaned through Explorations and Excavations", *An Integrated Approach to Marine Archaeology*, (ed.) S.R. Rao, NIO, Goa.

Patnaik, J.K., and Tripathy, B.K., 1993 "Ships and Shipping in Orissan Art", *Puratattva* No. 23, New Delhi.

Patnaik, P., 1993 "Odisara Loka Kathare Samudra Yatra", *Sagar O Sahitya*, (Oriya), (ed.), K.S.Behera, Cuttack.

Patnaik, S.K., 1991 "Routes in Ancient Orissa", *The Journal of the Orissan History*, Vol. IV, Bhubaneswar.

Pattanayak, A.K., and Patnaik, S.K., 1994 "Orissa and Southeast Asia — A Study of Ancient Relations up to 15th cent. AD", *The Role of Universities and Research Institutes in Marine Archaeology*, (ed.) S.R.Rao, NIO, Goa.

Pattanayak, A.K., and Patra, B., 1997 "Kalinga and the Sea", *An Integrated Approach to Marine Archaeology*, (ed.) S.R.Rao, NIO, Goa.

Pattanayak, A.K., and Sila, Tripati., 1997 "Role of Chilka Lake in the Maritime History of Orissa", *An Integrated Approach to Marine Archaeology*, (ed.) S.R.Rao, NIO, Goa.

Patra, B., 1996 "Trade Routes and Trade in Ancient Orissa", *Studies in History and Culture*, Vol. IV, (2), Berhampur.

Perumalil, A.C., 1942 "The India of the Early Greeks and Romans from the Time of Alexander's Invasion till the fall of Alexandria", *Journal of Bihar and Orissa Research Society*, Vol. XXVIII, Patna.

Pradhan, D., 1991 "Manikapatna: Ancient Port City on Chilika", *Kalingas, The Brave, Souvenir*, Bhubaneswar.

Prusty, H., *et al.*, 1995 "Dantapura, the Capital of Ancient Kalinga: a Reappriasal", *Studies in History and Culture*, Vol. III, (1), Berhampur.

Ramachandran, K.S., 1970 "Ancient Indian Maritime Ventures", *Indian's Contribution to World Thought and Culture, Vivekananda Commemoration Volume*, (ed.) Lokesh Chandra, Madras.

Raman, K.V., 1988 "Port Towns of Tamil Nadu—Some field Data and other prospects of Marine Archaeology", *Marine*

Archaeology of Indian Ocean Countries, (ed.) S.R. Rao, Goa.

Rao, K.N., 1988 "Development of Spits and Barrier at the Delta", *Monograph on short course on Modern Deltas*, Andhra University, Visakhapatnam.

Rao, R.S., 1931 "History of the Eastern Gangas of Kalinga", *Journal of Andhra Historical Research Society*, Vol. VI, (1), Rajahmundry.

– –, 1971-72 "The Historical Geography of Kalinga", *Journal of Andhra Historical Research Society*, Vol. XXXII, (1-4), Rajahmundry.

Rao, S.R., 1970 "Shipping in Ancient India", *Indian's Contribution to World Thought and Culture, Vivekananda Commemoration Volume,* (ed.) Lokesh Chandra, Madras.

Rath, P.C., 1947 "Maritime Activities of Kalinga", *Journal of Kalinga Historical Research Society*, Vol. I, (4), Bolangir.

Raut, L.N., and Patnaik, S.K., 1993 "Trade in Medieval Orissa: a study on Khalkatapatna Port", *The Journal of Historical and Social Analysis,* Vol. V, (10), Bhubaneswar.

Raut, L.N., & Sila, Tripati., 1993 "Traditional Boat-building centres around Chilika Lake of Orissa", *Journal of Marine Archaeology*, Vol. IV, NIO, Goa.

Rawlinson, H.G., 1908-1913 "Foreign Influences in the Civilization of Ancient India 900 B.C. to 400 A.D.", *Journal of Royal Asiatic Society*, Vol. XXXIII, London.

– –, 1975 "Early Contacts between India and Europe", *A Cultural History of India*, (ed.) A.L. Basham, Oxford.

Ray, H.P., 1989 "Early Maritime contacts between South and Southeast Asia", *Journal of Southeast Asian Studies*, Vol. XX, (1), Singapore.

– –, 1990 "Seafaring in the Bay of Bengal in the early centuries A.D.", *Studies in History*, Vol. VI, (1), Delhi.

– –, 1990-91 "In Search of Suvarnabhumi: Early Sailing Networks in the Bay of Bengal", *Bulletin of the Indo-Pacific Prehistory Association -10.*

– –, 1995 "Trade and Contacts", *Recent Perspectives of Early Indian History*, (ed.) R.Thapar, Bombay.

Ray, H.P., 1991 "The Identity of Huang Chih: An Ancient Indian Kingdom in intimate contact with Han China", *Indian Historical Review*, Vol. XVII, (1-2), New Delhi.

– –, 1994 "Orissa and Orissa trade in Chinese Historical Records", *Journal of Indian Ocean Studies*, Vol. II, (1), New Delhi.

Ritti, S.H., 1988 "Shipping in Ancient India", *Marine Archaeology of Indian Ocean Countries*, (ed.) S.R.Rao, NIO, Goa.

Roy, U.N., 1991 "History of the Brihatkatha-Sloka Samgraha on Marine activities of the Gupta Ages", *Recent Advances in Marine Archaeology*, (ed.) S.R.Rao, NIO, Goa.

– –, 1994 "Dronimukha and Lothal", *The Role of Universities and Research Institutes in Marine Archaeology*, (ed.) S.R. Rao, Goa.

Sahu, B.P., 1984 "Ancient Orissa Cultural Relations (Reflections on Archaeological Data)", *Indica*, Vol. XXI, (1), Bombay.

– –, 1994 "Situating Early Historical Trade in Orissa", Presented at the World Archaeological Congress 3, (4-11 December 1994), New Delhi.

Sahu, N.K., 1955 "Cultural Relations of Kalinga with South India and Ceylon" *Orissa Historical Research Journal*, Vol. III, (4), Bhubaneswar.

– –, 1977 "Historical Geography", *Sidelights on History and Culture of Orissa*, (ed.) M.N.Das, Cuttack.

– –, 1982 "Historical Geography of Orissa", *Souvenir - Orissa Sahitya Academy*, Silver Jubilee, Bhubaneswar.

– –, "Utkalki Nau Yatra Tatha Nau Vanijya" (Hindi), *Rashtrabhasha Rajat Jayanti Grantha.*

Samaddar, J.N., 1921 "Industrial and Trading Organisation in Ancient India", *Journal of the Bihar and Orissa Research Society*, Vol. VII, Patna.

Sarkar, H., 1987 "Emergence of Urban Centres in Early Historical Andhradesa", *Archaeology and History, Essays in Memory of Shri A.Ghosh,* (eds.) B.M. Pande and B.D. Chattopadhyaya, Delhi.

Sarkar, H.B., 1934 "The Homeland of Kaundiya of Funan and Tradition about his marriage", *Journal of Institute of Asian Studies*, Madras.

– –, 1972 "Bengal and Her Traffic routes in the Bay of Bengal and Southeast Asia (300 BC-300 AD)", *Journal of the Asiatic Society*, Vol. XIV, (2-4), Calcutta.

– –, 1990 "Gangetic Ports of Bengal and the Western World: (An Archaeological Survey)", *Researches in Indian History, Archaeology, Art, and Religion, U. Thakur Felicitation Volume*, (eds.) G. Kuppuram and K. Kumudamani, New Delhi.

Sarkar, R., and Sila, Tripati., 1993 "Boat-building technology of Bengal: An overview of Literary Evidences", *Journal of Marine Archaeology*, Vol. IV, NIO, Goa.

Sarma, I.K., 1989 "Salankayana coins from Ghantasala, District Krishna, Andhra Pradesh", *Ajaya Sri, Recent Studies in Indology*, (ed.) D. Handa, Vol. I, Delhi.

– –, 1991 "Rare Evidences on Maritime Trade on the Bengal coast of India", *Recent Advances in Marine Archaeology*, (ed.) S.R.Rao, Goa.

– –, 1991 "Ceramics and Maritime Routes of India: New Evidences", *Puratattva* No. XXI, New Delhi.

– –, 1997 "Indian Seafaring Traditions - Archaeological Perspectives", *An Integrated Approach to Marine Archaeology*, (ed.) S.R.Rao, NIO, Goa.

Sarmadhikari, R.K., 1984 "Some observations on the coins of East Bengal", *Indian Museum Bulletin*, Vol. XIX, Calcutta.

Saxena, P.S., & *et al.*, 1976 "Design and behaviour of sand traps in regions of high littoral drift", *Proceedings of 15th Conference of Coastal Engineering*, Vol. II, ASCE.

Seneviratne, S., 1981 "Kalinga and Andhra: the Process of secondary State Formation in Early India", *The Study of the State*, (eds.) H.J.M. Clalssen and P. Skalnik, The Hague.

Sengupta, G., 1996 "Archaeology of Coastal Bengal", *Tradition and Archaeology*, (eds.) H.P. Ray and J.F. Salles, New Delhi.

Sewell, R., 1904 "Roman Coins found in India", *Journal of the Royal Asiatic Society*, London.

Sila, Tripati, 1990 "Sea Goddesses of Orissa", *Journal of Marine Archaeology*, Vol. I, NIO, Goa

– –, 1991 "Ancient Ports of Kalinga", *Recent Advances in Marine Archaeology*, (ed.) S.R.Rao, NIO, Goa.

– –, 1993 "Ancient Ports of Orissa: Probable Causes of their Decline", *Puratattva* No. XXIII, New Delhi.

Sila, Tripati, Gudigar, P., Sundaresh, & Gaur, A.S., 1994 "A Preliminary study of Shipwrecks on the East Coast of India—Orissa and Andhra Pradesh", *Role of Universities and Research Institutions in Marine Archaeology*, (ed.) S.R.Rao, NIO, Goa.

Sila, Tripati & Rao, S.R., 1994 "Tamralipti: The Ancient Port of India", *Studies in History and Culture*, Vol. II, (1), Berhampur.

Sila, Tripati, and Patnaik, S.K., 1996 "Trade Routes and Communication Pattern of Ancient Orissa", *Gauravam, Recent Researches in Indology*, (Prof. B.K.Gururaja Rao Felicitation Volume), (eds.) K.V.Ramesh, *et. al.,* New Delhi.

Sila, Tripati., 1997, "Ports and Maritime Activities of Orissa (16th-19th century A.D.)", *Ship-building and Navigation in the Indian Ocean Region, AD 1400-1800*, (ed.) K.S.Mathew, New Delhi,

Sila, Tripati., 1999 "Traditional Boat-Building and Navigational Techniques of Southern Orissa", *Journal of the Royal Asiatic Society of Sri Lanka,* [New Series], Vol. XLII: 15-27.

Singh, G.P., 1996 "Trade and Commerce in Ancient India in the light of Jain and Buddhist Traditions bearing on its economic and cultural contacts", *Studies in History and Culture*, Vol. IV, (1), Berhampur.

Singh, M.M., 1961 "India's Overseas Trade as Known from the Buddhist Canon", *Indian Historical Quarterly*, Vol. XXXVII, Calcutta.

Sinha, B.K., 1992 "Khalkattapatna: A small Port on the Coast of Orissa", *New Trends in Indian Art and Archaeology*, (eds.) B.U. Nayak & N.C. Ghosh, New Delhi.

– –, 1993 "Excavations at Golbai Sasan, Dist. Puri, Orissa", *Puratattva,* XXIII, New Delhi.

Sircar, D.C., 1953 "The Madala Panji and the Pre-Suryavamsi History of Orissa", *Journal of Indian History*, Vol. XXXI, Trivandrum.

– –, 1953 "The Era of the Bhauma-Karas of Orissa", *Indian Historical Quarterly*, Vol. XXIX, Calcutta.

– –, 1953 "Some Minor Dynasties of Orissa", *Orissa Historical Research Journal*, Vol. II, (2), Bhubaneswar.

Sita Ramamma, J., 1997 "Maritime Contacts between Andhra and Southeast Asia", *An Integrated Approach to Marine Archaeology*, (ed.) S.R. Rao, NIO, Goa.

Sree Padma, B., 1991 "Kalingapatnam port through the Ages", *Recent Advances in Marine Archaeology*, (ed.) S.R. Rao, NIO, Goa.

– –, 1993 "Coins and Maritime Trade of Andhra Country" *Studies in South Indian Coins*, (ed.) A.V.Narasimha Murthy, Vol. III, Madras.

Subrahmanyam, B.R., & Sireesha, E.J., 1990 "Fossil Beaches and Palaeolithic evidences in Coastal Andhra", *Journal of Marine Archaeology*, Vol. I, NIO, Goa.

Subuddhi, U., 1985 "Inland Trade of Orissa in the Early Medieval Period (650-1200 A.D.)", *Journal of the Orissa Research Society*, No. 3, Bhubaneswar.

Supher, D.E., 1965 "Indian Boat types as a Cultural Geographic Problem", *Bombay Geographical Magazine,* Vol. XIII, (1), Bombay.

Thakur, U., 1970 "A Historical Survey of the Elements of Hindu culture in Burma", *India's Contribution to World Thought and Culture, Vivekananda Commemoration Volume*, (ed.) Lokesh Chandra, Madras.

Venkatarathnam, K., 1970 "Formation of the Barrier spit and other sand ridges near Chilka lake on the East Coast of India", *Marine Geology*, Vol. IX, (2), Amsterdam.

Wheeler, R.E.M., 1946 "Arikamedu: An Indo-Roman Trading station on the East Coast of India", *Ancient India No. 2*, Archaeological Survey of India, Delhi.

Yule, P., & *et al.,* 1987 "Sankarjang—a metals period burial site in the Dhenkanal Uplands of Orissa", *South Asian Archaeology*, Rome.

Secondary Works

English

Acharya, P., 1969 *Studies in Orissan History, Archaeology and Archives*, Cuttack.

Acharya, S.K., 1992 *Palaeography of Orissa from Third century BC to Twelfth century AD,* (Unpublished Ph. D. Thesis), Sambalpur University.

Adhya, G.L., 1966 *Early Indian Economics*, Bombay.

Agarawal, V.S., 1953 *India as known to Panini,* Lucknow.

Ahmed, E., 1972 *Coastal Geomorphology of India*, New Delhi.

Aiyangar, K.V.R., 1934 *Aspects of Ancient Indian Economics Thought*, Varanasi.

Allan, J., 1936 *Catalogue of the Coins of Ancient India*, London.

Allchin, B., & Raymond, A., 1968 *The birth of Indian Civilization*, Harmondsworth.

Anand, N.M., *et al.*, 1992 *Studies on Waves and Longshore Sediment Transport Along the Coast line of Chilka Lake*, NIO, Goa.

Apte, B.K., 1973 *A History of the Maratha Navy and Merchantships*, Bombay.

Asthana, S., 1976 *History and Archaeology of India's contacts with other countries (from Earliest times to the 3rd century B.C.)*, New Delhi.

Bagchi, P.C., 1929 *Pre-Aryan and Pre-Dravidian in India*, Calcutta.

– –, 1944 *India and China*, Calcutta.

Ballard, G.A., 1927 *Rulers of Indian Ocean*, London.

Banerjee, N., 1925 *Economic Life in Ancient India*, Allhabad.

Banerjee, R.D., 1930-31 *History of Orissa* (From earliest times to the British Period), 2 Vols., Calcutta.

Barnett, L.D., 1913 *Antiquities of India*, London.

Barua, B.M., 1934 *Bharhut*, Book I & II, Calcutta.

Basham, A.L., 1964 *Studies in Indian History and Culture*, Calcutta.

– –, 1971 *The Wonder that was India*, Calcutta.

Basham, A.L., (ed.) 1975 *A Cultural History of India*, Oxford University Press.

Behera, S.C., (ed.) 1982 *Interium Excavation Reports*, Sambalpur University, Sambalpur.

– –, 1982 *Rise and Fall of the Sailodbhavas*, Calcutta.

Bellwood, P.S., 1985 *Prehistory of the Indo-Malaysian Archipelago*, Sydney.

Bose, N.K., 1932 *Cannons of Orissan Architecture*, Calcutta.

Bose, P., 1926 *The Indian Colony of Champa*, Adyar.

– –, 1927 *The Hindu Colony of Cambodia*, Adyar.

Bowery, T.A., 1667-75 *Geographical Accounts of the Countries Round the Bay of Bengal*, Haklust Society, London.

Brown, C.J., 1922 *Coins of India*, Calcutta.

Brown, P., 1956 *Indian Architecture*, 2 Vols, Bombay..

Burnell, A.C., 1878 *Elements of South Indian Palaeography*, London.

Cady, J.F., 1964 *Southeast Asia: Its Historical Development*, New York.

Casson, L., 1973 *Ships and Seamanship in the Ancient World*, Princeton.

– –, 1989 *The Periplus Maris Erythraei*, Princeton.

Chakladhar, 1929 *Social Life in Ancient India*, Calcutta.

Chakravarti, H.P., 1966 *Trade and Commerce of Ancient India*, Calcutta.

Chandra, M., 1977 ·*Trade and Trade Routes in Ancient India*, New Delhi.

Chandra, S., (ed.) 1987 *The Indian Ocean, Exploration in History, Commerce and Politics*, New Delhi.

Chandramohan, P., 1989 Sediment Transport along the Indiän Coast, *Technical Report*, NIO, Goa.

Charlesworth, M.P., 1921 *Trade Routes and Commerce of the Roman Empire*, Cambridge.

Chatterji, B.R., 1933 *India and Java*, Calcutta.

– –, 1928 *Indian Cultural Influence in Cambodia*, Calcutta.

Chattopadhyay, B., 1994 *An Introduction to the Maritime History of India*, Calcutta.

Chhabra, B.Ch., 1950 *Expansion of Indo-Aryan Culture*, Delhi.

Coedes, G., 1971 *The Indianized States of Southeast Asia*, Honolulu.

Collins, M., 1907 *The Geographical data of the Raghuvamsa and the Dasakumaracharita*, Leipzig.

Coomaraswamy, A.K., 1965 *History of Indian Art and Indonesian Art*, London.

Cowell, E.B., (tr.) 1895-1907 *The Jatakas*, 6 Vols., Cambridge.

Cunningham, A., 1963 *The Ancient Geography of India*, Varanasi.

Dani, A.H., 1968 *Indian Palaeography,* 2nd Edition, New Delhi.

Das, B., 1978 *The Bhaumakara and Their Times*, New Delhi.

Das, B.S., 1978 *Studies in Economic History of Orissa from Ancient Times to 1833*, Calcutta.

Das, D.N., 1977 *The Early History of Kalinga, A Socio-Economic and Cultural History of Coastal Orissa*, Calcutta.

Das, H.C., & *et al.*, (ed.) 1976 *Buddhism and Jainism*, Cuttack.

Das, H.C., 1985 *Cultural Development of Orissa*, Calcutta.

Das, K.B., & Mahapatra, L.K., 1979 *Folklores of Orissa*, National Book Trust, New Delhi.

Das, M.N., 1949 *Glimpses of Kalinga History*, Calcutta.

– –, (ed.) 1977 *Sidelights on History and Culture of Orissa*, Cuttack.

Das, S.K., 1925 *Economic History of Ancient India*, Calcutta.

Dawson, J., 1928 *A Classical Dictionary of Hindu Mythology and Geography, History and Literature*, London.

Dey, N.L., 1927 *The Geographical Dictionary of Ancient and Medieval India*, New Delhi.

Dehejia, V., 1979 *The Early Stone Temples of Orissa*, New Delhi.

Deloche, J., 1994 *Transport and Communication in India*, Vol. II (water transport), New Delhi.

Devi, S.M., 1978 *Economic Condition of Ancient India (from 750 to 1200 A.D.)*, New Delhi.

Dikshit, M.G., 1949 *Etched Beads in India*, Poona.

– –, 1969 *History of Indian Glass*, University of Bombay.

Dikshitar, V.R., 1932 *The Mauryan Polity*, Madras.

Douglas, J.S., 1952 *The Story of the Oceans*, New York.

Edgarton, W.E., 1933 *Ancient Egyptian Ships and Shipping*, Chicago.

Eliot, H.M., 1922 *Hinduism and Buddhism*, London.

Elliot, W., 1896 *Coins of Southern India*, London.

Eschmann, A., *et al.*, (ed.) 1978 *The Cult of Jagannath and the Region Traditions of Orissa*, New Delhi.

Fabri, C., 1974 *History of the Art of Orissa*, Calcutta.

Fairservis, W. Jr., 1971 *The Trade Routes of India*, New York.

Fergusson, J., 1910 *History of Indian and Eastern Architecture*, Vol. I & II, London.

Ganguly, D.K., 1975 *Historical Geography of Ancient Orissa*, Calcutta.

Ganguly, M.M., 1912 *Orissa and Her Remains*, Calcutta.

Geiger, W., (ed. & tr.) 1908 *Mahavamsa*, Pali Text Society, London.

Gerini, G.E., 1974 *Researches on Ptolemy's Geography of Eastern Asia, Further India and Indo-Malaya Peninsula*, Delhi.

Ghose, B.K., 1848 *The History of Pooree*, Calcutta.

Ghosal, U.N., 1927 *Ancient Indian Culture in Afghanistan*, Calcutta.

– –, 1957 *Studies in Indian History and Culture*, Calcutta.

Ghosh, A., 1973 *The City in Early Historical India*, Simla.

– –, (ed.) 1989 *An Encyclopaedia of Indian Archaeology*, 2 Vols, New Delhi.

Gibbon, E., 1912 *The Decline and the Fall of the Roman Empire*, London.

Giles, H.A., 1923 *The Travels of Fa-Hien*, Cambridge.

Glover, I.C., 1989 *Early Trade between India and Southeast Asia*, Hull.

Gode, P.K., 1953 *Studies in Indian Literary History*, Bombay.

Gopal, L., 1965 *The Economic Life of Northern India*, Delhi.

Gopalachari, K.,1941 *Early History of the Andhra country*, Madras.

Gorakshkar, S., and Desai, K., 1989 *The Maritime Heritage of India*, Bombay.

Greenhill, B., 1976 *The Archaeology of the Boat*, London.

Gupta, P., *Geography from Ancient Indian Coins and Seals*, New Delhi.

Gupta, P.L., 1965 *Roman Coins from Andhra Pradesh*, Hyderabad.

Griffth, J., 1896 *The Paintings in the Buddhist Cave Temples of Ajanta*, London.

Hall, D.G.E., 1968 *History of Southeast Asia*, London.

Hall, H.R., 1927 *The Ancient History of Near East*, London.

Hall, K.R., 1985 *Maritime trade and State Development in Early Southeast Asia*, Honolulu.

Hamilton, W., 1990 *A Geographical Statistical and Historical Description of Hindustan and the adjacent Countries*, 2 Vols., Calcutta.

Haque, M.A., 1980 *Muslim Administration of Orissa* (1568-1751 AD), Calcutta.

Higham, C., 1989 *The Archaeology of Mainland Southeast Asia*, Cambridge.

Hourani, G.F., 1975 *Arab Seafaring in the Indian Ocean in Ancient and Early Medieval Times*, New York.

Hunter, G., 1966 *Southeast Asia: Race, Culture and Nation*, London.

Hunter, W.W., 1872 *A History of Orissa*, 2 Vols, London.

Jagadeb, G.C., 1977 *Utkal Empire Under Ganga Kings*, Bhubaneswar.

Jain, J.C., 1947 *Life in Ancient India as depicted in the Jain Canons*, Bombay.

Jha, A.K., (ed.) 1991 *Coinage, Trade, and Economy*, Anjaneri.

Jit, N.K., 1984 *The Agrarian Life and Economy of Orissa*, Calcutta.

Joshi, A., 1979 *New Light on Cultural Heritage of Orissa*, Cuttack.

Kangle, R.P., (ed.) 1986 *The Kautilya Arthasastra*, New Delhi.

Kanchan, R.K., 1990 *Hindu Kingdoms of Southeast Asia*, Delhi.

Kane, P.V., 1930-62 *History of Dharmasastra*, 4 Vols., Poona.

Kosambi, D.D., 1956 *An Introduction to the Study of Indian History*, Bombay.

– –, 1965 *The Culture and Civilization of Ancient India*, London.

Krishna Rao, B.V., 1942 *The History of the Early Dynasties of Andhradesa*, Madras.

– –, 1983 *The Proto and Early Historical Cultures of Andhra Pradesh*, Hyderabad.

Krishna Sastry, V.V., Subrahmanyam, B., and Rao, N.R., 1992 *Thotlakonda (A Buddhist Site in Andhra Pradesh)*, Department of Archaeology and Museums, Series No. 68, Hyderabad.

Kulke, H., *et al.*, (ed.) 1978 *Orissa, A Comprehensive Bibliography of an Indian State*, Bhubaneswar.

Lahiri, N., 1992 *The Archaeology of Indian Trade Routes*, Delhi.

Law, B.C., (ed.) 1925 *Dathavamsa*, Lahore.

– –, 1941 *India as Depicted in Early Texts of Buddhism and Jainism*, London.

– –, 1967 *Historical Geography of Ancient India*, Paris.

Le, Mar R., 1954 *The History of Southeast Asia*, London.

Mahapatra, P.R., 1984 *Some Aspects of the Economic Life of Orissa*, Bhubaneswar.

– –, 1986 *Archaeology in Orissa*, 2 Vols., Delhi.

Mahtab, H.K., 1959-1960 *History of Orissa*, 2 Vols., Cuttack.

Maity, S.K., 1957 *Economic Life of Northern India in the Gupta Period, 300-550 A.D.*, Calcutta.

Majumdar, B.C., 1925 *Orissa in the Making*, Calcutta.

Majumdar, N.G., 1929 *Inscriptions of Bengal*, Rajshahi.

Majumdar, R.C., 1927 *Champa*, Lahore.

– –, 1944 *Hindu Colonies in the Far East*, Calcutta.

– –, 1960 *Classical Accounts of India*, Calcutta.

– –, (ed.) 1970 *The Classical Age*, Bharatiya Vidya Bhavan, Bombay.

– –, (ed.) 1971 *Vedic Age*, Bharatiya Vidhya Bhavan, Bombay.

– –, 1986 *Suvarnadvipa*, (reprint) Delhi.

Majumdar, S.N., 1924 *Ancient Geography of India*, Calcutta.

Malalasekera, G.D., 1937-38 *Dictionary of Pali Proper Names*, 2 Vols., London.

Margabandhu, C., 1985 *Archaeology of the Satavahana-Kshtrapa Times*, Delhi.

Marshall, J., 1931 *Mohenjo-Daro and the Indus Civilization*, 3 Vols, London.

– –, 1936 *A Guide to Sanchi*, Delhi.

Marshall, J., & Foucher, A., 1940 *The Monuments of Sanchi*, Calcutta.

Mansingh, M., 1962 *History of Oriya Literature, Sahitya Akademy*, New Delhi.

Mehta, R.N., 1939 *Pre-Buddhist in India*, Bombay.

Mendis, G.C., 1938 *Early History of Ceylon*, Calcutta.

Mishra, B., 1934 *Orissa Under the Bhauma Kings*, Calcutta.

– –, 1934 *Dynasties of Medieval Orissa*, Calcutta.

Mishra, K.C., 1971 *The Cult of Jagannath*, Calcutta.

Mishra, P.K., and Samal, J.K., (eds.) 1997 *Comprehensive History and Culture of Orissa*, Vol. I, (1-2), New Delhi.

Mishra, Y.K., *Socio-Economic and Political History of Eastern India*, New Delhi.

Misra, P., 1970 *The Chilka Lake*, Government of Orissa, Cuttack.

Mital, A.C., 1962 *An Early History of Orissa*, Banaras Hindu University, Varanasi.

Mitra, D., 1971 *Buddhist Monuments*, Calcutta.

– –, 1978 *Bronzes from Achutarajapur, Orissa*, Delhi.

Mitra, K.C., 1886 *Orissa Past and Present*, Calcutta.

Mitra, R.C., 1954 *The Decline of Buddhism in India*, Visvabharati.

Mitra, R.L., 1961 *The Antiquities of Orissa*, 2 Vols., Calcutta.

Mookerji, R.K., 1912 *A History of Indian Shipping*, Bombay.

Mookherji, R.K., 1943 *Chandragupta Maurya and His Times*, Madras.

Mukherjee, P., 1940 *The History of Medieval Vaishnavism in Orissa*, Calcutta.

– –, 1953 *The History of the Gajapati Kings of Orissa and their Successors*, Cuttack.

Mukherjee, P.K., 1931 *Indian Literature in China and the Far East*, Calcutta.

Mukherjee, R.K., 1956 *Ancient India*, Allahabad.

Mukherjee, T.B., 1967 *Inter-state Relations in Ancient India*, Delhi.

Nandargikar, G.R., (ed. & tr.) 1897 *Raghuvamsa*, Bombay.

Narain, A.K., 1957 *The Indo-Greeks*, Oxford.

Nayak, A.K., 1987 *Trade and Commerce in Ancient Orissa*, (Unpublished M.Phil. Thesis), Kuruksetra University.

Needham, J., 1954 *Science and Civilization in China*, Cambridge.

Nema, S.R., 1978 *Political History of the Somavamsi Kings of South Kosala and Orissa*, New Delhi.

Nigam, J.S., 1993 *A Brief Note on the excavations at Manikapatna*, (Unpublished), Bhubaneswar.

Niyogi, P., 1962 *Contributions to the Economic History of Northern India*, Calcutta.

Panda, A.K., 1987 *Four Hundred Years of Orissa*, Calcutta.

Panda, C.B., 1963 *History of Andhra-Satavahana Empire*, Delhi.

Panikkar, K.M., 1955 *Geographical Factors in Indian History*, Bombay.

Panigrahi, K.C., 1961 *Archaeological Remains at Bhubaneswar*, Calcutta.

– –, 1961 *Chronology of the Bhaumakara and the Somavamsis of Orissa*, Bhopal.

– –, 1981 *History of Orissa*, Calcutta.

Panikkar, K.M., (ed.) 1951 *India and the Indian Ocean*, Delhi.

– –, 1957 *India and China: Cultural Relations*, Bombay.

Paul, P.L., 1910 *Early History of Bengal*, Calcutta.

Pathak, S., *Brahmanical Religion in Ancient Orissa*, New Delhi.

Pattanayak, A.K., 1988 *Religious Policy of the Imperial Gangas*, Delhi.

Paul, P.L., 1910 *Early History of Bengal*, Calcutta.

Peterson, P., 1905 *A Collection of Prakrit and Sanskrit Inscriptions*, Bhavanagar.

Phayre, A.P., 1883 *History of Burma*, London.

– –, 1882 *Coins of Arakan of Pegu and Burma*, London.

Phipps, J., 1840 *Papers Relative to Shipping in India*, Calcutta.

Ping, N., 1988 *Contact between Orissa and Southeast Asia in Ancient and Medieval Times*, (Unpublished Ph.D. Thesis), Sambalpur.

Pleyte, C.M., 1901 *Indonesian Art*, The Hauge.

Pradhan, A.C., 1985 *A Study of History of Orissa*, Calcutta.

Pragiter. F.E., 1913 *Purana Text of the Dynasties of the Kali Age*, London.

– –, 1962 *Ancient Indian Historical Tradition*, Delhi.

Prasad, P.C., 1977 *Foreign Trade and Commerce in Ancient India*, New Delhi.

Raffles, T.S., 1830 *The History of Java*, London.

Raghavan, M.D., 1964 *India in Ceylonese History, Society and Culture*, New Delhi.

Rajaguru, S.N., 1968-72 *History of the Gangas*, 2 Vols., Bhubaneswar.

– –, 1958-66 *Inscriptions of Orissa*, Bhubaneswar.

Rao, S.R., 1973 *Lothal and the Indus Civilization*, Bombay.

– –, 1978 *Progress and Prospects of Marine Archaeology in India*, Goa.

Raman, K.V., 1968 *Excavations at Pumpuhar, Handbook published by 2nd World Tamil Conference*, Madras.

Rapson, E.J., 1897 *Indian Coins*, Strassburg.

– –, 1908 *Catalogue of the Coins of the Andhra Dynasty, the Western Ksatrapas, the Traikutaka Dynasty and the Bodhi Dynasty*, London.

– –, (ed.) 1962 *Cambridge History of India* (Ancient India), Vol. I, Delhi,

Rath, A.K., 1987 *Studies on Some Aspects of the History and Culture of Orissa*, Calcutta.

Rath, B.K., 1983 *Cultural History of Orissa*, (C. AD 885-1110), Delhi.

Raut, L.N., 1988 *Socio-Economic Life in Medieval Orissa*, Calcutta.

Rawlinson, H.C., 1916 *Intercourse between India and the Western World from the earliest times to the fall of Rome*, Cambridge.

Ray, A., 1983 *Life and Art of Early Andhradesa*, Delhi.

Ray, B.C., 1960 *Orissa under the Marathas*, Allahabad.

– –, 1981 *Orissa Under the Mughals*, Calcutta.

Ray, H.P., 1986 *Monastery and Guild: Commerce Under the Satavahanas*, Delhi.

– –, 1994 *The Winds of Change*, New Delhi.

Ray, H.P., and Salles, J.F., (eds.) 1996 *Tradition and Archaeology: Early Maritime contacts in the Indian Ocean*, New Delhi.

Ray, H.P., 1993 *Trade and Diplomacy in India-China Relations: A Study of Bengal during the Fifteenth Century*, New Delhi.

Ray, J.C., 1948 *Ancient Indian Life*, Calcutta.

Ray, N.R., 1932 *Brahmanical Gods in Burma*, Calcutta.

Ray, P.K., 1975 *Prachi Valley*, Archaeological Survey Report, Bhubaneswar.

Raychoudhary, H.C., 1950 *Political History of Ancient India*, Calcutta.

Rea, A., 1894 *South Indian Buddhist Antiquities*, Madras.

Rose, J.H., 1926 *The Mediterranean in the Ancient World*, Cambridge.

Sachau, E.C., 1983 *Alberuni's India*, 2 Vols., New Delhi.

Sah, A.P., 1976 *Life in Medieval Orissa*, Varanasi.

Sahai, B., 1986 *The Ports of India*, New Delhi.

Sahoo, K.C., 1976 *Literature and Social Life in Medieval Orissa*, Ranchi.

Sahu, N.K., 1958 *Buddhism in Orissa*, Cuttack.

– –, 1964 *Utkal University History of Orissa*, Vol. I, Cuttack.

Sahu, N.K., Mishra, P.K., & Sahu, J.K., 1981 *History of Orissa*, Cuttack.

Samaddar, J.W., 1922 *Lectures on the Economic Condition of Ancient India*, University of Calcutta.

Sarkar, H.B., 1934 *Indian Influence on the Literature of Java and Bali*, Calcutta.

– –, 1970 *Some Contributions of India to the ancient Civilization of Indonesia and Malaysia*, Calcutta.

– –, 1971-72 *Corpus of the Inscriptions of Java*, Vol. I & II, Calcutta.

– –, 1985 *Cultural Relations Between India and Southeast Asia*, New Delhi.

– –, 1986 *Trade and Commercial Activities of the Southern India in the Malayo-Indonesian World*, Calcutta.

Sarkar, J.N., 1975 *Studies in the Economic life in Mughal India*, New Delhi.

Sarma, B.K., 1983 *Somavamsi Rule in Orissa*, Calcutta.

Sarma, I.K., 1980 *Coinage of the Satavahana Empire*, Delhi.

– –, 1988 *Studies in Early Buddhist Monuments and Brahmi Inscriptions of Andhradesa,* Nagpur.

– –, 1992 *South Indian Coinage, A Review of Recent Discoveries*, Madras.

Sastri, I.C., (ed.) 1917 *Yuktikalpataru*, Calcutta.

Sastri, K.A.N., (ed.) 1939 *Foreign Notices of South India*, Madras.

– –, (ed.) 1957 *A Comprehensive History of India*, Vol. II, Bombay.

– –, 1972 *South India and Southeast Asia*, Mysore.

Shamasastri, R., 1967 *Kautilya's Arthasastra*, Mysore,

Sastri, T.G., (ed.) 1925 *Aryamanjusrimulakalpa*, 3 Vols., Trivandrum.

Schlingloff, D., 1988 *Studies in the Ajanta Paintings*, Delhi.

Schoff, W.H., (ed.) 1912 *Periplus of the Erythraean Sea*, New York.

Seckel, D., 1964 *The Art of Buddhism*, London.

Sharma, B.N., 1966 *Social Life in Northern India*, Delhi.

Singh, M., 1965 *The Cave Paintings of Ajanta*, London.

Singh, M.R., 1972 *Geographical Data in the Early Puranas*, Calcutta.

Singhal, D.P., 1972 *India and World Civilization*, 2 Vols., Calcutta.

Sircar, D.C., 1942 *Select Inscriptions bearing on Indian History and Civilization,* Calcutta.

– –, 1960 *Studies in the Geography of Ancient and Medieval India*, Delhi.

Smith, V.A., 1924 *The Early History of India*, Oxford.

Soper, A.C., 1959 *Literary Evidence for Early Buddhist Art in China*, Ascona.

Spate, O.H.K., 1954 *India and Pakistan*, London.

Sridharan, K., 1965 *A Maritime History of India*, Delhi.

Srivastava, B., 1968 *Trade and Commerce in Ancient India*, Varanasi.

Subba Rao, N.S., 1911 *Economic and Political Conditions in Ancient India*, Mysore.

Subrahmanyam, K.R., 1932 *Buddhist Remains in Andhra and the Andhra History between (225-610 A.D.)*, Madras.

Subrahmanyam, R., 1964 *Salihundam, Buddhist Site in Andhra Pradesh*, Hyderabad.

Subramanyam, R.C., 1957 *The Suryavamsi Gajapatis of Orissa*, Andhra University, Waltair.

Subuddhi, U.K., 1978 *The Bhaumakaras of Orissa*, Calcutta.

Su, Jiging, (ed.) 1981 *Records of Islands*, (reprint), Beijing.

Swami, S., 1949 *Hindu Culture in Greater India*, Delhi.

Syamchaudhuri, N.K., 1977 *Social Structure of Car Nicobar Islanders*, Calcutta.

Takakusu, J., 1982 (tr.) I- tsing's, *A Record of the Buddhist Religion as Practised in India and Malaya Archipelago 671-695 A.D.*, New Delhi.

Tawney, C.H., (tr.) 1928 *The Kathasaritsagara*, London.

Thapar, R., 1963 *Asoka and the Decline of the Mauryas*, New Delhi.

– –, 1973 *History of India*, Vol. I, New Delhi.

Tiwari, S.P., 1985 *Comprehensive History of Orissa*, Calcutta.

Torr, C., 1894 *Ancient Ships*, Cambridge.

Toynbee, G., 1973 *A Sketch of the History of Orissa*, Calcutta.

Tozer, H.F., 1935 *History of Ancient Geography*, Cambridge.

Tripathy, M.P., 1969 *Development of Geographic Knowledge in Ancient India*, Varanasi.

Tripathy, S., 1986 *Early and Medieval Coins and Currency system of Orissa*, Calcutta.

Twany, C.H. & McCrindle, J.W., (tr.) 1936 *Megasthenes Accounts and Periplus of the Erythraean Sea*, London.

Vasu, N.N., 1911 *Archaeological Survey of Mayurbhanj*, Vol. I, Calcutta.

Vasu, S.C., 1962 *Astadhyayi of Panini*, Delhi.

Vincent, W., 1807 *The Commerce and Navigation of the Ancients in the Indian Ocean*, London.

Vogel, J.P., 1946 *Buddhist Art in India, Ceylon and Java*, Oxford.

Wales, H.G.Q., 1951 *The Making of Greater India*, London.

Warmington, E.H., 1974 *The Commerce Between the Roman Empire and India*, Delhi.

Watters, T., 1973 *On Yuan Chawang's Travels in India*, 2 Vols, New Delhi.

Wheeler, R.E.M., 1955 *Rome beyond the Imperial Frontiers*, New York.

– –, 1968 *The Indus Civilization*, 3rd edition, Cambridge.

Wijesimha, L.C., 1909 *Mahavamsa*, Part-1, Colombo.

Wolters, O.W., 1967 *Early Indonesian Commerce: A Study of the Origin of Sri Vijaya*, New York.

Yeats, J., 1882 *Technical History of Commerce*, 3rd Edition, London.

Zimmer, H., 1955 *The Art of Indian Asia*, 2 Vols, New York.

Sources in Oriya

Acharya, P. M., 1975 *Odissara Itihasa*, Cuttack.

Behera, K.S., (ed.) 1993 *Sagar O Sahitya*, Cuttack.

Champatiray, K., 1953 *Paika Kheda*, Cuttack.

Das, K.B., 1977 *Lokagalpa Sanchayana*, Orissa Sahitya Academy, Bhubaneswar.

Das, Nilakanta, 1972 *Konark*, Cuttack.

Das, Siba Prasad, 1959 *Atitare Odisa*, Cuttack.

Kabi, Asit, 1985 *Fakir Mohananka Krutire Samakalina Samaj Chitra*, Cuttack.

Kar, B., 1973 *Prachina Utkalara Nau Vanijya*, Cuttack.

Mohanty, A.B., (ed.) 1952-53 *Labanyavati*, Cuttack.

— —, (ed.) 1969 *Madala Panji*, Utkal University Publication, Bhubaneswar.

Mahapatro, K.N., 1975 *Tosalira Itihasa*, Cuttack.

Mahatab, Harekrishna., 1977 *Odisa Itihasa*, Vol. I, Cuttack.

Mansingh, Mayadhara, 1967 *Odiya Sahityara Itihasa*, Cuttack.

Mishra, Krupasindhu., 1979 *Utkal Itihasa*, Cuttack.

Mohanty, B., 1976 *Odisara Paricaya*, Bhubaneswar.

Mohanty, P.C., 1984 *Fakira Mohananka Sahityare Samakalina Odisa Chitra*, Cuttack.

Mohanty, Surendra., 1981 *Fakira Mohana Samikhya*, Cuttack.

Panigrahi, K.C., 1962 *Itihasa O Kimvadanti*, Utkal University, Bhubaneswar.

Rajaguru, S.N., 1993 "Prachin Abhilekhare Samudra Yatrara Suchana", *Sagar O Sahitya*, (ed.) K.S. Behera, Cuttack.

Sahu, N. K., 1974 *Odiya Jatira Itihasa*, Bhubaneswar.

Senapati, F.M., 1963-65 *Fakir Mohan Granthavali*, Vol. I-II, Cuttack.

Singha, Jagabandhu., 1982 *Prachina Utkala*, Vols. I-II, Cuttack.

Journals, Proceedings, Reviews and Gazetteers

Ancient India, Archaeological Survey of India, New Delhi.

Antiquity, Cambridge.

Annual Report of Archaeological Survey of India, New Delhi.

Annals of the Bhandarkar Oriental Research Institute, Poona.

Art and Letters, London.

Anthropological Society of Orissa, Bhubaneswar.

Asian Perspectives, Honolulu.

Asiatic Society Monthly Bulletin, Calcutta.

Bihar and Orissa District Gazetteers, Cuttack, Puri and Balasore.

Bharati, Journal of Utkal University, Bhubaneswar.

Bulletin of the Indo-Pacific Prehistory Association, Canberra.

Epigraphia Indica, Archaeological Survey of India, New Delhi.

Imperial Gazetters of India, London.

Indian Archaeology—A Review, Archaeological Survey of India, New Delhi.

Indian Antiquary, Delhi.

Indian Culture, Calcutta.

Indian Economic and Social History Review, New Delhi.

Indian Historical Quarterly, Calcutta.

Indian Journal of History of Science, New Delhi.

Indian Historical Reviews, New Delhi.

Indian Museum Bulletin, Calcutta.

Indica, Bombay.

International Journal of Dravidian Linguistic, Trivandrum.

Islamic Culture, Hyderabad.

Jhankara (Oriya), Cuttack.

Journal of the Andhra Historical Research Society, Rajahmundry.

Journal of Ancient Indian History, Calcutta.

Journal of the American Oriental Society.

Journal of the Asiatic Society, Calcutta.

Journal of the Asiatic Society of Bengal, Calcutta.

Journal of the Bihar Research Society, Patna.

Journal of the Bihar and Orissa Research Society, Patna.

Journal of the Bombay Branch of the Royal Asiatic Society, Bombay.

Journal of Coastal Research, Florida.

Journal of the Greater India Society, Calcutta.

Journal of Indian History, Trivandrum.

Journal of Indian Ocean Studies, New Delhi.

Journal of Kalinga Historical Research Society, Bolangir.

Journal of Marine Archaeology, NIO, Goa.

Journal of Marine Research, New Haven.

Journal of the Numismatic Society of India, Varanasi.

Journal of the Orissa Research Society, Bhubaneswar.

Journal of the Royal Asiatic Society of Bengal, Calcutta.

Journal of the Royal Asiatic Society, London.

Journal of the Royal Asiatic Society of Sri Lanka, Colombo.

Journal of the Royal Asiatic Society of Great Britain and Ireland, London.

Journal of South Asian Studies, London.

Journal of Southeast Asian Studies, Singapore.

Journal of the University of Bombay, Bombay.

Journal of the United Provinces Historical Society, Lucknow.

Marine Geology, Amsterdam.

Memoirs of the Asiatic Society of Bengal, Calcutta.

Modern Reviews, Calcutta.

Orissa Historical Research Journal, Bhubaneswar.

Orissa Review, Bhubaneswar.

Proceedings of Asiatic Society of Bengal, Calcutta.

Proceedings of Indian Academy Science, Bangalore.

Proceedings of the Indian History Congress.

Proceedings of Orissa History Congress, Bhubaneswar.

Puratattva, New Delhi.

Quarterly Review of Historical Studies, Calcutta.

Science Today, New Delhi.

South Asian Studies, New Delhi.

South Indian Inscription, Madras.

Studies in History, New Delhi.

Studies in History and Culture, Berhampur.

The Journal of Orissan History, Bhubaneswar.

The Journal of Historical and Social Analysis, Bhubaneswar.

Transactions of the American Philological Association, New Haven.

Utkal Historical Research Journal, Bhubaneswar.

Utkal Prasanga (Oriya), Bhubaneswar.

Index

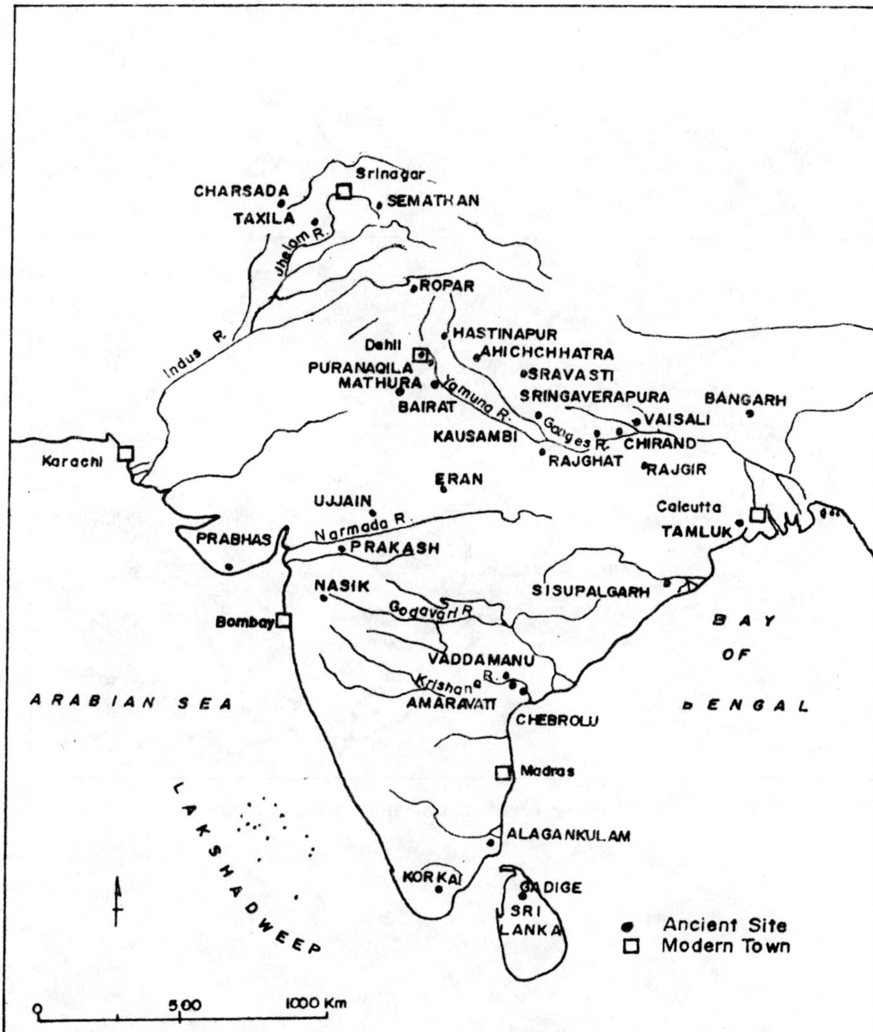

Fig. I. Silver Punch Marked Coins & Northern Black Polished ware

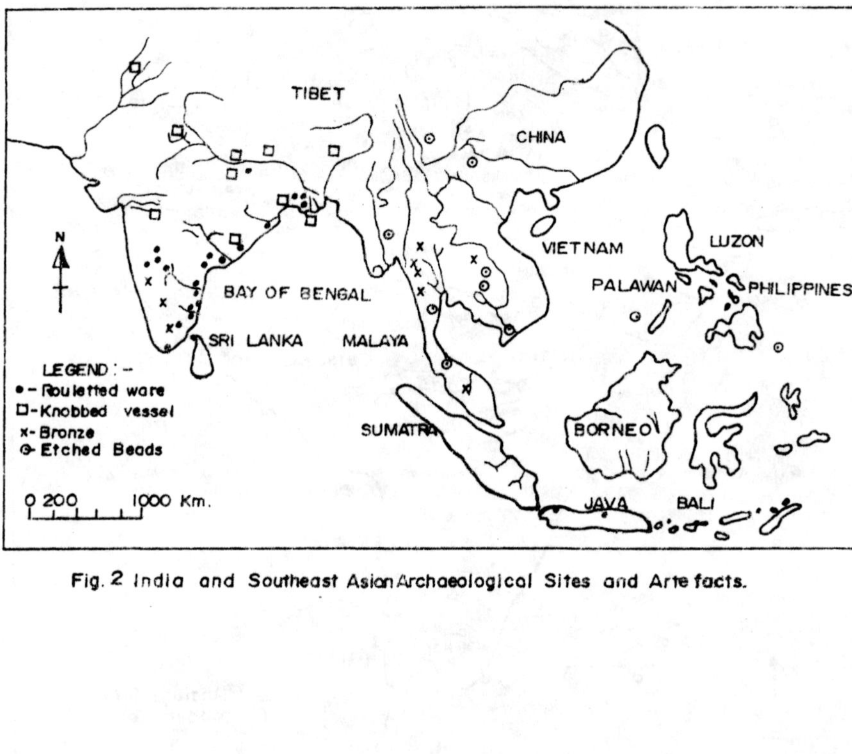

Fig. 2 India and Southeast Asian Archaeological Sites and Artefacts.

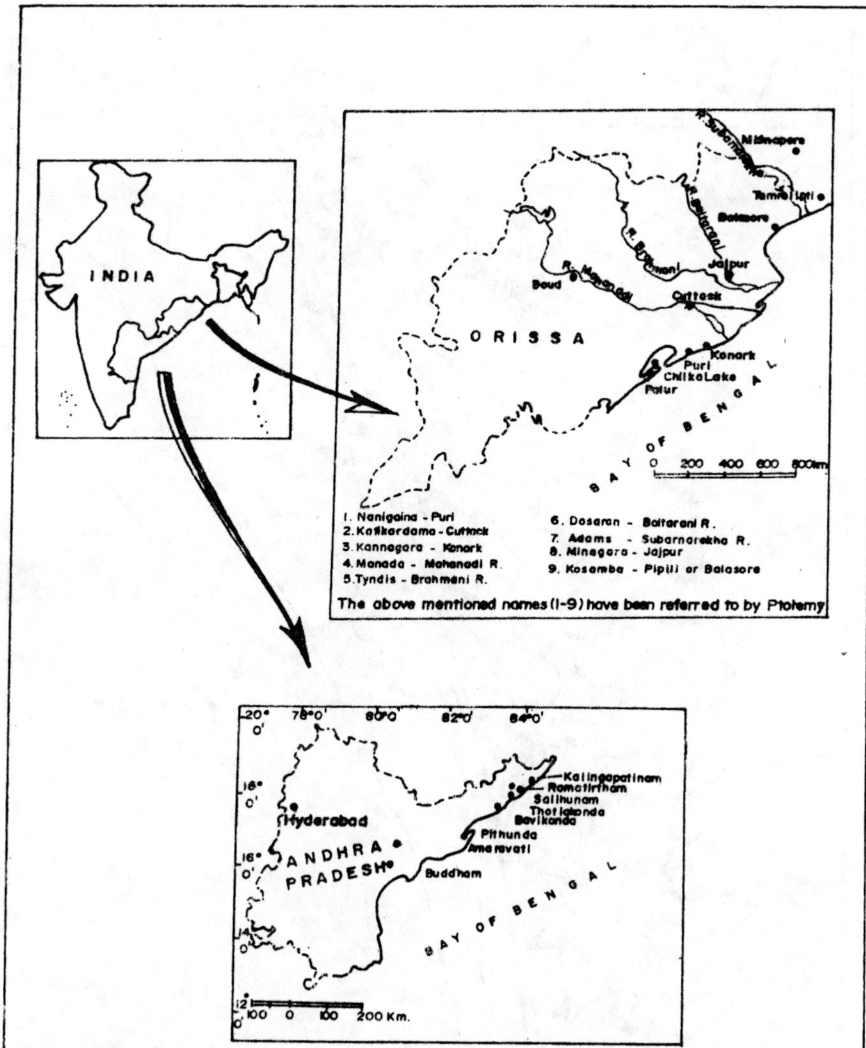

Fig. 3. Ancient ports of Kalinga and other Bhuddhist sites.

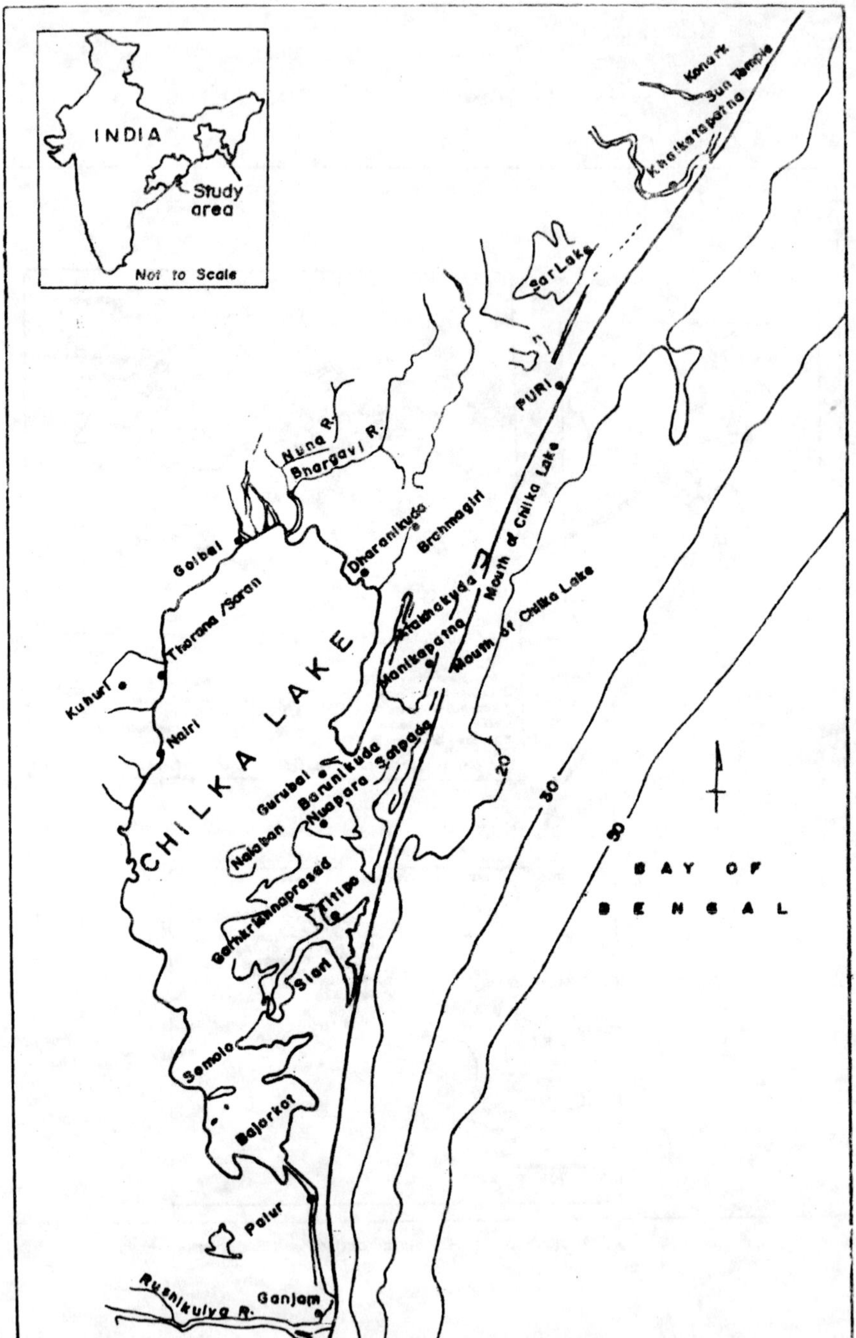

Fig. 4. Ancient Ports and Historical Sites around Chilka Lake.

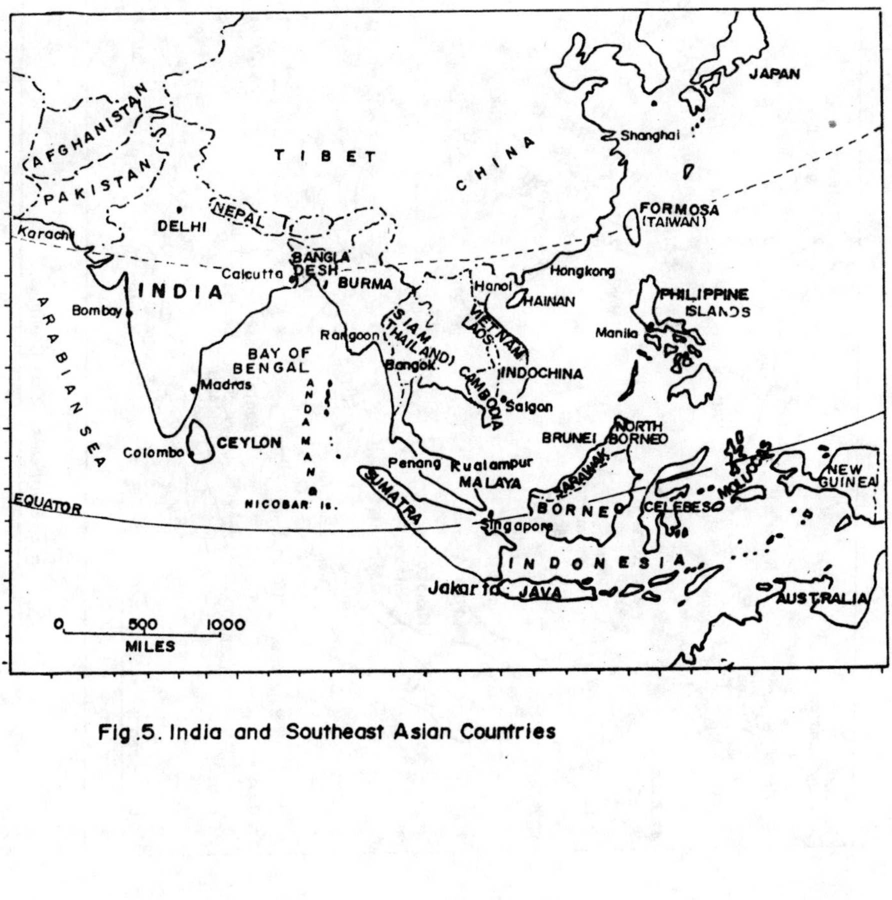

Fig.5. India and Southeast Asian Countries

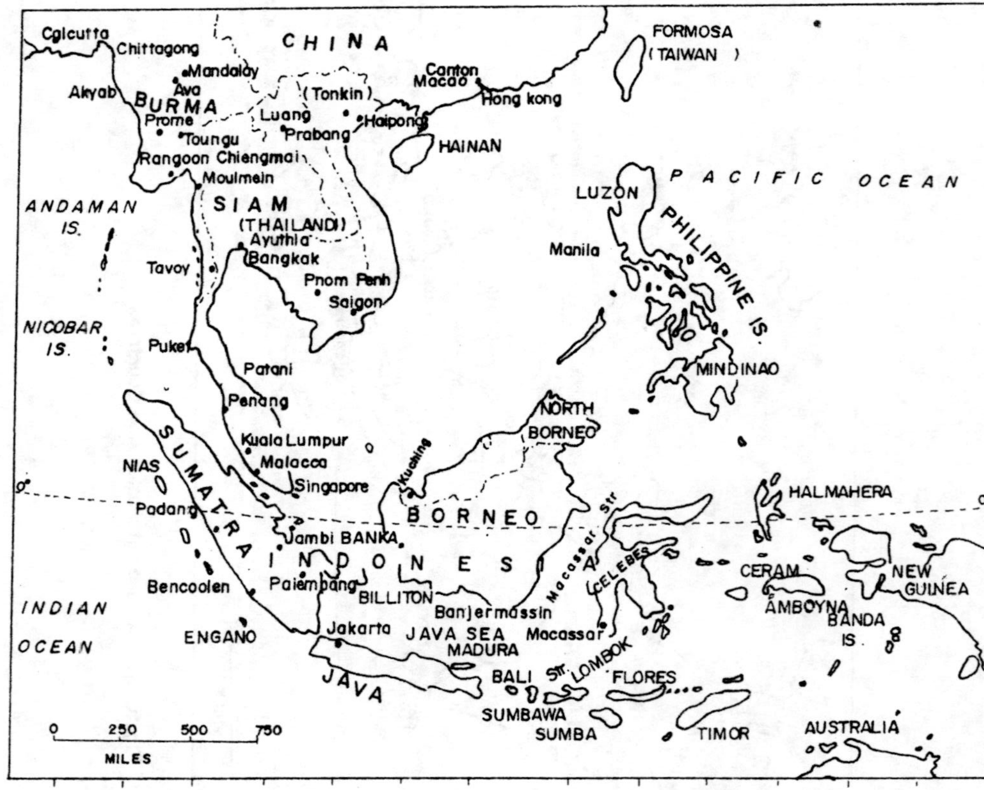

Fig. 6. Southeast Asian Countries.

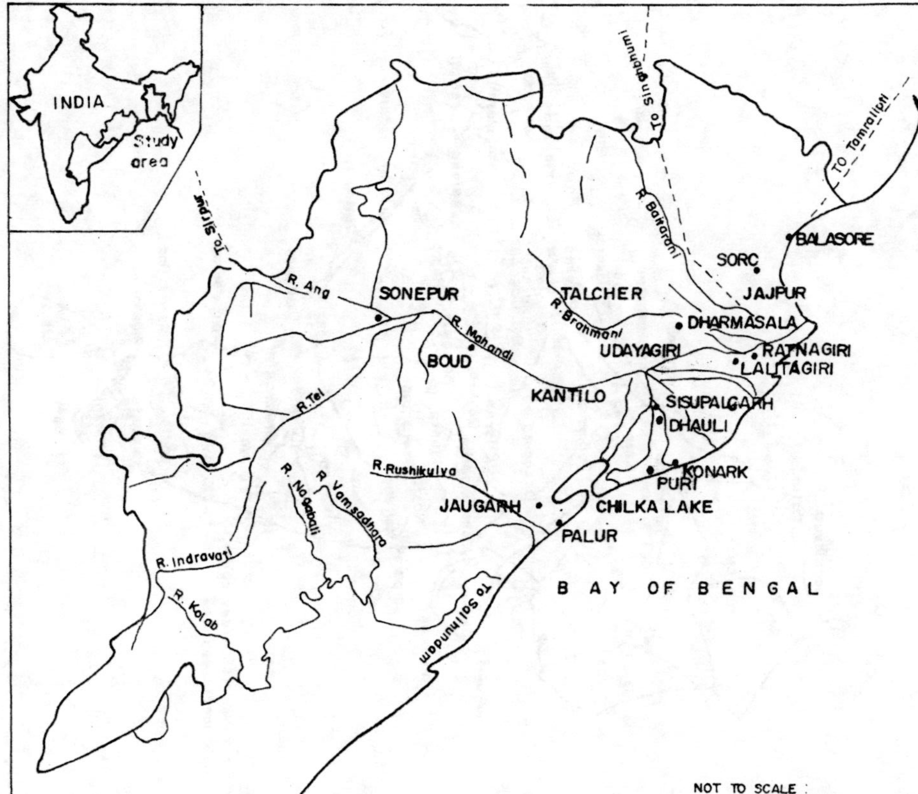

Fig. 7. Ancient trade routes and rivers of Orissa.

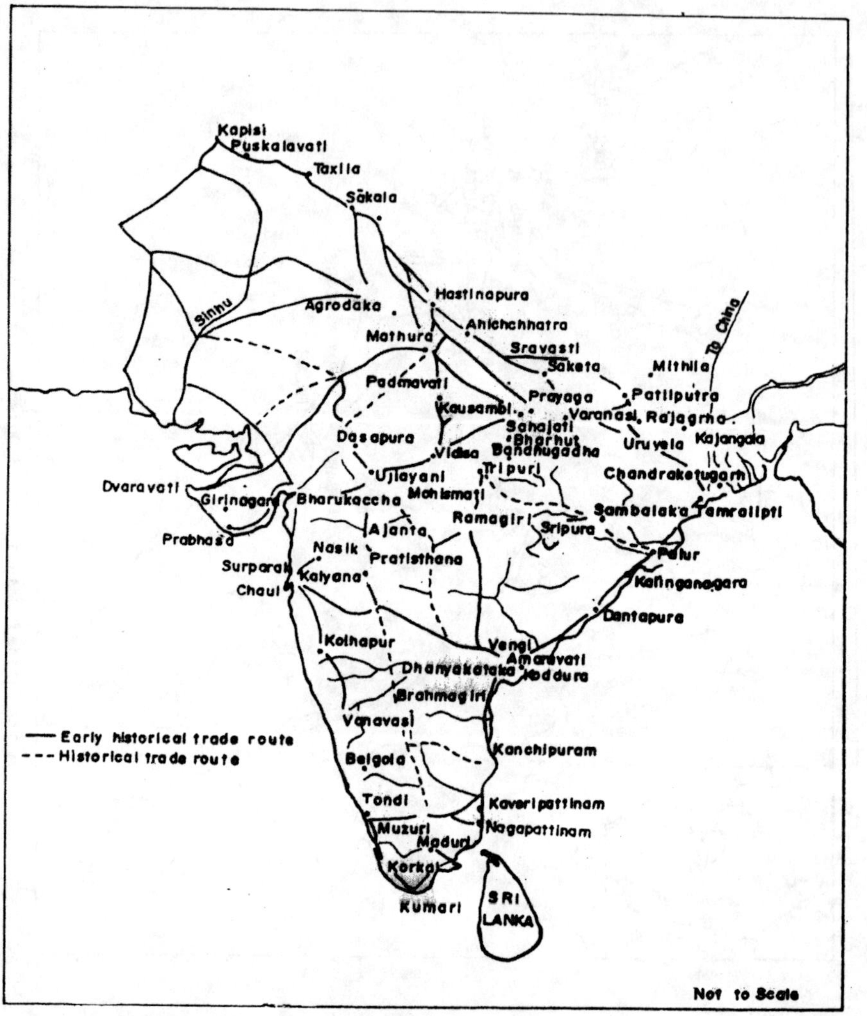

Fig. 8. Trade Routes and ancient Towns of India:

Fig. 9. Routes of Ancient India.

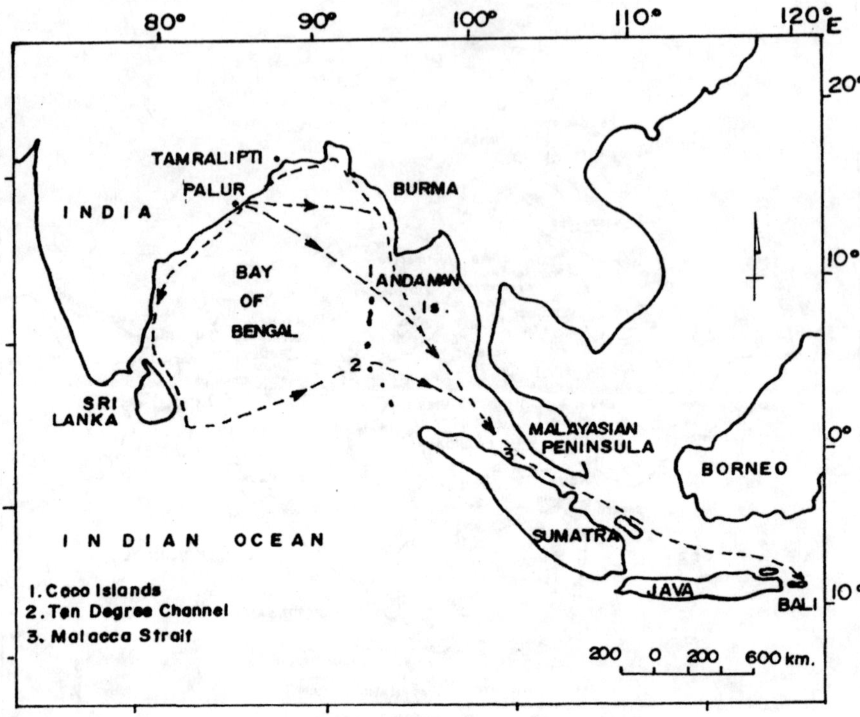

Fig. 10. Sea Route from Kalinga to Southeast Asian Countries.

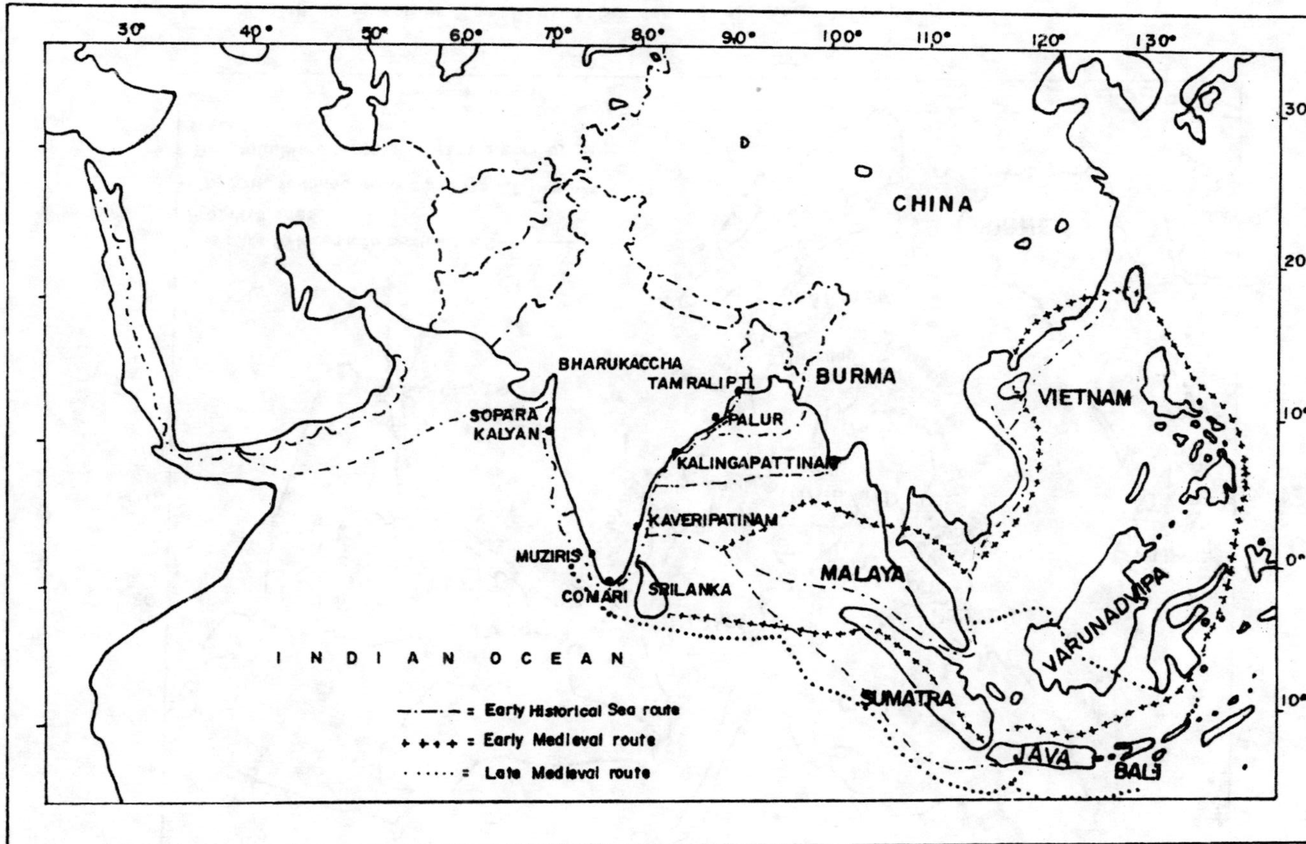

Fig. II. Maritime Trade Routes of India & Southeast Asia.

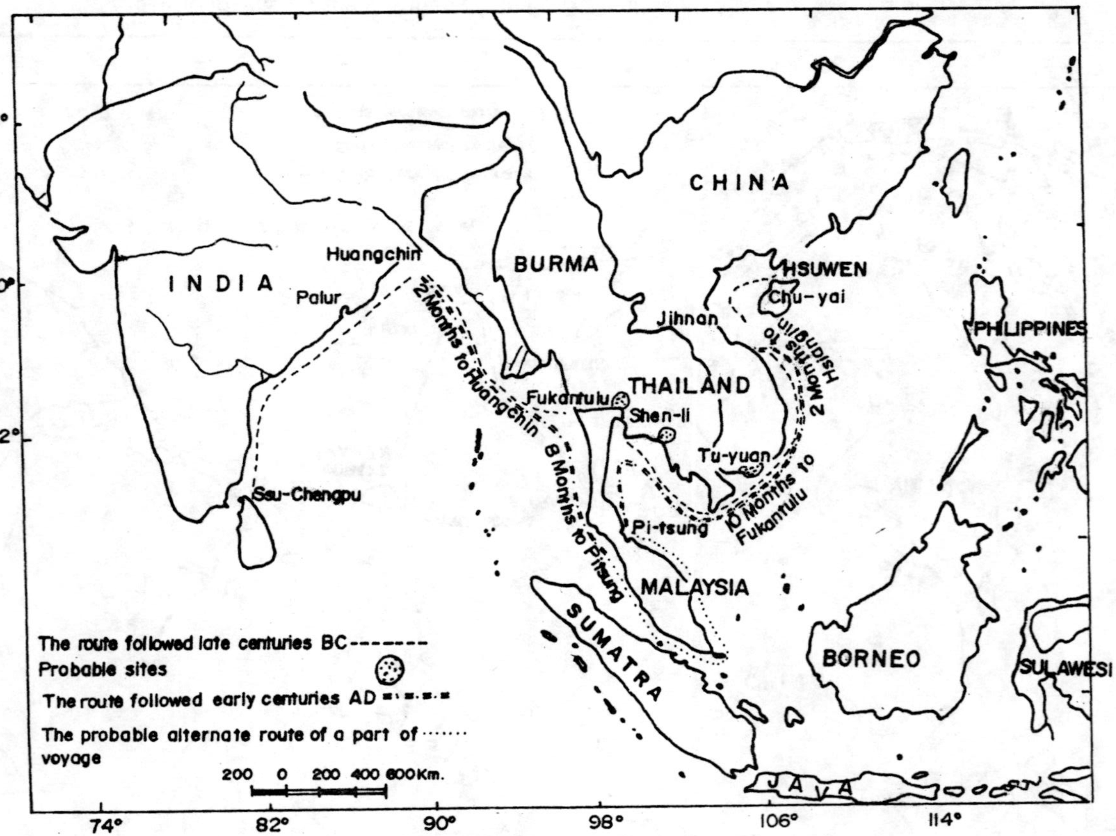

Fig.12. Possible Sea Routes Between India and China.

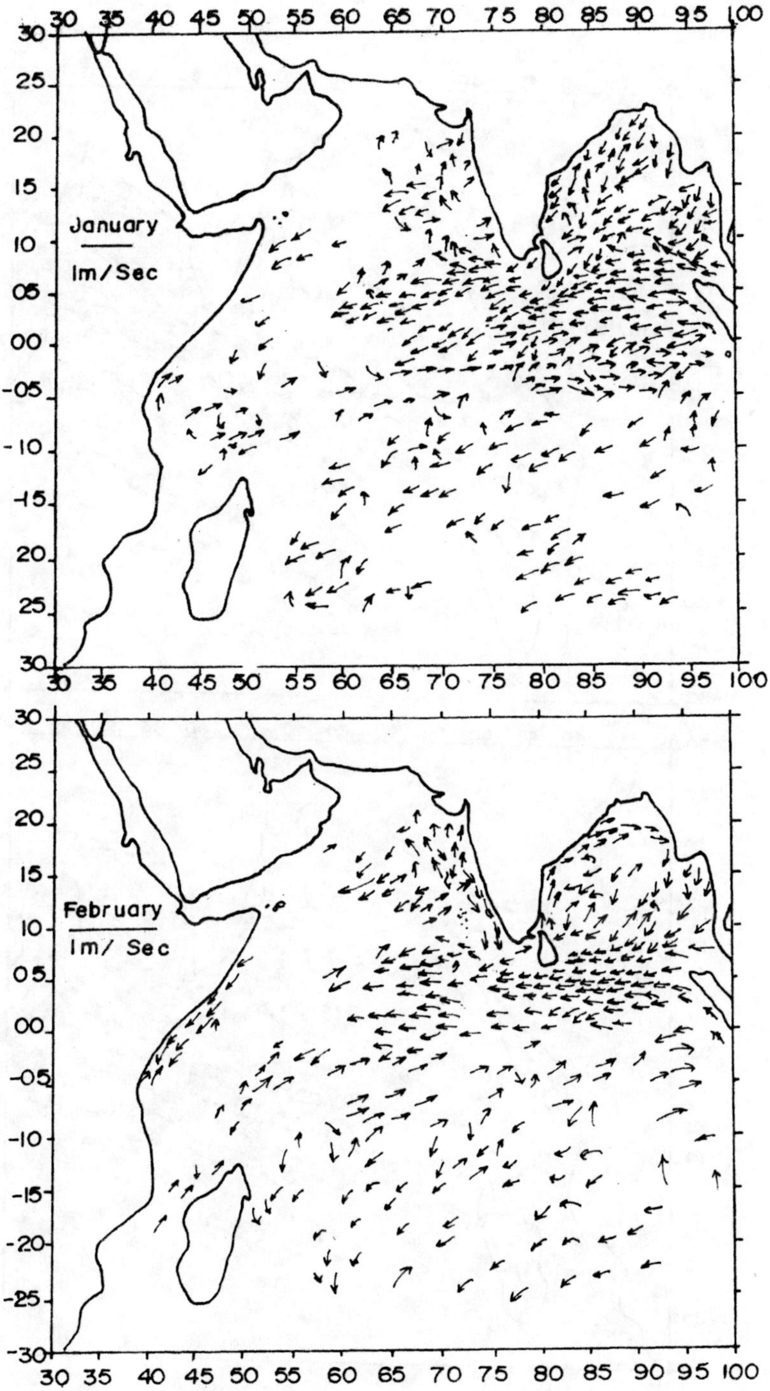

Fig. 13. A: Indian Ocean surface currents during January and February.

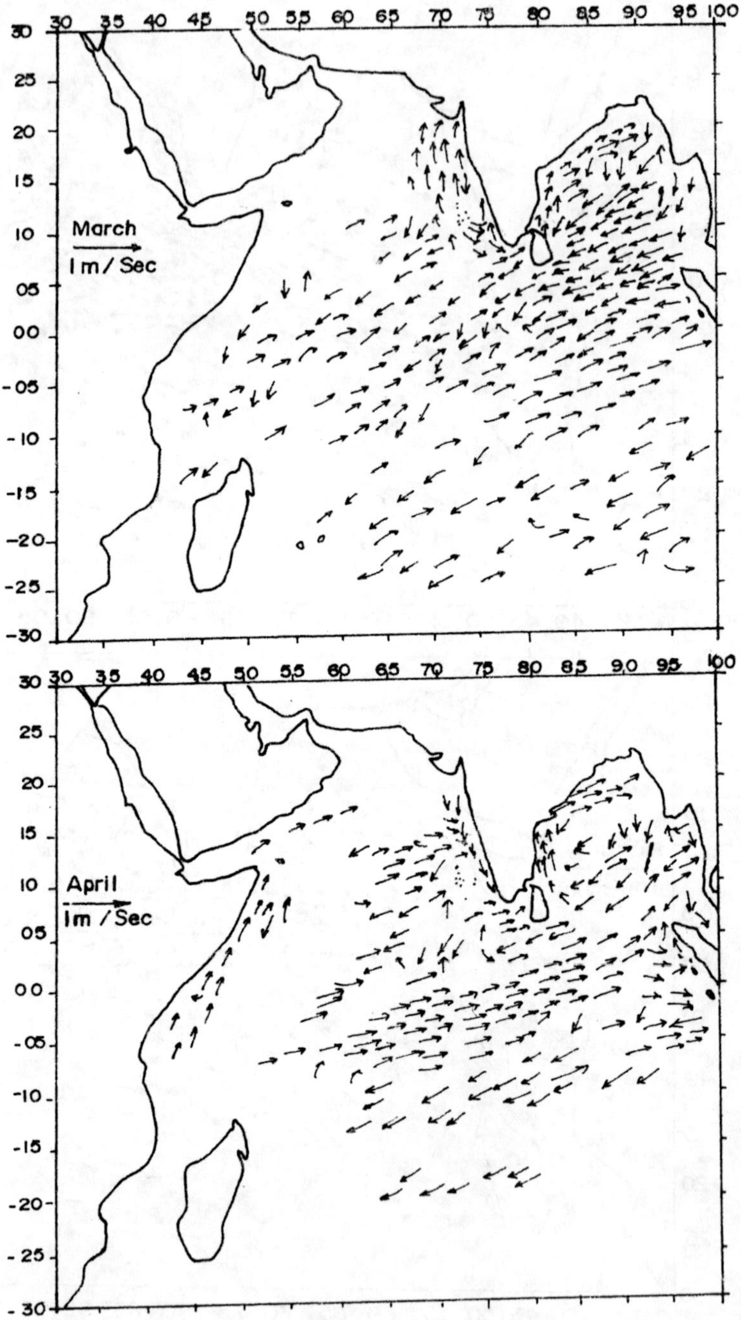

Fig. 13. B : Indian Ocean surface currents during March and April.

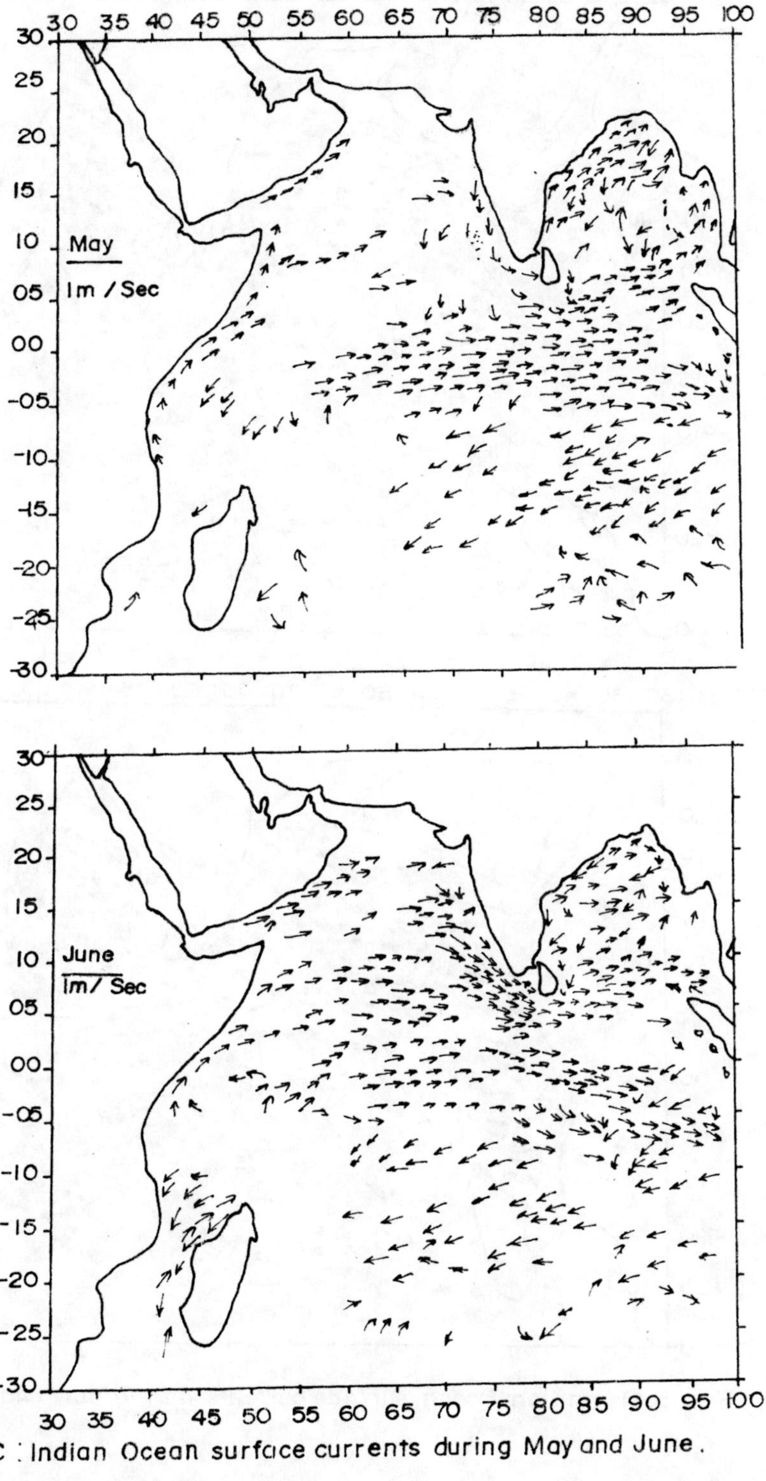

Fig. 13 C : Indian Ocean surface currents during May and June.

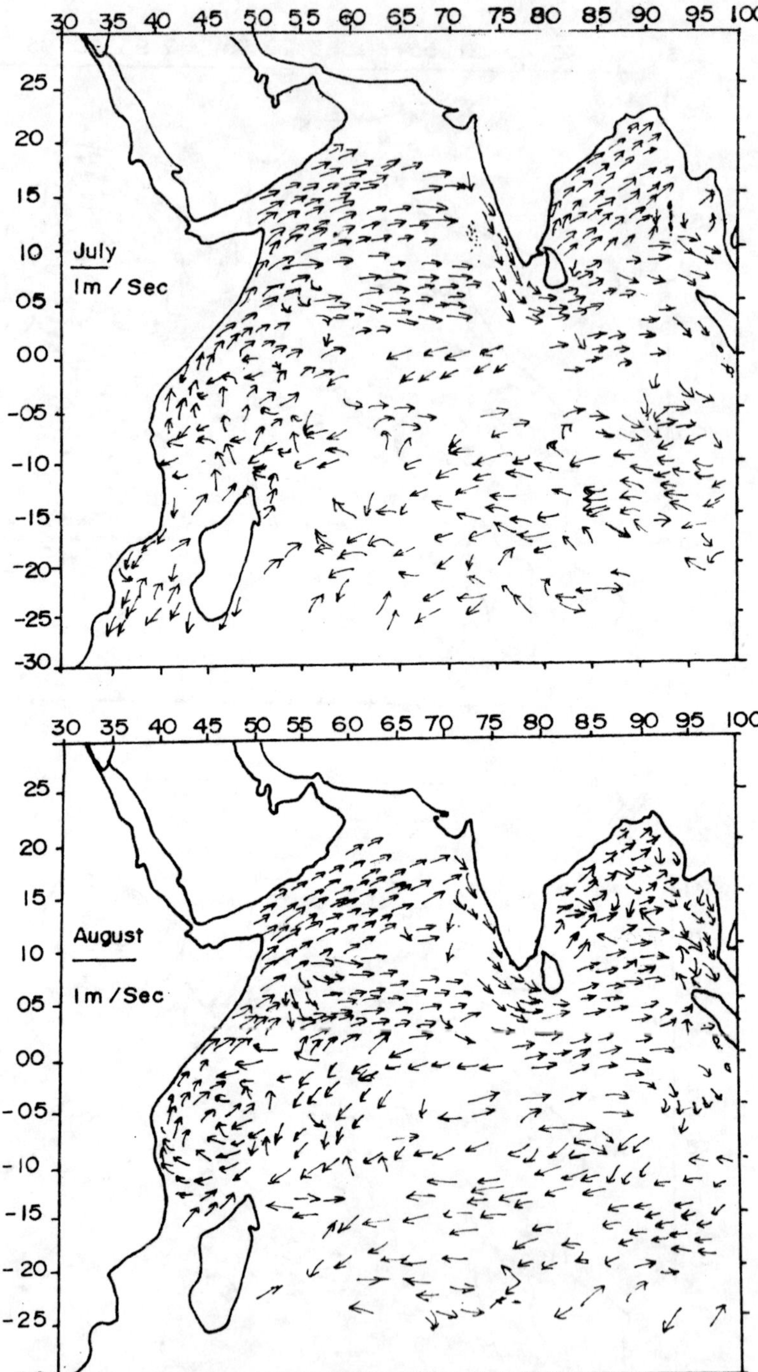

Fig. 13. D : Indian Ocean surface currents during July and August.

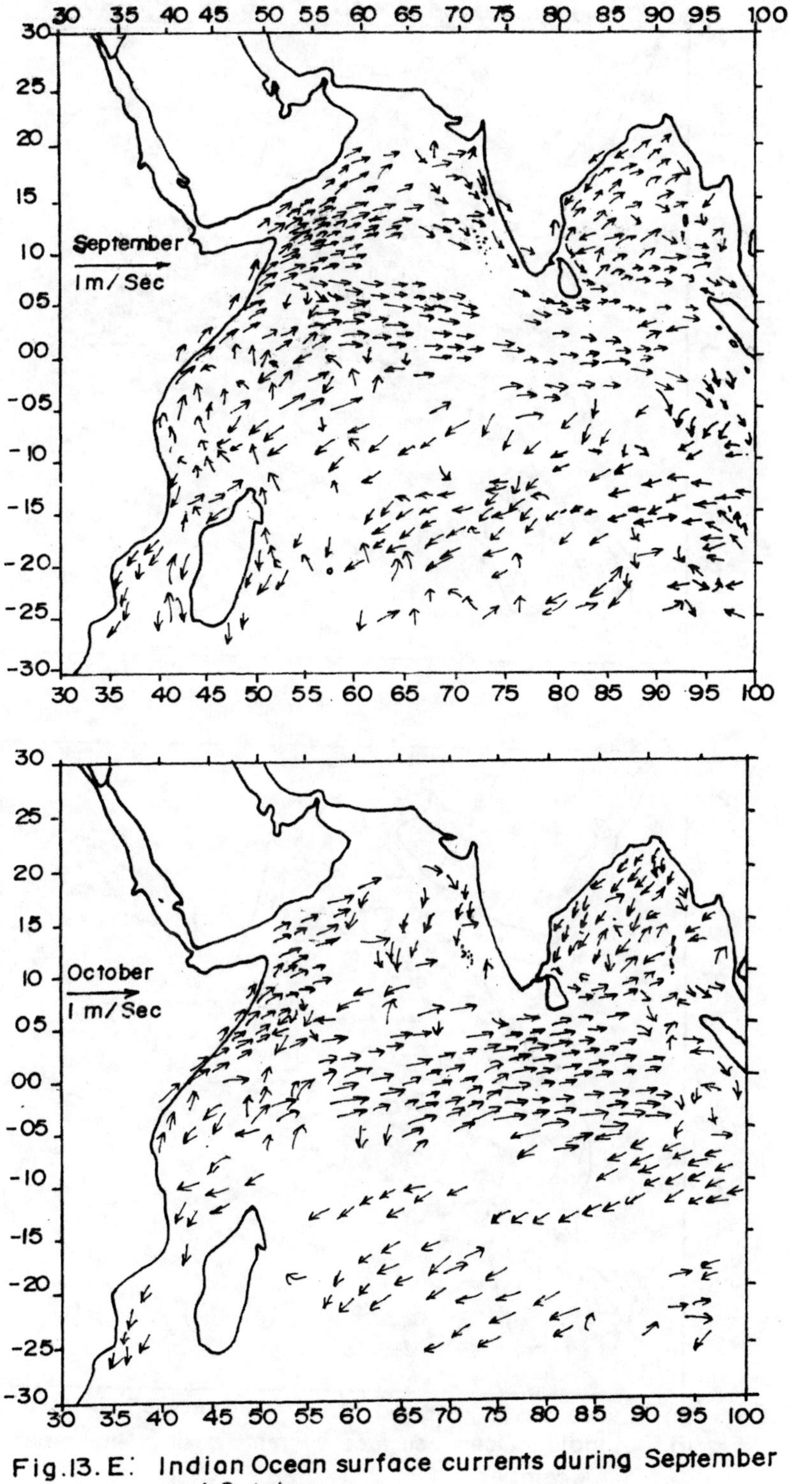

Fig.13.E: Indian Ocean surface currents during September and October.

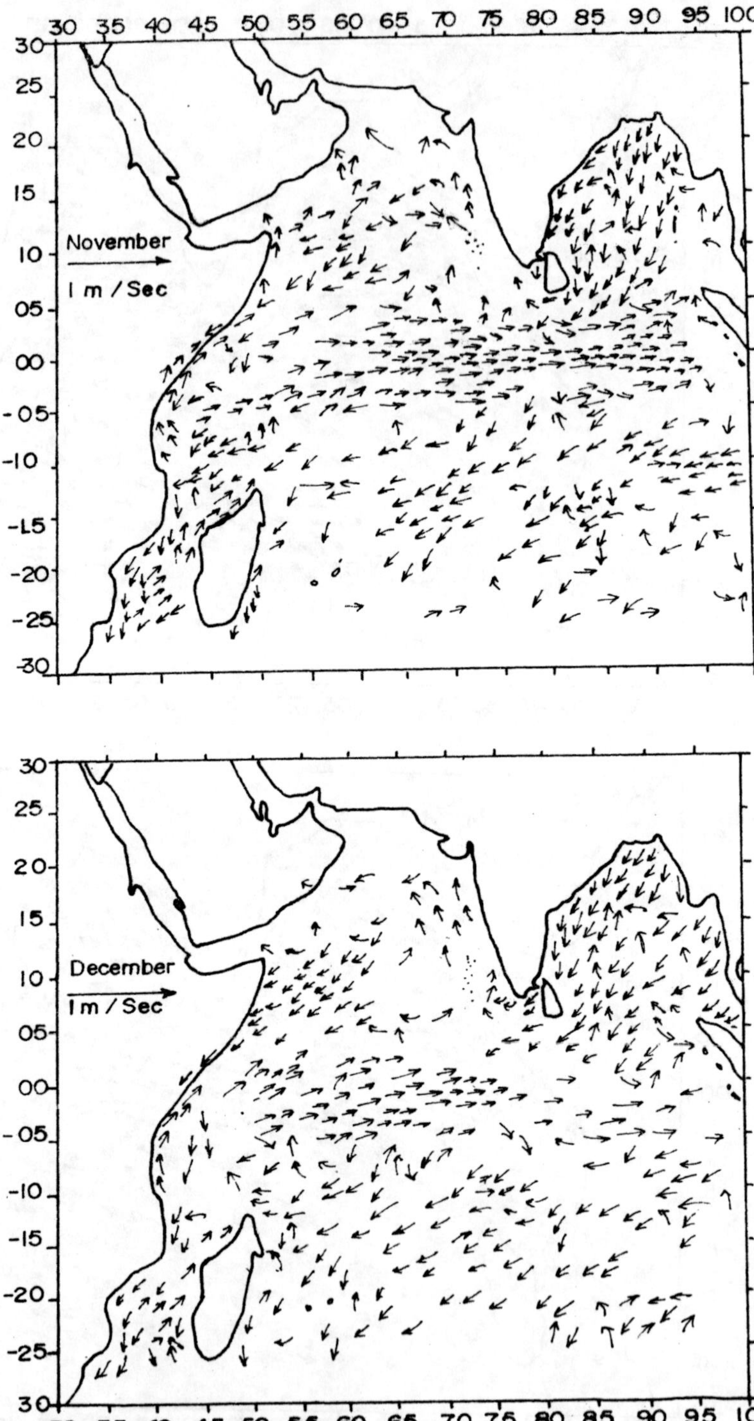

Fig. 13.F : Indian Ocean surface currents during November and December.

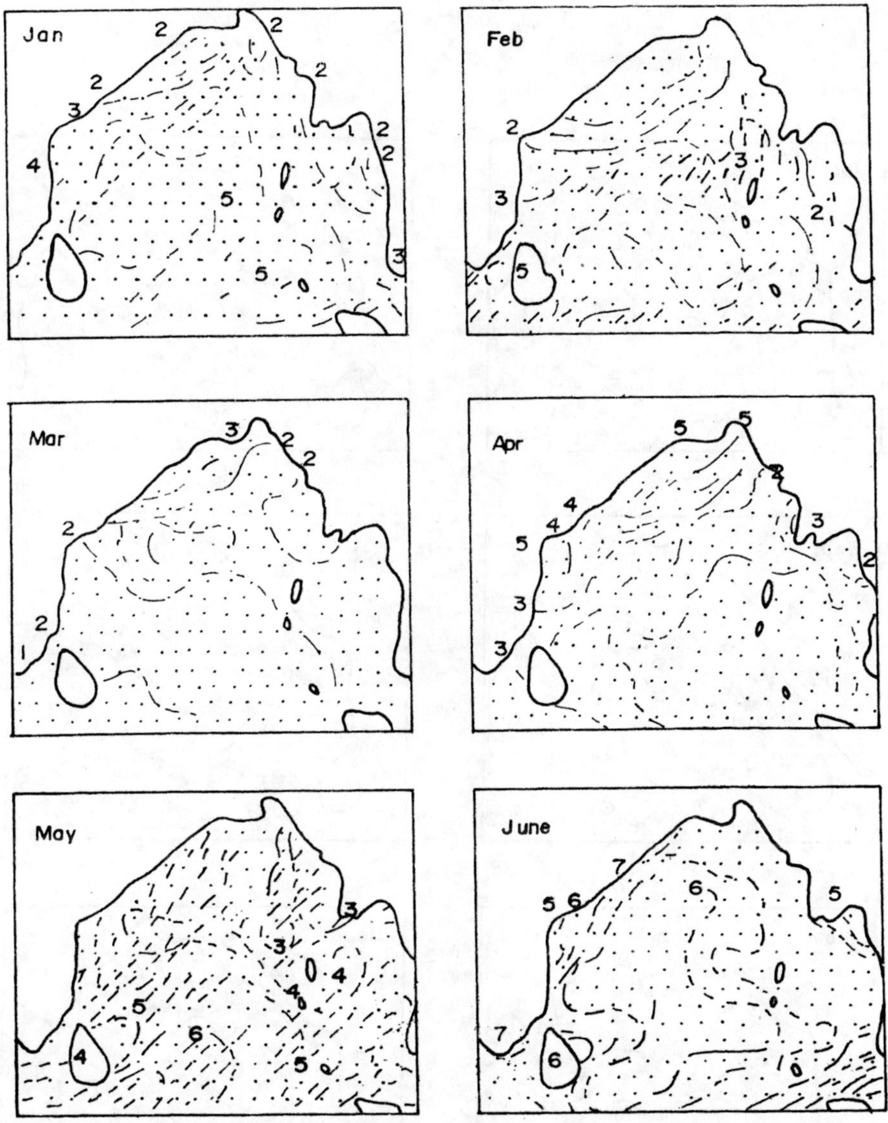

Fig. 14. A. Climatological wind field over the Bay of Bengal for January to June.

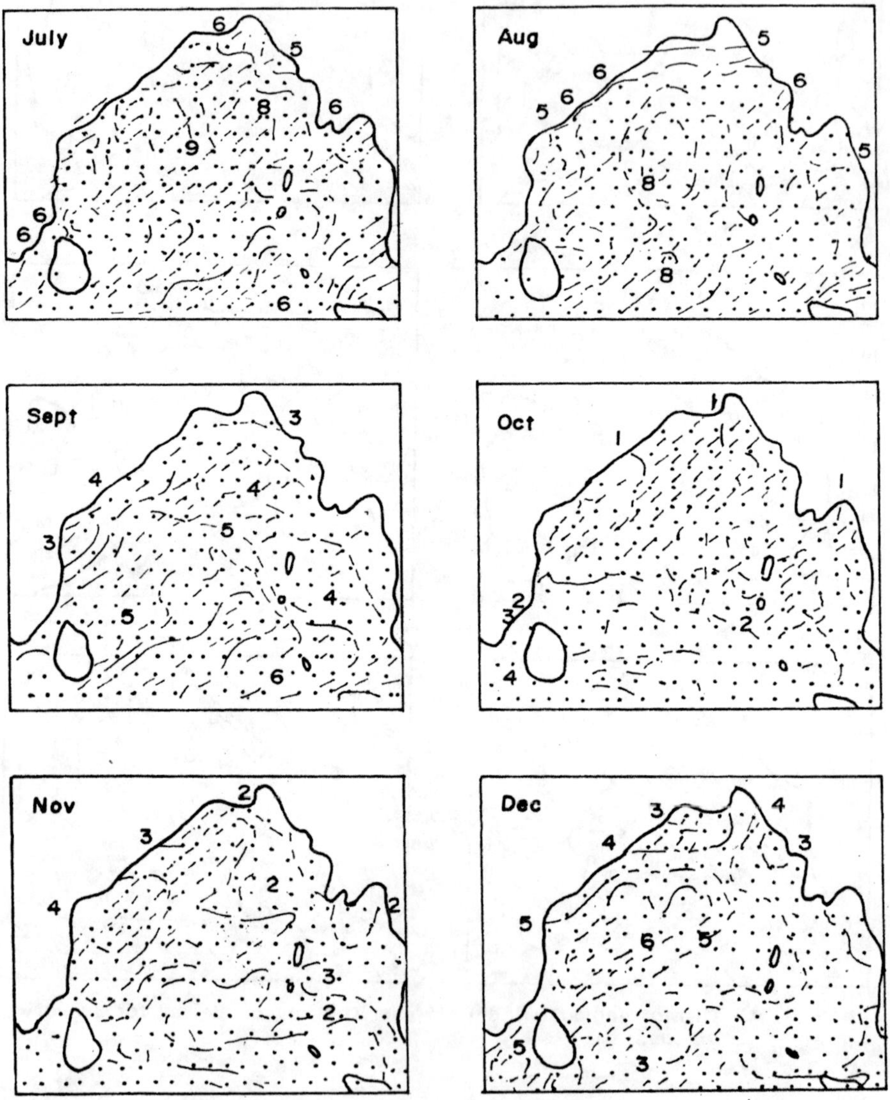

Fig. 14. B. Climatological wind field over the Bay of Bengal for july to December.

I(a). Andhra Coin Minted about 200 AD by King Satakarni showing a Sailing Vessel with Two Masts

I(b). Andhra Coin Minted about 200 AD by King Satakarni showing a Sailing Vessel with Two Masts

II. Boat Carrying Elephants, Orissa State Museum, Bhubaneswar

III. Four Headed Bhairava Dancing in Ecstasy on a Boat, Konark Temple, 13th century AD

IV. African Animal Giraffe Carved on Konark Temple, 13th century AD

V(a). A Boat Scene at Bharhut depicting evidence of Nautical Activity, 2nd century AD

V(b). Whale Attacking a Boat, 2nd century AD, Bharhut

VI. Boat Scene of Aurangabad Cave No. 7, 8th-9th century AD

VII(a). Indian Adventurers Sailing out to Colonise Java, 8th century AD

VII(b). Indian Adventurers Sailing out to Colonise Java, 8th century AD

VIII. Depiction of Boat and other Art Motifs from Sanchi Stupa, 2nd century BC

IX. Royal Pleasure Boat of Madhyamandira Type with a Cabin in the centre, Ajanta, 6th century AD

X. Boat with High Prow Stern and Three Oblong Masts, 6th century AD, Ajanta.

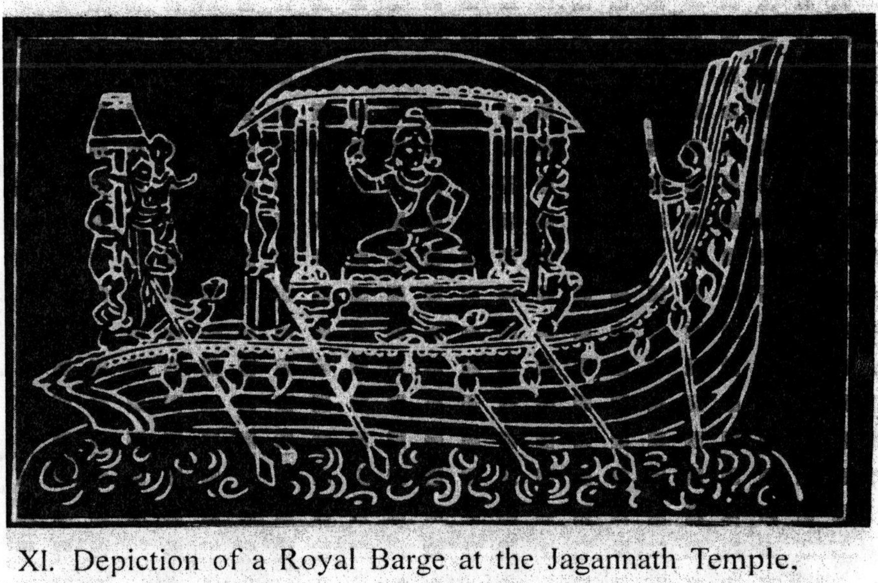

XI. Depiction of a Royal Barge at the Jagannath Temple, Puri.

XII(a). Boat Motifs Carved in the Ushavilasha Manuscript of Sisusankar Das, (Oriya) 18th century AD.

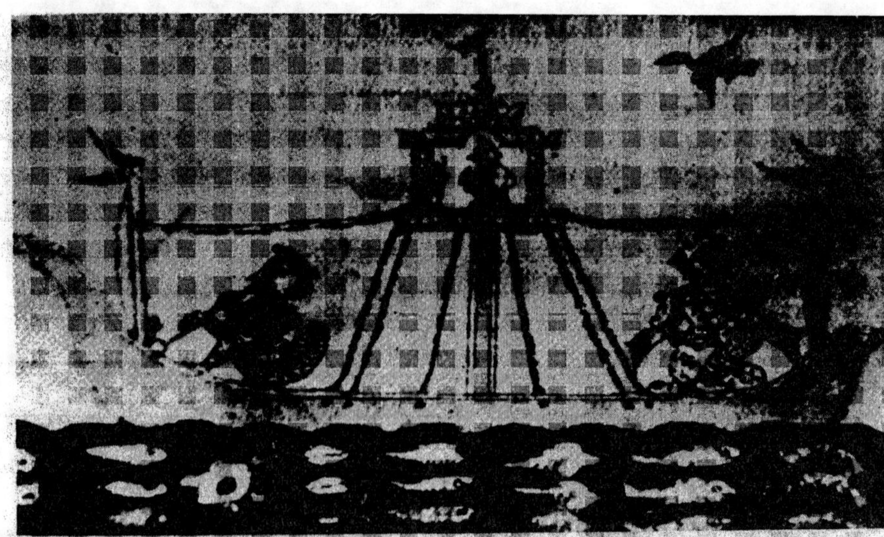

XII(b). Boat Motifs Carved in the Ushavilasha Manuscript of Sisusankar Das, (Oriya) 18th century AD.